LAWYER'S FORENSIC MEDICINE

LAWYER'S GUIDE TO FORENSIC MEDICINE

Second Edition

**Bernard Knight, CBE, MD, DSc (Hon),
LLD (Hon), BCh, MRCP, FRCPath, Dip Med Jur**
Barrister of Gray's Inn
Emeritus Professor of Forensic Pathology,
University of Wales College of Medicine

With compliments of the author
Bernard Knight.

Cavendish
Publishing
Limited

London • Sydney

Published in Great Britain 1998 by Cavendish Publishing Limited, The Glass House, Wharton Street, London WC1X 9PX, United Kingdom.
Telephone: +44 (0) 171 278 8000   Facsimile: +44 (0) 171 278 8080
E-mail: info@cavendishpublishing.com
Visit our Home Page on http://www.cavendishpublishing.com

First published by William Heinemann Medical Books 1982

Knight, Bernard
Lawyer's Guide to Forensic Medicine – 2nd edn
1. Medical jurisprudence
I. Title
614.1

ISBN 1 85941 159 2

Printed and bound in Great Britain

PREFACE

The 16 years that have elapsed since the first edition of this book have seen many changes which require significant updating of the text. Some entries have been deleted and others added, to reflect the changing priorities in the interface between medicine and the law.

This book has apparently filled a previously vacant niche in lawyer's libraries – on one occasion, I had the uncomfortable experience of standing in the witness box while both prosecuting and defence counsel, as well as the judge, quoted passages to me from their own copies.

Due to restrictions of space, the text is sometimes telegraphic and does not purport to be of great literary quality but, hopefully, the content is useful, comprehensible and free from unexplained medical jargon.

Within this small compass, it is impossible to provide references to all topics, but a list of standard forensic medical texts is provided, which will direct the reader to the relevant literature.

Bernard Knight

Lisvane, Cardiff

1998

CONTENTS

Contents

Contents

PART I: ANATOMICAL DRAWINGS

Figure 1: **Anatomical directions**

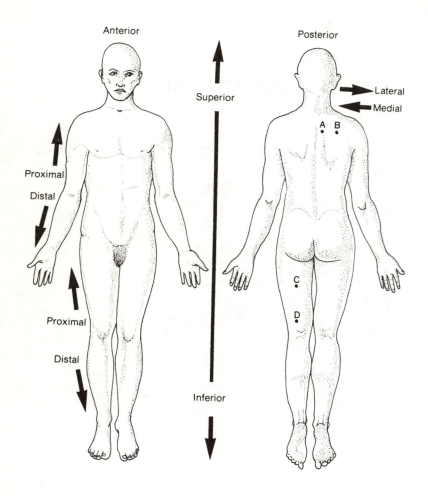

A is medial to B
Bis lateral to A
C is proximal to D
D is distal to C

Figure 2:   **Structures of the thorax and upper abdomen (anterior view)**

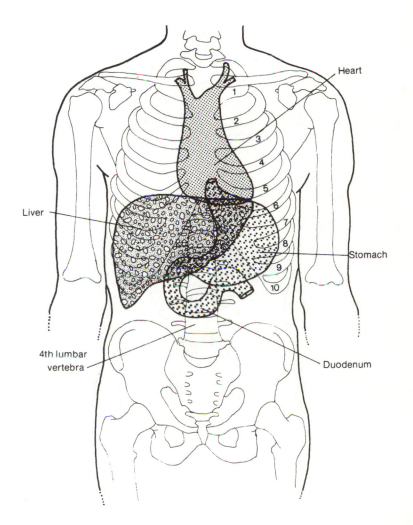

Figure 3: **Structures of the thorax and upper abdomen (posterior view)**

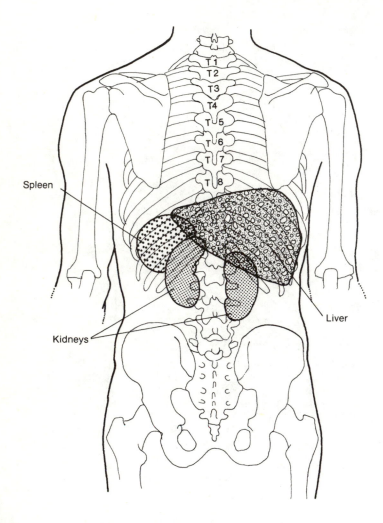

Figure 4: **Posterior view of kidneys and spleen (showing relationship to pleural cavity)**

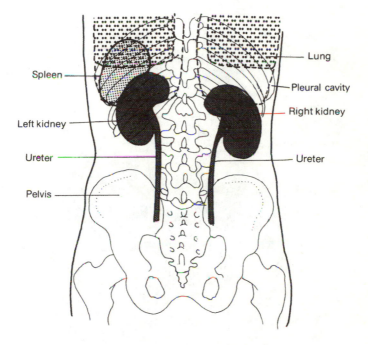

Figure 5: **Structures of the thorax and neck**

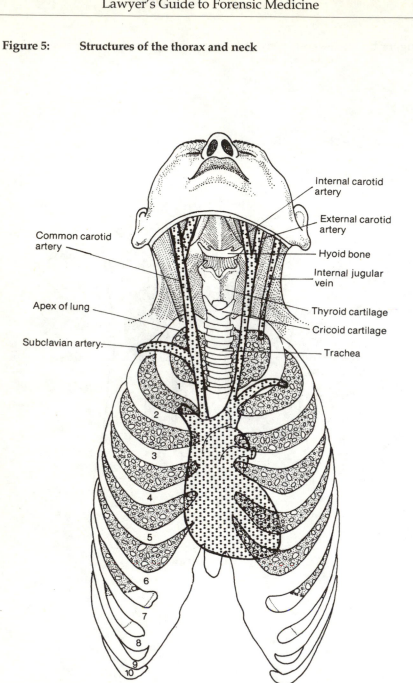

Figure 6: **The aorta and its branches**

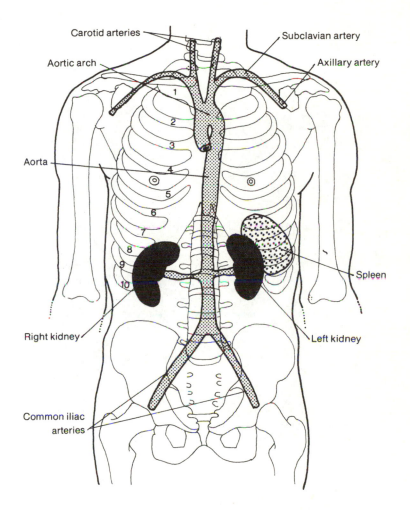

Figure 7: **Surface outlines of the heart and lungs**

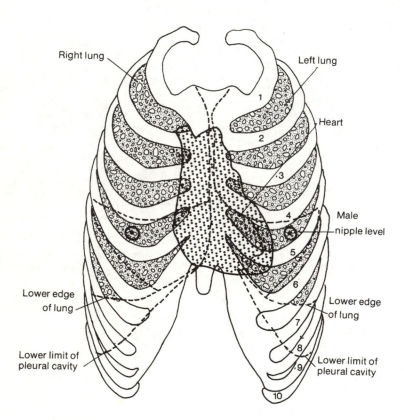

Figure 8:   **Surface markings of the heart**

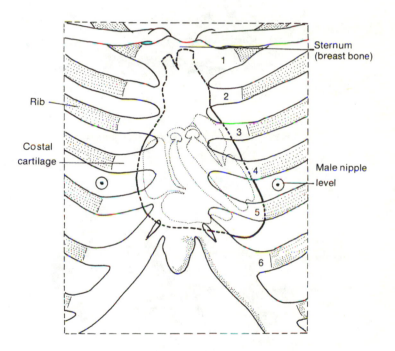

Figure 9: **Relationships of female and male genital organs**

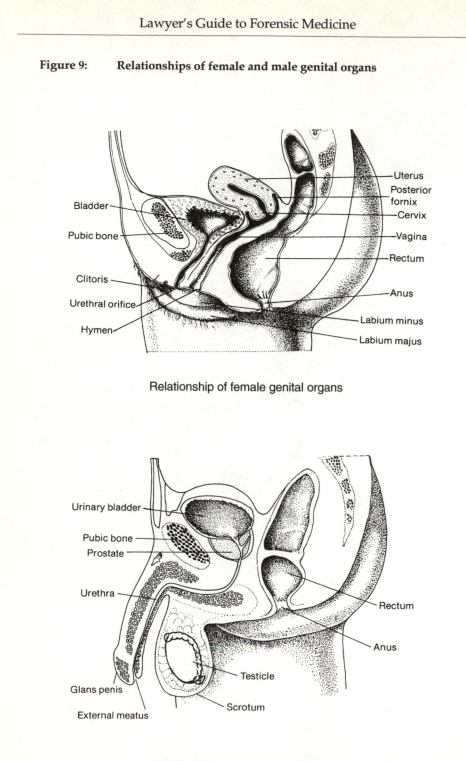

Relationship of female genital organs

Relationship of male genital organs

PART II: ALPHABETICAL ENTRIES

ABDOMINAL INJURY

A blow or kick upon the abdomen can cause severe, even fatal internal injury. There need not be any mark on the skin, especially if clothing is interposed. Though bruising or abrasions may be seen externally, rupture of internal organs can occur with no visible skin mark.

Most common injuries

Rupture of the spleen (qv) which lies in the left upper part of the abdomen. Fatal haemorrhage may occur from impact on the upper left abdomen or lower ribs.

Rupture of the intestine (qv), especially in children as part of child abuse syndrome. The upper small intestine may be lacerated or even divided where it crosses the projection of the spinal column, due to direct blows in the centre or upper part of the abdomen. This can be delayed if the injury first makes the intestinal wall non-viable, then it tears a day or two later.

The mesentery, the membranous root of the intestine may be lacerated in a similar fashion, leading to severe haemorrhage.

Rupture of the liver (qv) often occurs in traffic accidents and falls from a height due to heavy impact on the abdomen or lower chest. Also seen in kicks to the abdomen.

Rupture of the stomach or large bowel, but this happens less often than the above.

In all these instances, severe illness or death may be due to:

(a) haemorrhage into the peritoneal cavity (the free space around the organs), especially from liver, spleen and mesentery; or

(b) infective or chemical peritonitis, with shock when intestine or stomach is perforated into the abdominal cavity.

Rarely, death may occur instantaneously from a blow in the central abdomen: this is due to cardiac arrest from so called 'vagal inhibition' (qv) and where there are no external or internal signs of violence, the diagnosis rests upon the circumstances and exclusion of other causes.

ABORTION

Synonymous with the older term 'miscarriage', meaning the expulsion of a pregnancy from the womb before the 24th week of gestation. Later than this, the process is usually called a premature birth, though these are not legal definitions.

A considerable proportion – up to 40% – of fertilised ova fail to proceed to full term, most of them aborting at such an early stage that pregnancy may not even have been apparent.

The causes of natural abortion include any severe general illness in the mother, but especially acute fevers, congestive heart disease, hypertension with kidney disease, etc. In spite of these risks, a large proportion of pregnancies in ill women do not abort, though the strain of the pregnancy may cause further deterioration in the health of the woman.

A defect in the ovum or foetus is one of the most common causes of aborting, this being a genetic safety device to reduce the incidence of malformed individuals. Abortion may be at a very early stage when the actual defect is indiscernible.

Trauma and violence is rarely a factor, though it can be grounds for litigation if alleged to have been precipitated by some accident or assault. As the incidence of natural abortion is said to be of the order of 10% of all recognisable pregnancies, it can never be definitely stated that a particular traumatic event was the inevitable cause, though a close association in time will naturally strengthen the probability.

Induced abortion

This may be illegal or medically induced under permissive legislation (for Britain, the Abortion Act 1967).

Methods employed include the following:

Dilatation of the neck of the womb and curettage (scraping) of the products of conception. Usually performed by medically trained persons, either legally or, rarely now in Britain, criminally.

Suction aspiration. The removal of the foetus and membranes by suction through a tube inserted into the womb via the cervix. Now the most common, rapid and complication-free method, usually employed during termination of early pregnancy by legitimate means. A very rare complication is air embolism (qv), though in theory this should not occur.

Hysterotomy. The opening of the womb by surgical operation through the abdomen, similar to a Caesarean section. Usually used in the later stages of pregnancy. Sterilisation is often performed at the same time.

Drugs. Usually ineffective and taken by the woman herself in an effort to abort. A wide and largely useless pharmacopoeia exists, such as herbal remedies, purgatives, quinine. Substances such as lead and ergot may have some effect but are dangerous to the mother. Medical drugs like pituitrin and prostaglandin are effective, but only near full term as inducers of labour.

External physical stimuli. Riding, bicycling, hot baths, enemas and violence to the abdomen are all without effect, but severe violence may cause injury, sometimes fatal, to the mother.

Uterine syringing. Formerly the most common means of effective illegal abortion, using a Higginson enema syringe to inject fluid into the uterus through the neck of the womb (cervix). The purpose is to peel off the pregnancy sac from the walls of the womb by fluid pressure: once loosened, it is expelled by the uterus. Effective, but potentially dangerous method.

Injection of irritant substances into the womb through the cervix. Performed legally and illegally by use of such substances as Utus paste, which causes expulsion of the displaced and irritated embryo sac.

Hazards of abortion

Infection. Formerly the most common complication, especially of criminal abortion. With antibiotics and greater involvement of medical and nursing operators, the incidence is greatly reduced. Anaerobic infection by gas-gangrene-type bacteria is a particular danger.

Haemorrhage can occur from vaginal damage or perforation from inept technique, especially by the woman herself. Damage to the neck of the womb or the womb itself also a hazard. The placental bed of the pregnancy sac may bleed profusely, especially in later pregnancy.

Air embolism (qv) from Higginson syringing was one of the most common fatal sequelae of illegal abortion, though now almost unknown in Britain.

Rapid shock effects of abortion. Not common, but may be immediate from cardiac arrest due to interference with the neck of the womb (see 'Vagal inhibition').

Poisoning (for example, toxic effects of substances such as permanganate of potash applied to the neck of the womb) or antiseptics containing phenolic substances douched into the vagina or syringed into the cervix.

Figure 10:   **Hazards of abortion**

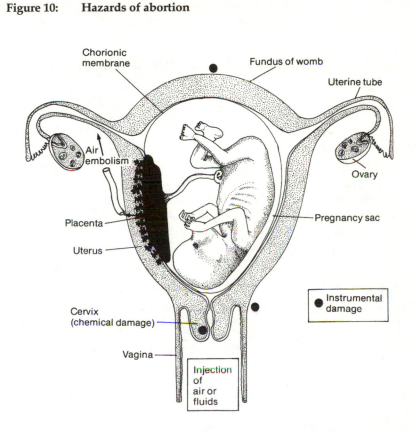

ABORTION LEGISLATION

Offences Against the Person Act 1861 did not contemplate any exclusion for medical reasons. Section 58 made it a felony for a woman (if she be pregnant) or any other person (whether she was pregnant or not) to procure or intend to procure an abortion. Section 59 concerned the supply of poisons or instruments for the purpose of abortion.

Pharmacy and Medicine Act 1941 made it unlawful to advertise goods in terms calculated to lead to their use in abortion.

Infant Life (Preservation) Act 1929 first mention that medical abortion might not be unlawful – 'no person shall be found guilty of an offence unless it is proved that the act was not done in good faith for the purpose only of preserving the life of the mother'.

The later Abortion Act and Human Fertilisation and Embryology Act make it impossible for a medical practitioner to be charged under the 1929 Act.

Abortion Act 1967 (as amended by the Human Fertilisation and Embryology Act 1990)

It is not unlawful for a registered medical practitioner to terminate a pregnancy provided that two registered medical practitioners form the opinion in good faith:

(a) that the pregnancy has not exceeded the 24th week and that continuance of the pregnancy would involve greater risk than if the pregnancy were terminated, of injury to the physical or mental health of the pregnant woman or any existing child of her family; or

(b) that the termination is necessary to prevent grave permanent injury to the physical or mental health of the pregnant woman; or

(c) that the continuation of the pregnancy would involve risk to the life of the pregnant woman greater than if the pregnancy were terminated; or

(d) that there is a substantial risk that if the child were born, it would suffer from physical or mental abnormalities as to be seriously handicapped.

Notes

(a) Any two doctors may so certify and the actual operation may be carried out by a third doctor. However, it is most common for a general practitioner and a consultant obstetrician to certify, and frequently the latter is the operator.

(b) In assessing the risk to the woman or to her family, account must be taken of her actual or reasonably foreseeable environment.

(c) The termination of pregnancy may only be carried out either in a National Health Service hospital or in premises approved for the purpose by the Secretary of State.

(d) In an emergency, the opinion of one doctor is sufficient only on the grounds that abortion is immediately necessary to save the life or prevent grave permanent injury to the pregnant woman.

(e) Documentation must comply with the requirements of the Abortion Regulations (1968), the termination being notified to the appropriate Chief Medical Officer. These must be completed either before or within 24 hours of the completion of the operation. Records must be retained for at least three years.

(f) Conscientious objection to taking part in abortions is to be upheld amongst medical and nursing staff, except when the operation is necessary to save the life or avoid grave damage to the woman.

(g) The 1990 amendment placed an upper limit of 24 weeks' gestation (in place of the previous 28) only on the first ground for termination. There is no time limit on the three subsequent grounds.

ABRASIONS

These are the most superficial type of wounds, in which the injury does not penetrate through the full thickness of the skin. A pure abrasion therefore does not bleed, as no blood vessels are present in the epidermis (the upper layer of the skin), but in most cases the injury, unless merely a very superficial scrape, does involve the tips of the corrugated papillae of the underlying dermis and therefore some bleeding usually occurs.

Figure 11:   Characteristics of abrasions

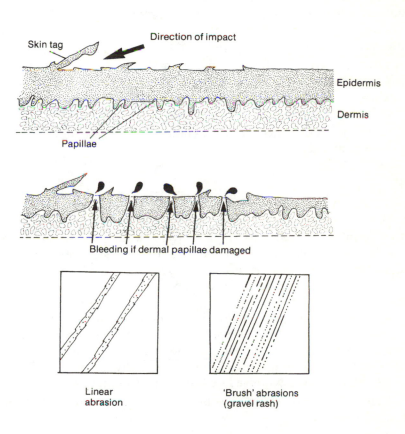

Abrasions are also called 'scratches' or 'grazes', the former referring to a single linear abrasion and the latter to multiple parallel abrasions due to a tangential contact with a rough surface. A 'gravel rash' is a colloquial term for a graze caused by sliding impact with a road surface, often seen in traffic injuries and to a lesser degree in simple falls to the ground. These multiple parallel marks are also known as 'brush abrasions'.

In these and other abrasions, the direction of the injury can often be determined by close inspection of the ends of the scratches, where tags of skin will be piled up at the end furthest from the initial point of contact. Where a weapon or object hits the skin, its direction will be towards the skin tags, whereas if a moving body skids along a rough surface, the direction will be away from the end of the graze that shows skin tags.

Abrasions take the imprint of the object which caused them better than bruises and a clear pattern may be imprinted on the skin (see 'Patterned injuries').

After death, extensive abrasions become leathery and dark reddish brown, especially where friction has occurred as in grazes and ligature marks. In the living, drying of the surface scab, where present, may also heighten the prominence of an abrasion after a few hours or a day.

Abrasions are sometimes caused on the assailant when a victim is attacked, due to defence actions by the victim. In such instances, forensic examination of finger-nail scrapings may reveal fragments of skin which can be DNA analysed, to assist in the identification of the assailant.

Abrasions frequently occur in association with bruises (qv) and lacerations (qv) to form mixed lesions.

ADIPOCERE

A long term post-mortem change in body fat, leading to partial preservation of the soft tissues. Fats are converted to adipocere, a crumbly grey material, which may persist for many years as an alternative to the usual putrefaction. The cheeks, breasts and buttocks are most obviously preserved, but patchy conversion of any part of the body fat may occur. Features may even be recognisable if facial fat is preserved. The process usually needs a wet environment, either in water or in damp burials, but this is not invariable. The adipocere may retain bullet holes or other evidence of violence usually lost during putrefaction. Adipocere formation usually takes several months to occur, but may happen within a few weeks in the right conditions.

Chemically, adipocere is a complex mixture of waxes and soaps due to the action of water on body fat. Fatty acids are a predominant constituent. The water necessary for conversion may be provided from the original body water, so a damp environment is not absolutely essential.

AGE ESTIMATION

Required in both living and dead, either for identification or for determining age of criminal responsibility, inheritance, in sexual offences, marriage, employment, immigration, military service, etc – also in foetuses and infants to determine the stage of maturity (see 'Foetus').

Up to about age 25, development of the skeleton affords a reasonably accurate means of age determination. The bones mature by developing 'ossification centres', which are foci of chalky calcium in the cartilage

Figure 12:   Development of the femur

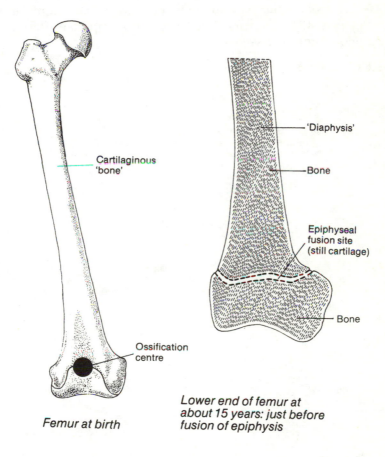

Cartilaginous 'bone'

'Diaphysis'

Bone

Epiphyseal fusion site (still cartilage)

Bone

Ossification centre

Femur at birth

Lower end of femur at about 15 years: just before fusion of epiphysis

precursors. These progressively enlarge and eventually fuse together at relatively constant ages, the last being between 20–25 years. These ossification centres, usually at 'epiphyses' or growing ends of the bones, can be detected by X-ray in the living as well as by direct exposure in the dead. Textbooks of forensic medicine and of radiology give tables for the times of appearance and fusion, but caution must be employed in the degree of accuracy expected, as girls tend to fuse up to one year earlier than boys and, in the tropics, there may be two to three years advance in bony changes compared to Europe. The advice of an experienced radiologist, pathologist or anatomist is necessary as to the expected degree of accuracy in any given circumstance.

Other most useful tools are the teeth, especially in children. The first set of teeth ('milk' or 'deciduous' teeth) begin to appear at about the sixth month after birth and the second set of permanent teeth begin to erupt at about six years. The last tooth is the 'wisdom' tooth or third permanent molar, which may not appear until 20–25 years. Where the issue is important, the opinion of a forensic odontologist is essential.

Figure 13:   Development of the teeth

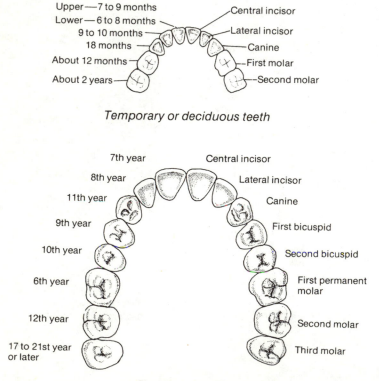

Upper — 7 to 9 months — Central incisor
Lower — 6 to 8 months — Lateral incisor
9 to 10 months — Lateral incisor
18 months — Canine
About 12 months — First molar
About 2 years — Second molar

Temporary or deciduous teeth

7th year — Central incisor
8th year — Lateral incisor
11th year — Canine
9th year — First bicuspid
10th year — Second bicuspid
6th year — First permanent molar
12th year — Second molar
17 to 21st year or later — Third molar

Permanent teeth

After 25 years, the determination of age becomes very imprecise, compared with children, where accuracy measured in weeks can be attained by special dental techniques. Certain specialised tests of teeth may give an age in the mature adult to within five to seven years, but only on dead subjects. Once the skeleton is fully matured at about 25 years, accuracy only of the nearest decade can be expected in the living, based on general appearances and the onset of degenerative changes. In the skeleton of the dead, special techniques such as pubic bone examination may give a much better result, but expert anthropological advice is required. Considerable space is devoted to this subject in standard textbooks of forensic pathology which should be consulted for details, but it is vital to appreciate the inherent inaccuracies, especially in the mature living person, and to accept the biological variations (sexual, ethnic, nutritional and individual) in the development of children, especially where body height and weight are concerned.

AIDS

Acronym for Acquired Immune Deficiency Syndrome, where the body's immunological defences are impaired by the action of HIV (human immune deficiency virus). This loss of defence is against foreign material, including bacteria, fungi, other micro-organisms and tumour cells, and particularly reduces the T-lymphocytes, the major defensive mechanism.

This allows a range of opportunist infections to thrive, including candidiasis, cytomegalic virus, cryptosporosis, pneumocystis carinii pneumonia, tuberculosis, etc. In addition, a type of cancer, called Kaposi's sarcoma may develop, due to the loss of the normal destruction of malignant cells by the immune system.

It should be noted that death is not from HIV itself, but of the consequences of HIV infection, which is a spectrum of secondary infections constituting AIDS. There may be a number of years between infection with HIV and the development of AIDS – a period now able to be prolonged by drug treatment – and some persons with HIV infection seem not to go on to develop AIDS.

AIR EMBOLISM

Introduction of air or other gas into circulatory system. Small amounts may be tolerated but, beyond a threshold volume (which is very variable from case to case), bubbles in heart, brain or coronary arteries may cause death.

Causes

Induced criminal abortion from the use of a Higginson enema syringe, now a very rare event. Here, instead of fluid, air is inadvertently pumped into the womb and penetrates the open veins of the separated placental bed to gain access to the circulation. Can be a very rare complication of therapeutic abortion by suction (see 'Abortion').

Surgical operations on the neck or chest, above heart level, where air may be sucked into opened veins. Thyroid operation is most common circumstance, though rare. Cut throat also an uncommon cause. The induction of artificial pneumothorax and pneumoperitoneum also carry risks of embolism.

During transfusion, where bottle empties and air enters vein – especially if being introduced under pressure from gas cylinder. The introduction of flexible plastic containers has greatly reduced this danger.

A few homicidal instances, where air is deliberately introduced by syringe into arm veins; usually so called 'mercy killings' by doctors, for example, the *Sander* and *Montemerano* cases in the USA.

In divers, when rapid decompression allows gas bubbles to form.

Diagnosis

This is best made by radiology (bubbles seen in heart and large blood vessels). At autopsy, a special technique is needed. It is not necessary to open the chest and heart under water. After X-rays, the large veins and right side of the heart must be carefully palpated and examined for contained bubbles. Once the vessels and chambers are opened, the bubbles rapidly vanish. The diagnosis must exclude gas formed by decomposition. There are many difficulties in interpretation, for instance, false bubbles may be seen in brain surface vessels. Radiology is the only really reliable method of detection, either before or after death. Volume of air needed is a matter of controversy: as little as 10 ml has been fatal, while over 100 ml has been survived. Other authorities say that 60–100 ml is a minimum fatal volume.

AIR-GUN INJURIES

Air-rifles and pistols can cause lethal injuries, either in the .177 or .22 inch calibres. Most deaths occur from penetration of the skull and brain, especially in children and young persons, the pellet being able to traverse the entire width of the interior of the skull and impact against the further side. Though the slug is small, a wide track of damage may be present in the brain substance, as with all projectile injuries.

A common, usually non-fatal, injury is damage to the eye, frequently causing blindness in that eye.

As well as head injuries, the pellet can penetrate the chest and cause death or severe injury from damage to the heart or great blood vessels.

Some control over air weapons was brought in as a result of several deaths in children. This was the Air-Guns and Shotguns, etc, Act 1962, now incorporated in later Firearms Acts. This made it an offence for a child under 14 years to have an air weapon or ammunition and for anyone under 17 years to have an uncovered gun in a public place.

The Firearms (Dangerous Weapons) Rules 1969 make the maximum allowable muzzle energy of an air-rifle 16 joules (12 ft/lb) and a pistol 8 joules (6 ft/lb).

AIR PASSAGE OBSTRUCTION
(see also 'Choking')

Blockage of back of throat (pharynx), voice box (larynx), windpipe (trachea) or lung tubes (bronchi) by foreign objects or material. For external obstruction due to constriction of neck, obstruction of nose and mouth, etc, see 'Suffocation', 'Strangulation'.

Main causes

Internal blockage of air passages is usually due to food material, toys, dentures, extracted teeth, blood, etc. There are two types of food obstruction:

Food just eaten, before it is swallowed into stomach. Common in senile and mentally defective people, including children. Also in the so called 'café coronary' (qv), confused with heart attacks whilst eating. In all these cases, the food is fresh and undigested. It may impact in the entrance to the voice box (at the glottis) or in the windpipe and cause death either by asphyxia, due to blockage of air, or (much more often) from sudden reflex cardiac arrest (qv).

Food regurgitated from stomach, the so called 'aspiration of vomit', or 'inhalation of stomach contents'. Considerable caution is required in accepting such a diagnosis from post-mortem findings, unless corroborated by clinical observation. Many pathologists use this as a cause of death, though it may not be possible to prove. Spurious aspiration of vomit is often really due to agonal or even post-mortem spillage of stomach contents into air passages. Regurgitation is common in death throes; also post-mortem handling of body by porters and undertakers has been shown to move stomach contents into larynx. A quarter of all autopsies reveal some gastric contents in the air passages, but this cannot be accepted as genuine unless someone saw the aspiration take place during life. Only true proof of aspiration at post-mortem is acid digestion in lungs, with a cellular reaction seen under the microscope: not visible unless aspiration occurred some time before death, probably in excess of many minutes after entry of vomit into lungs.

The mere finding of food particles in the lungs under the microscope is not evidence of death from aspiration; it can be sucked down during the dying process – and if artificial respiration has been given it has no significance at all.

Other causes

Other causes of air passage blockage include gags in the back of the mouth; though these may allow breathing via nose passages at first, mucus and swelling in the nasal passages may close the airway later and cause death. Seen in tied-up watchmen during robbery, etc.

Inhalation of teeth after extraction, false teeth, small toys and other objects may also block air passages. Blood from facial and mouth injuries, especially in unconscious victims of assault, may also block air tubes. There may or may not be 'asphyxial signs' of blue face, petechial haemorrhages in eyes. These are frequently absent in choking, due to the rapid death from cardiac arrest.

ALCOHOL (ETHYL)

A very complex toxicological and physiological subject: much uncertainty and controversy surrounds the relationship between the amount taken and the behavioural effects, due to great variation in a number of factors, including the following.

Absorption

Alcohol is normally rapidly absorbed after drinking, both from the stomach lining and especially from the first part of the intestine (duodenum and jejunum). The rate of absorption differs according to various factors.

Presence of food in the stomach. A full stomach dilutes the swallowed alcohol and reduces its contact with the stomach wall, so absorption is slowed. A fatty meal retards absorption, partly by delaying the transfer of stomach contents into the intestine where alcohol absorption is maximal. Persons who have had a stomach operation, such as partial gastrectomy or a gastro-jejunostomy (usually for peptic ulcers) will absorb alcohol more quickly, as the swallowed drink will almost immediately enter the upper intestine where absorption is more rapid.

The concentration of the alcohol. About 20% alcohol in the drink is optimal for quick absorption. Very strong liquor may irritate the stomach wall and slow absorption by production of mucus on the lining. Very weak alcohol naturally has less active substance per volume for absorption and so raises the blood level more slowly. Large volume drinks, such as beer, absorb more slowly than small volume spirits because the bulk prevents the alcohol from reaching the walls of the stomach or intestine, which is a prerequisite for absorption.

Carbon dioxide bubbles. In 'aerated' diluents for drinks (lemonade and tonic, etc), these are said to increase the rate of absorption. Sparkling wines, such as champagne, may have the same enhancing effect on absorption, probably due to the large surface area of the bubbles carrying alcohol molecules to the stomach wall.

Personal variation. Marked variation exists in the rate of absorption, including the build of a person, the length of the intestinal canal and the size of the stomach (both related to area of absorptive surface) and other unknown idiosyncratic factors, such as the proportion of alcohol which passes unabsorbed through the intestinal canal. Habitual drinkers appear to have the ability to destroy alcohol more quickly.

All these factors make it impossible accurately to calculate the blood level at a certain time after a certain amount of drink, but a generalisation would be that after a single 'dose' of alcohol on an empty stomach, a maximum blood level is reached within 30–60 minutes, though, if the dose is large, this time may be prolonged up to a couple of hours. If taken as spirits the level will peak rapidly, but diluted drink, such as beer or alcoholic drink on a full stomach, will be partly eliminated during the period of absorption and thus a much lower, longer peak will occur.

Elimination of the alcohol

Once absorbed, the alcohol will be progressively lost because of:

(a) excretion in the breath, urine and sweat; this amounts to less than 10% of the total;

(b) destruction by chemical processes in the tissues, mainly the liver, accounting for the major part of elimination.

These processes begin as soon as the first alcohol appears in the blood from absorption, so the maximum blood level is a dynamic equilibrium between the rates of absorption and elimination. Naturally, further intake of drink after the first will escalate the absorption phase and will soon overtake the maximum rate of elimination, which is generally taken to be about 9–15 ml per hour (about the amount in a small whisky) and a figure of about 15 mg per 100 ml of blood is an acceptable rule of thumb for the drop in blood alcohol per hour once absorption has ceased, though more recent research favours a figure of 18 mg/100 ml/hour.

However, this figure is by no means sacrosanct and must vary greatly in different persons, especially habitual drinkers, who are able to eliminate alcohol much faster. Normal rates of between 11–25 mg/100 ml/hour have been found experimentally and it is said that the rate is especially irregular during the first few hours after the cessation of drinking – the period in which most medico-legal interest lies.

Chronic alcoholics (not intermittent 'binge' drinkers) can eliminate much faster, even up to 40 mg/100 ml/hour.

Alcohol diffuses evenly throughout all the water in the body. It attains a higher level in the urine, due to selective withdrawal of water by the kidneys. The excess is in the ratio of between 1.2:1 to 1.4:1, a mean of 1.3:1 being usually quoted.

Naturally, where urine alcohol is used as a quantitative measure, any stored urine in the bladder before drinking began must be emptied to avoid a dilution effect: hence the requirement under the Road Traffic Act for a second sample to be collected after a minimum of 20 minutes. Though a level of 107 mg/100 ml is accepted as the minimum level for conviction under this Act, urine/blood ratios are not constant enough for the use of urine as a reliable indicator of the blood level.

Breath alcohol is a much better index, as there is an immediate equilibrium established between blood and 'alveolar air' – air in the smallest air sacs of the lungs; 2,100 ml of alveolar air contain the same amount of alcohol as 1.0 ml of blood, though accuracy is reduced by the dilution with dead-space air from the large bronchial tubes which has not been equilibrated with blood and also by the change in temperature of the air as it is expired. However, many countries accept the ratio as good enough for the establishment of minimum blood concentrations for road traffic testing.

Because alcohol diffuses into all the body water, but not into fat, women attain a higher blood concentration (20–30% greater) than men, for a given dose of alcohol in persons of the same weight. This does not depend on overt obesity, but on the 'pannunculus adiposus', a layer of fat under the skin.

Because of all these variables, it is not possible accurately to back-calculate either the amount of alcohol taken from a knowledge of the blood alcohol, nor the likely blood level to be expected from the drinking of certain amounts of liquor. Different persons will have different biochemical responses to alcohol and even the same person will have different responses at different times, especially in relation to their dietary habits. Therefore the over-optimistic tables of conversion which were formerly relied upon cannot be justified, except as the roughest of guides where large potential errors may have to be admitted.

Even more than the unforeseeable biochemical results, the physiological and behavioural sequelae cannot be related with any accuracy to the amount of drink taken.

The physiological effects of alcohol

Alcohol is entirely depressant in effect and the apparent stimulatory action of small-to-moderate amounts is due to depression of the inhibitory control of the highest centres in the brain, giving rise to the social lubricant of loquaciousness and other apparently stimulant effects. 'Sobriety disguiseth man' (wrote de Quincey), but once this removal of inhibition is past, a further rise of alcohol levels causes progressive descent through stupor to coma, and finally death from paralysis of the lower brain functions of breathing control.

It is impossible to relate behaviour to levels of blood alcohol, except in the very broadest terms, but judgment, co-ordination and reaction time may be impaired by low levels in the region of 20–40 mg/100 ml. A number of jurisdictions have minimum levels for motor vehicle driving much lower than the British 80 mg/100 ml, which at the time of writing is under consideration for lowering to 50 mg.

On ordinary clinical testing, as opposed to sophisticated techniques, few signs can be detected below about 80–100 mg/100 ml, though many people may show euphoria, garrulousness, loss of concentration, etc, after reaching 50–70 mg/100 ml.

From 100–150 mg/100 ml, flushed face, poor sensory perception and slight incoordination may be expected and from this range up to 250 mg/100 ml, the whole range of behavioural abnormalities and progressive signs will be present.

These include impaired mental ability, yawning and sighing, reddened eyes, tremor and incoordination, impaired gait and staggering, dilated pupils, heavy breathing and possibly vomiting. However, great variation occurs in different people and in the same person at different times. General health and specific illness can markedly affect the level of impairment.

During the Blennerhassett research before the introduction of evidential breath testing, it was found that most volunteers became nauseous and sick by 150 mg/100 ml.

Over 200 mg/100 ml, severe drunkenness is likely to be present, except in habitual drinkers who may appear relatively normal up to very high blood levels, though objective signs are usually present.

Vomiting, incoherence, circulatory collapse with pallor and sweating lead up to the dangerous levels of 350–400 mg/100 ml, where coma may ensue and death can take place at any point from here onwards.

Occasionally, levels of 500–600 mg/100 ml may be seen in habituated drinkers, though death is likely at these levels, in spite of many reported exceptions, which can exceed 1000 mg/100 ml.

Natural disease may mimic or exaggerate the effects of alcohol. The following non-exhaustive list comprises the most common conditions:

Carbon monoxide poisoning, especially in motor vehicles.

Diabetes: either high or low blood sugar states. The latter, due to excess insulin-like drugs or loss of a meal, may be the closest mimic of all to drunkenness.

A cerebral vascular defect, such as a 'stroke' or incipient vascular catastrophe.

Head injury, often related either to a traffic accident or some assault where intoxication may be co-existent.

Epilepsy, including the pre- or post-fit state.

Kidney or liver failure and other toxic biochemical states.

Intoxication with drugs other than alcohol, especially narcotics, barbiturates, other hypnotics, antihistamines, etc.

Numerous neurological and psychiatric conditions.

ALCOHOL (METHYL)

A common industrial chemical, which has often given rise to illness and death when drunk either accidentally or deliberately. It is broken down in the body much more slowly than ethanol and can thus accumulate even from a moderate intake.

Some chronic abusers drink methylated spirit, often flavoured with cheap wine (red Biddy, etc) and appear to be less sensitive to its toxic effects. Methylated spirit is duty-exempt ethyl alcohol denatured by the addition of about 9% methyl alcohol, together with offensive-tasting substances such as naphtha, pyridine and a violet dye.

Industrial and surgical spirit consist of ethyl alcohol and about 5% methyl, without the other disgustants.

Pure methyl alcohol has been used as a motor antifreeze and deaths have occurred from its drinking, between 60–200 ml being a fatal dose. Lower blood levels than ethyl alcohol are dangerous or fatal, 80 mg/100 ml being a dangerous level. It persists in the blood for several days, being excreted and destroyed much more slowly than ethanol. The general effects are similar, but it has a specific effect on the optic nerves, causing failure of vision and sometimes permanent blindness. Muscle weakness, cramps, abdominal pains, depression of breathing and toxic damage to liver and kidneys are characteristic.

AMNESIA

Loss of memory, either transient or permanent. An extremely common defence to criminal actions, obviously over-used in proportion to the amount of true amnesia seen in clinical practice.

Post-concussional (retrograde) amnesia. There is a delay in imprinting sensations and experiences into the memory. This is a protective mechanism to prevent a later disturbing appreciation of traumatic events, for example, the memory of being hit by a car. Thus after recovery from any concussion due to head injury, there is a period of amnesia for events prior to the concussion, which may vary from a few seconds to a few hours. This is the most common type of genuine loss of memory. It may also be seen after electric shock.

Alcoholic amnesia is very common, occurring in between 60–80% of chronic alcoholics, as well as the acutely drunk.

Epilepsy (qv).

Many toxic, infective and drug-induced causes.

Hypoglycaemia. Low blood sugar, either as an inherent state or in uncontrolled diabetics on insulin.

Failure of registration of sensation as in (a) above, but due to emotion, fear, repression of guilt, hysteria and numerous psychiatric conditions.

Amnesia is not likely to be due to organic causes if it is an isolated instance.

AMPHETAMINES
(see also 'Ecstasy')

Drugs originally developed to dispel fatigue by stimulating brain activity: later used in obesity to reduce appetite. The side effects and misuse by addiction led to amphetamine use being abandoned in legitimate medicine and it is no longer prescribed or legally manufactured in Britain. Now a well known illicit drug, often known as 'speed'. Its clandestine manufacture is relatively simple, as is its even more popular derivative 'ecstasy'.

Though rarely fatal except in large doses, amphetamine can lead to marked psychological disturbances. The acute phases of ingestion show restlessness, insomnia, excitability, impaired judgment and distorted sense of time. Psychotic states, similar to schizophrenia, may ensue with continued usage and withdrawal may bring depression and suicidal tendencies.

A cyclic misuse is common, in which the stimulant effect of amphetamine is alternated with barbiturates, dependence forming to both substances. As well as amphetamine itself, usually in the form of its sulphate, a wide range of chemicals with similar properties exists, including methylamphetamine, dextro-amphetamine, methyl phenidate, phenylephrine and many others, all of which may be misused.

All these drugs produce a rise in blood pressure, which may induce a sudden cardiovascular catastrophe, such as a cerebral haemorrhage. Though rarely producing direct fatal poisoning, 30 mg has been reported as causing death, though the toleration of addiction may allow several hundred milligrams per day to be ingested.

ANAESTHETIC DEATHS

Usually a misnomer, as most deaths are associated with an anaesthetic, rather than due to it.

Deaths during or soon after surgical procedures may be due to:

(a) the disease or injury for which the operation was performed, especially if the operation was a 'heroic' attempt at saving the life;

(b) a poor preoperative condition of the patient: usually the operation will again be an urgent procedure, otherwise it would have been delayed until the patient's condition could be improved;

(c) other concomitant diseases, such as heart or lung complaints, other than the condition for which the operation is being performed. Again, the situation would usually be urgent enough for this risk to be taken, after a 'risk-benefit' assessment;

(d) some accident or other defect in the surgical technique, rather than an anaesthetic mishap. Such a defect need not be negligent, for example, where anatomical or other complications exist;

(e) a true anaesthetic death is due to the effects of the anaesthetic agent itself – relatively rare – or, more often, to a defect in its administration.

Disease or injury cause the largest proportion of deaths associated with surgical operations. Surgical mishaps include gross haemorrhage from slipped ligatures, uncontrolled oozing and damage to blood vessels from clamps and sharp instruments. Accidental perforation of an organ, removal of the wrong organ or part of an organ and air embolism (qv) also contribute to this group.

Deaths during surgical operations, or other diagnostic procedures requiring an anaesthetic, are customarily referred to the coroner in England and Wales if they occur during the anaesthetic or within 24 hours of its administration. In Scotland, there is a statutory duty to report 'anaesthetic' deaths to the Procurator Fiscal, by means of a completed standard questionnaire.

Other jurisdictions have varying, but broadly similar requirements for cases in which surgical procedures and anaesthetics may have contributed to death.

It should be noted that the '24 hour' rule in England and Wales is not exclusory, in that any death, however long after a medical or surgical intervention, where a doctor thinks that the procedure may have contributed, should be reported to the coroner, for example, a pulmonary embolism (qv) two weeks after operation.

True anaesthetic deaths and mishaps vary according to the method employed.

Local anaesthesia

This depends upon the deadening of nerves supplying the operation zone by the injection of a cocaine-like substance or a synthetic homologue. Widely used in dentistry and minor operations, but increasingly advocated for major surgery because of the speed of recovery and lack of complications seen in general anaesthesia. To reduce the spread of the local anaesthetic beyond the operative zone, a substance such as adrenaline is usually added to constrict the blood vessels of the area – this may give rise to dangers in itself. Dangers of local anaesthesia include 'hypersensitivity' to the drugs, especially if they diffuse away from the operative area. It is said that most alleged hypersensitivity is really overdosage, but there are undoubtedly cases in which an individual idiosyncrasy can give rise to a severe or fatal reaction.

Straight overdosage of the agent or vasoconstrictive additive is probably the most common hazard: accidental injection into a blood vessel, instead of into the tissues or nerve sheath, may also give sudden death or dramatic adverse reactions, usually by poisoning the respiratory centres in the brain or the heart. Where local anaesthetics are sprayed or injected onto highly absorptive surfaces such as the interior of the nose or throat, the sudden absorption may again give rise to serious or fatal effects.

In essence, the dangers usually consist of sudden over-absorption of either an excessive dose or of too rapid absorption of a dose which would have been safe if spread over a longer period. The overall rate of complications from local anaesthesia is about 1:2000, rarely fatal in nature.

Spinal and epidural anaesthesia

A variety of local anaesthesia, where the drug is either injected into the fluid around the lower spinal cord or into the nerve roots outside the dura, the sheath around the spinal cord (epidural anaesthesia). Either method achieves sensory numbing of the lower part of the body; commonly used in childbirth.

The dangers of true spinal anaesthesia are that the agent may diffuse upwards and involve vital centres in the upper part of the cord: it thus cannot be used for operations above the abdomen. It also paralyses the nerves controlling blood vessel tension and may lead to dangers from low blood pressure.

Other dangers exist from contamination of syringes and apparatus by sterilising and cleansing agents such as phenols and detergents, which can cause permanent paraplegia and tetraplegia (paralysis of two or four limbs) or even death. A number of older litigation cases arising from this cause led to spinal anaesthesia falling into relative disrepute for some years.

To avoid these dangers, epidural anaesthesia was developed, especially for childbirth. The dangers are less but still exist, being mainly that of permanent nerve paralysis, the risks of which are calculated to be about 1 in every 10,000 anaesthetics.

General anaesthesia

The abolition of pain by producing total unconsciousness. Basically a controlled narcosis which paralyses the upper centres of the brain by administering substances which reduce the oxygen uptake, for example, barbiturates or nitrous oxide gases. Numerous substances are now used, for example, halothane, cyclopropane, trichlorethylene, etc.

All anaesthetics have risks but, relative to the millions given each year, the dangers are small and are usually due to factors other than the inherent toxicity of the actual anaesthetic agent itself. The greatest danger is 'hypoxia' or 'anoxia', that is, a reduction or absence of oxygen supply to the patient due to negligent administration or equipment failure. This may lead to death or permanent brain damage, with a vegetable-like survivor.

Such mishaps are usually due to an error in administration or to malfunction of the equipment, such as a wrongly connected or filled gas cylinder, incorrect or blocked tube connections or defective supervision by the anaesthetist.

During anaesthesia, the autonomic nervous system is depressed less than other parts. This leads to an increased sensitivity to vagal stimuli, which may lead to sudden heart stoppage (see 'Vagal inhibition'). This is more likely to occur if there is any degree of oxygen lack. Such stimuli might arise from errors in introducing tubes into the air passages, vomit entering the air passages and other anaesthetic techniques. The detailed discussion of the many risks is a matter for expert anaesthetic opinion, but the following particular hazards must be mentioned.

Halothane anaesthesia, though a widely used and very effective technique, has acquired a reputation for causing liver damage in a small proportion of cases, especially where several separate anaesthetics using halothane have been administered, even widely spaced in time. A number of surveys have been carried out on its use, but with no constancy of agreement on the risks.

Malignant hyperpyrexia (qv) may also occur after certain anaesthetics and relaxant agents, including halothane and suxamethonium.

Ether and chloroform, now of historical interest only in most parts of the world, had the dangers of inflammability for the former and liver damage for the latter.

Cyclopropane is a powerful and useful gas, but again has the dangers of fire and explosion.

A number of anaesthetic agents are directly toxic to the heart muscle and may precipitate irregularities and fatal arrest, though these major complications are rare except when administered by inexperienced staff who fail to monitor and anticipate the various permutations of danger signs. A large British survey (Lunn and Mushin) indicated that the majority of deaths was due to inexperience of the anaesthetist and failure to adopt proper precautions when indicated. It has been calculated that deaths associated with general anaesthesia comprise about 0.2–0.6% of administrations, but that those attributable directly to the anaesthetic procedure rather than other factors are only between 0.03 and 0.1%.

The autopsy on a death associated with anaesthesia is often unhelpful in providing positive information, except where death has been due to factors other than the anaesthetic, for example, surgical complications. Toxicological analysis for residual anaesthetic agents is rarely useful and is difficult to interpret. The pathologist can usually assist by excluding certain factors, but the overall investigation of an anaesthetic death depends heavily upon clinical records and a review of the procedure by an experienced anaesthetist.

ANEURYSMS

A swelling on a blood vessel, usually an artery. It arises at a point of weakness, due to the internal blood pressure distending the vessel wall, much as a motor inner-tube will swell at one point if overinflated. Beyond a threshold point, the swelling will burst, causing an aneurysmal rupture, often a fatal event.

Figure 14:   Types of arterial aneurysm

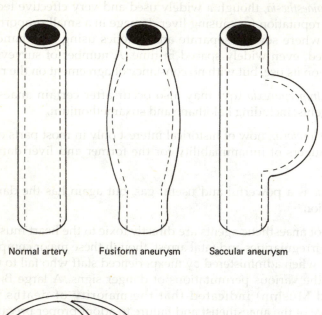

Normal artery   Fusiform aneurysm   Saccular aneurysm

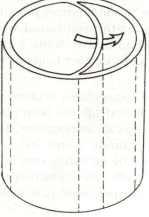

Dissecting aneurysm
(split in wall)

Berry (cerebral)
aneurysm of
Circle of Willis

Causes

Atheromatous degeneration. The most common variety, most frequently in the aorta (qv). Due to degeneration of the wall from atheroma, athero-sclerosis or 'hardening of the arteries' – all synonyms for the common fibro-fatty breakdown of the wall. Aneurysms of the aorta may rupture and form a huge haemorrhage in the back of the abdomen, with often rapidly fatal results. A slow leak may be repaired surgically, by a synthetic bypass or graft transplantation.

Dissecting aneurysm. Softening of the central zone of the aortic wall due to 'medio-necrosis', a degenerative condition. A potential space may form, like the filling in a sandwich. If blood under high pressure finds it way into this space (usually by tearing through a patch of atheroma in the lining) then a cleavage plane will open and fill with blood. This may strip the aortic wall from pelvis to heart and kill the patient by bursting through into the pericardium (bag around the heart) causing a haemopericardium or cardiac tamponade, which rapidly embarrasses the heart's action by preventing filling of the chambers.

Syphilitic aneurysm. A complication of tertiary syphilis, now very rare in Britain due to the treating of primary and secondary syphilis. Almost always affects the arch of the aorta and may produce a large bulge which may rupture.

Traumatic aneurysm. Due to firearm, explosive or other wounds damaging an arterial wall, often in a limb. Sometimes a false connection is made with an adjacent vein, causing an arterio-venous aneurysm or anastomosis.

Mycotic aneurysm. Due to an infection, usually blood-borne, damaging the wall.

Berry, congenital or cerebral aneurysm (see also 'Subarachnoid haemorrhage'). This is a small swelling on an artery at the base of the brain on the Circle of Willis (qv). Rupture is a common cause of sudden headache, collapse and death in young and middle-aged adults. Though called 'congenital', the aneurysms are not present at birth, but develop as age and blood pressure increase. They arise at points of weakness in the structure of the wall of brain arteries, usually at junctions. The relationship of exertion, trauma and alcohol in rupture of a berry aneurysm has profound medico-legal connotations.

AORTA

The main artery of the body, leading out of the heart to supply all tissues. Shaped like a round handled walking stick, it begins at the aortic valve at the upper border of the heart, behind the upper part of the breast bone. It curves backwards and downwards to run along the front of the spine in the chest, penetrates the diaphragm to enter the back of the abdomen and divides into two large branches to the legs, at a level just below the umbilicus.

Figure 15:   Position of aorta

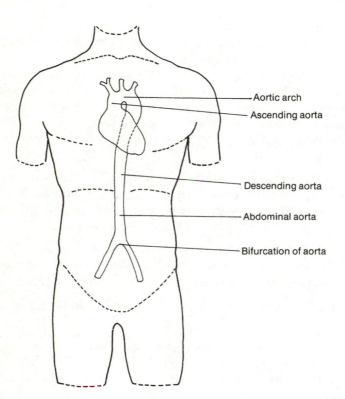

Medico-legal importance

Stab wounds of the chest may perforate the aorta, leading to rapid death unless surgical repair is possible. On the right side of the upper part of the breast bone (sternum), the aorta is very near the surface and here even a small penknife can cause a fatal wound. As the pressure in the aorta rises to 120 mm mercury with each heart beat (and over 200 mm mercury in persons with hypertension), any defect in the wall will bleed torrentially and rapidly fill either the sac around the lung (pleural cavity) or the bag around the heart (pericardium), causing a cardiac tamponade. Stab wounds of the chest may only bleed internally and several pints may fill the chest cavity without any significant amount leaking externally.

Diseased swellings of the aorta, called 'aneurysms' (qv) are common causes of natural sudden death when they burst.

In traffic accidents, in occupants in motor cars, a severe deceleration injury may lead to aortic tearing, which is often the cause of death. In such a whiplash, the spine is violently flexed and extended (bent in a forward and backwards direction) and the aorta may be ripped as it follows this distortion. Another mechanism may be the abrupt traction of the heart on the root of the aorta during violent deceleration. Where the descending aorta joins the spine (at the level of the junction of the curved arch of the aorta with the straight section) the tethering of the straight part to the spine may lead to transverse horizontal tears in the lining and other layers of the aortic wall. These may be multiple and appear as rungs of a ladder when viewed from the inside. The full thickness of the aortic wall may be torn, in which case the blood under high pressure will leak out into the surrounding body cavities, usually the pleural space in the chest.

ARM-LOCK DEATHS

See 'Neck-hold deaths'.

ARTERIES

Vessels supplying oxygenated blood to the tissues (with the exception of the pulmonary arteries which convey blood from the heart to the lungs and are thin-walled as the pressure is relatively low). Arteries are thick-walled to resist high pressure within, which varies between 70–120 mm mercury in the normal person (see 'Blood pressure').

The arterial wall contains muscle and elastic fibres to accommodate pulsation at every heart beat. The vessels all originate from the aorta (qv) and branch progressively down to the smallest branches or 'arterioles', which are microscopic in size, but still retain elastic fibres. From these the final distributing branches arise, the capillaries.

In the condition of 'hypertension' or high blood pressure, the arterial walls thicken to resist the increased internal strain.

Some arteries, notably the carotids in the neck, have intrinsic nerve endings to detect and measure pressure changes These have great forensic importance, as external pressure, as in manual strangulation (qv), may cause sudden death from heart stoppage.

Tearing or laceration of a large artery causes torrential haemorrhage and death if not rapidly staunched. The time of survival depends on the size of the artery, the size and nature of the defect and the age and condition of the victim. Paradoxically, if an artery is completely transected, the bleeding may be less than if partly torn, as the severed vessel can retract due to its muscle and elastic tissue, thus reducing or even stopping the rate of blood loss.

ASBESTOSIS

See 'Pneumoconiosis'.

ASPHYXIA

An unsatisfactory term which has come to mean 'deprivation of air', though the literal meaning is 'absence of pulsation', which in some ways is often nearer the truth. More exact modern terms for lack of air (essentially oxygen) are 'hypoxia' for partial, and 'anoxia' for total deprivation.

In a medico-legal context, true asphyxia refers to mechanical deprivation of air by obstruction of the gas exchange system.

May be due to:

(a) *lack of oxygen in the surrounding gaseous environment,* for example, a closed room with a gas fire or a ship's tank that has been sealed for a long period (see 'Suffocation');

(b) *blockage of the external breathing orifices* (see 'Smothering');

(c) *blockage of the internal air passages* (see 'Choking');

(d) *pressure on the neck* which may block the air passages (see 'Strangulation', 'Throttling'); or

(e) *fixation of the chest* preventing breathing movements (see 'Traumatic asphyxia').

Other causes of asphyxia, not usually involved in forensic issues, are as follows:

Disease of the lungs, such as extensive pneumonia, industrial lung diseases such as pneumoconiosis or some infant conditions which prevent gas transfer across the lung membranes.

Figure 17:   Causes of mechanical asphyxia

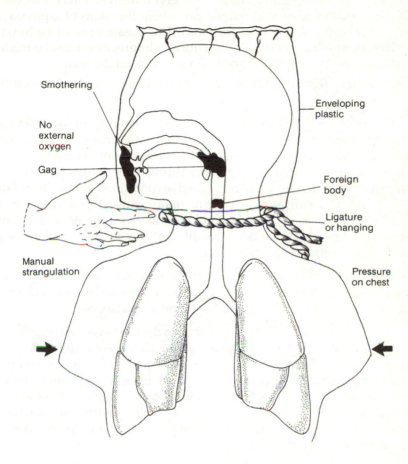

Chronic heart failure, which fail to shift the oxygen-laden blood around the body.

Severe anaemias and other blood disorders which cause a deficiency in the oxygen-carrying capacity of the blood.

Some forms of poisoning which either prevent oxygen-carrying by the blood (see 'Carbon monoxide') or prevent uptake of oxygen by the body cells (for example, cyanide).

However, mechanical obstructions provide most medico-legal problems, discussed under the various headings given above. There has been a considerable shift of opinion in recent years about the 'signs of asphyxia' and the true role of asphyxia in these conditions. The 'classic signs' of asphyxia are now suspect and in many cases a very critical interpretation must be made, as artefacts and non-specific appearances can easily cloud the issues.

The 'classical' signs of asphyxia, both in the living and dead, are outlined below.

Congestion (reddening of skin and tissues) and *cyanosis* (purplish coloration). This can be due to both blockage of veins preventing blood returning to the heart, as in pressure around the neck, and to depletion of oxygen in the blood which has been prevented from passing through the lungs. However, it is such a non-specific finding (seen in congestive conditions such as heart failure and very commonly after deaths from many causes) that alone, it is of negligible significance. Above a strangulation mark on the neck, it has more significance if the rest of the body is pale, but this is due to obstruction of returning blood, rather than oxygen lack.

Fluidity of the blood and over-distension of the right side of the heart; these are utterly non-specific signs which may be related to many modes of death and even to post-mortem changes – of no significance whatsoever.

Petechial haemorrhages (qv). These may occur in the face, eyes and membranous coverings of heart and especially lungs (where they were formerly known as Tardieu's spots). Many 'petechiae' are post-mortem artefacts and many apparent petechiae are not haemorrhages at all. Even when genuine, they can be seen in greater or lesser numbers on the lungs in many autopsies and their significance is now very much in doubt, unless numerous and when associated with other signs of mechanical asphyxia. Alone, they are meaningless as an indicator of asphyxia.

Bleeding from nostrils or ears. This is a consequence of raised pressure in the veins of the head after constriction of the neck and is not related to asphyxia itself.

It will be seen that most of the 'classical signs', which veteran US pathologist Lester Adelson calls the 'redundant quintet', are signs of raised venous pressure from pressure on the neck. The most florid signs occur in 'traumatic asphyxia', where venous return is prevented by fixation of chest movements. Most other signs are due to strangulation and the signs are therefore due not to oxygen lack, but to raised pressure in obstructed veins.

Adelson, whose account of the forensic interpretation in his book *Pathology of Homicide* (1974, Springfield, Illinois: Charles Thomas), is the best exposition of the subject, admirably summarises thus:

Figure 16:   Classical features in strangulation

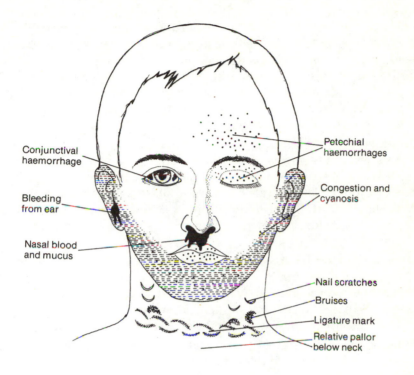

Conjunctival haemorrhage

Petechial haemorrhages

Bleeding from ear

Congestion and cyanosis

Nasal blood and mucus

Nail scratches

Bruises

Ligature mark

Relative pallor below neck

The general signs of asphyxia, either singly or in combination, are merely consistent with, though not diagnostic of asphyxia. To establish that death occurred from mechanical asphyxia, reliable local indications of lethal obstructing trauma must be demonstrable. In other words, the pathologist must find unequivocal evidence of the means by which the airway was obstructed.

The time taken for 'asphyxia' to occur is a matter of controversy and uninformed theorising. At least half the cases of strangulation die quickly with a pale face, due to rapid, even almost instantaneous death from carotid artery pressure (see 'Strangulation').

If death is due to 'pure' asphyxia, such as an irrespirable atmosphere or a plastic bag over the head, without the added factor of pressure on blood vessels, then the time factor is a matter of conjecture, as no controls have been measured in the human for obvious reasons.

To attain the signs of venous obstruction described above, probably a minimum of 15–30 seconds unremitting pressure is necessary. This will produce congestion, blueness and small haemorrhages in the eyes. Pure blockage of the windpipe or larynx is hardly possible without pressure on blood vessels, so 'pure' asphyxia from neck pressure is not seen. As breath can be held for several minutes, death could not occur from pure asphyxial neck pressure for at least a minute, but this is of little practical moment in strangulation, because of the co-existence of the other factors which can precipitate death at any time from zero seconds to the full blown asphyxial picture of congestion and bleeding.

In suffocation and choking, where external pressure is not a factor, then pure asphyxia can occur, but again they produce a very variable time scale. Many sudden obstructions of the air passages cause instant death from cardiac arrest (for example, café coronary (qv)), as can obstruction of the face with plastic bags. At the other end of the spectrum, survival from complete obstruction has occurred after three, four or even more minutes, where relief has been forthcoming.

Thus it is impossible to be dogmatic about the length of time required to produce an asphyxial death, a matter often led in criminal trials where the determination of an assailant may be an important issue in the prosecution or defence. All that is safe to say in medical evidence is that where signs of pressure on the neck or obstruction of the air passages are present, then:

(a) if the face is pale and there are no small haemorrhages in the eyes or skin, death must have been very rapid due to cardiac arrest;

(b) if congestive/asphyxial signs are present, then obstruction or pressure must have been maintained for at least a quarter of a minute. This estimate is arbitrary, but is a reasonable minimum time.

ASPIRIN POISONING

Acetyl-salicylic acid is one of the oldest and most widely used analgesics (pain relievers). Though generally very safe, it is toxic in large amounts and some persons have an idiosyncratic sensitivity to normal doses (varying from a rash to sudden death).

Recent research has shown that aspirin has a mild tranquillising effect as well as analgesic: it also has the effect of reducing blood-clotting ability, which may lead to dangerous bleeding from stomach ulcers or even from an intact stomach.

Forensically, aspirin was formerly a common suicidal agent in Britain but fatalities are now rarely seen. It is still used as a suicidal gesture method, especially in teenage girls. It also causes accidental poisoning in children.

The medicinal dose in adults is 1–2 tablets of 300 mg each, but far larger doses are given for rheumatic and arthritic conditions. The lethal dose varies enormously and some persons who swallow a whole bottle of 100 tablets (30 gm) may suffer no more than ringing in the ears. However, this dose may often be fatal, though nausea and vomiting may be self-protective by removing the substance from the stomach.

Deaths in children have been reported after only a few tablets. The clinical symptoms of aspirin toxicity include nausea, tinnitus (ear ringing), sweating, confusion and shock. The breathing may first be stimulated, then depressed. Bleeding from the stomach or bowel may occur. Severe acidosis of the blood, which might mimic diabetic acidosis, can develop.

The blood level of toxic doses is also variable, but above 50–90 mg/100 ml the danger of death exists, though patients on long term salicylate treatment may tolerate similar levels without ill effect. A particular danger of aspirin overdosage is delayed death. A person may present at hospital with minimal symptoms, such as tinnitus, and be discharged from casualty after examination, only to die at home during the next few hours or even a day later. This has been cause for negligence allegations against doctors, and all cases of undoubted aspirin overdosage should be admitted for overnight observation.

Autopsy appearances may reveal gastric irritation and perhaps signs of bleeding in the stomach lining. Other organs and serous membranes may also have haemorrhagic manifestations, but nothing specific may be found in examination, the diagnosis resting upon the history and analyses of body fluids.

AUTOPSY

Now the most common name for a full post-mortem examination by a pathologist. The latter term is still very frequent in Britain, but elsewhere is not synonymous with an autopsy, as it may mean merely an external scrutiny of a body.

'Autopsy' strictly means 'seeing for oneself'. A better term is 'necropsy', an examination of the dead, a word gaining acceptance, especially in America.

An autopsy is performed to achieve one or more of the following objectives:

(a) to determine the cause of death;

(b) to determine the nature and extent of disease;

(c) to record and describe any injuries and to offer an interpretation as to their mode of infliction;

(d) to estimate the time since death;

(e) to assist in identifying the deceased where this is in doubt;

(f) to estimate the expectation of life in certain cases where injuries have prematurely terminated life;

(g) in the new-born, to determine whether live birth occurred; and

(h) to obtain samples and fluids for analysis and other ancillary investigations.

The law concerning permission for autopsy varies widely in different jurisdictions, but basically there are two types: *clinical or medico-legal*.

The *clinical autopsy* is to investigate the extent of disease and the effectiveness of treatment and often to utilise the results in medical audit or research. This type of autopsy almost invariably requires some form of consent, either ante mortem from the deceased or post-mortem from the relatives (see 'Human Tissue Act 1961').

The *medico-legal or forensic autopsy* is at the behest of law enforcement authorities where the cause of death is unnatural, suspicious or unknown. Here, permission is not required in most jurisdictions, the autopsy being ordered by legal authority. In England and Wales, this authority is contained in the various Coroner's Acts and Rules (qv).

BARBITURATES

A group of hypnotic drugs used to induce sleep or sometimes anaesthesia, or to sedate and quieten agitated or epileptic patients. Formerly prescribed in vast quantities as 'sleeping pills', but active restraints by doctors and safer alternatives have made their legitimate prescribing rare in Britain, although they are easily available on the illicit market.

There are four types of barbiturate (see below), related to their speed of action: all are derivatives of barbitone or barbituric acid.

Long acting, such as barbitone or phenobarbitone. Therapeutic dose of phenobarbitone is about 50–100 mg, fatal dose upwards of 1–4 g, but with great variation. Blood levels in coma and death are of the order of 5–8 mg/100 ml.

Intermediate acting, such as amylobarbitone, butobarbitone and allobarbitone. Therapeutic dose 50–200 mg, dangerous dose around 1–2 g. Blood levels in fatal or comatose cases between 2–5 mg/100 ml.

Short acting, such as pentobarbitone and cyclobarbitone. Therapeutic doses between 200–400 mg, dangerous dose about 1 g. Blood levels in coma about 1 mg/100 ml.

Ultra short acting drugs given as intravenous injection for induction of general anaesthesia or short anaesthetics for dental and minor operations. Examples are thiopentone (Pentothal) and methohexobarbitone.

The short acting barbiturates, such as cyclobarbitone and quinalbarbitone, may cause death from heart failure (ventricular fibrillation) within 20 minutes in large doses. Other drugs cause extended coma which may result in death from respiratory depression. In long coma, bronchopneumonia may be the mode of death: blisters on the skin are sometimes seen (see 'Blisters').

BESTIALITY

Sexual connection with animals. In English law, it is an offence under the Sexual Offences Act 1956 and can be committed by either man or woman, if intercourse *per vaginam* occurs.

In Scotland, this is a common law crime and appears to be applicable only to men.

Medical aspects are similar to those relevant in rape, but modified by physical disparity depending upon the size of the animals concerned. Forensic science evidence is more important than medical aspects; it is concerned with the detection of human and animal semen and blood, species differentiation of animal blood, semen, hairs, faeces, etc. Both serological and microscopic testing used, especially DNA.

BITE MARKS

Present on the skin in some cases of assault, especially sexual and in child abuse.

In sexual assaults, there may be actual bites or less severe 'love bites', the latter often taking the form of multiple suction marks (a shower of small pin-head haemorrhages sometimes in the shape of pursed lips). Actual bites may be deep and sometimes sadistic. Common sites are the side of the neck and the breasts. Nipples may be injured or even bitten off.

The teeth in any bites may cause bruising, abrasion or lacerations depending upon the force used. Bites may occasionally be inflicted on the thighs, abdomen, buttocks or vulva and where more severe than mere sexual enthusiasm, indicate a sadistic element. Increasingly, they are being seen in sporting injuries, especially to ears in rugby matches. Occasionally, police officers are bitten during attempted arrests.

Bites are not infrequently seen in battered child syndrome, usually inflicted by the mother. They may be on any part of the body, but especially arm, leg, buttock or cheek. Usually not as severe as in sexual cases, but may leave a clear imprint of the teeth.

In any bite mark, observation and measurement may match up with the dentition of the assailant or exclude alleged assailants. In child abuse syndrome, the excuse is sometimes made that the bite was due to a pet dog or another child of the family. The pattern of the bite can be compared with the spacing and shape of the suspect's teeth.

Photography of the bite is essential before it fades, as it is to have an examination performed by a dentist skilled in forensic work (a forensic odontologist). Casts (rubber or PVC, etc) can be made of marks if still palpable. Also swabs of the area may reveal the DNA pattern of the assailant from the saliva.

Occasionally, bite marks may have a forensic aspect if left in objects at the scene of a crime, for example, in cheese, apples, chewing gum, etc, which again may help to identify the culprit.

BLACK EYE

Bruising in the loose tissues of the upper and/or lower eyelids, medically termed a 'peri-orbital haematoma'.

Most often due to a direct blow in the eye, frequently from a fist. Unlikely to occur from a fall onto a flat surface, as the arch of the eyebrow, cheek bone and nose protect the eye itself. However, if there are abrasions, bruises or lacerations on these surrounding areas, it is possible that a black eye can occur from impact, including a fall, with an object larger than a fist.

Fist blows causing a black eye frequently also damage the skin over the upper edge of the cheek bone, the nose (especially the bridge, which may be fractured) and the eyebrow, which may be split.

As well as bruising in the lids, there may be marked swelling of the tissues, which can close the eye. This does not appear immediately, as can the bruising, but may take minutes or hours to develop. The bruising may increase over hours, but some is always apparent immediately after injury.

Figure 18:   **Production of black eye**

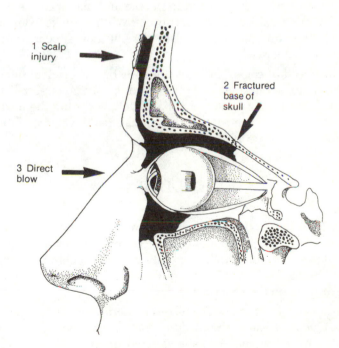

Though a black eye usually heals completely, there can be internal damage to the eye, such as a detached retina or dislocated lens or haemorrhages into the vitreous. These are more common in children, as part of child abuse syndrome (qv).

A kick in the eye region can obviously cause a black eye, but there is usually more surrounding damage than from a fist blow, such as laceration of the cheek and eyebrow and perhaps fractures of the facial skeleton.

A black eye can occur from causes other than a direct blow in the eye:

(a) A bruise or laceration of the forehead or scalp above the eye may allow blood to track downwards under the scalp. It flows by gravity over the eyebrow ridge and can then accumulate in the loose tissues of the eyelids. This process takes hours or a day or more to complete.

(b) A severe head injury, especially a fall onto the back of the head, may cause a fracture of the front of the base of the skull (see 'Contre-coup'). Blood can then leak down into the interior of the eye sockets from damaged brain membranes and appear in the white of the eye and the eyelids, causing blackening and often swelling of the lids. In such cases, the victim is usually unconscious.

A black eye, from whatever cause, will undergo the usual colour changes of any bruise. When fresh, it is dark red to purple and may increase in intensity in the first day or so as more blood accumulates – the bruise 'coming out'. In fatal cases, in common with bruises elsewhere, it may appear more marked one or more days after death.

In life, the speed of colour changes depends on the original intensity and individual variations, but a green-brown colour may be expected in two to three days, passing through paler green and yellow during the next week or so until fading occurs. The rate of these changes is very variable and is markedly slowed in old people (see 'Bruises').

BLADDER

The urinary bladder, in the lower abdomen, behind the pelvic bone, is a roughly spherical organ which can enlarge to many times its empty size by virtue of its elastic, muscular wall. Normally protected behind the pubis, a full bladder can rise to the level of the umbilicus and be vulnerable to rupture from blows or kicks on the abdomen.

Two tubes enter the back of the bladder, the *ureters*, bringing urine from the kidneys. One tube leaves the bladder, the *urethra*, conveying urine to the outside. In the male this may become sheared or ruptured by severe pelvic injury, either pelvic fractures or kicks in the genitals.

BLISTERS

Dome-shaped swellings on the skin, formed in the thickness of the epidermis, the outer layer. They contain fluid, but may be collapsed and empty either during life or after death. Blisters may be formed ante or post-mortem.

Main types of forensic interest

Burns. Blisters of any size may occur in medium-severity burns. Less severe burns do not blister, more severe destroy the skin. Burn blisters may occur before or after death and it is often difficult or impossible to differentiate between them if they occur peri-mortally (at the time of death). This has important forensic importance, related to the possibility of a dead body being disposed of in a fire. Classical differentiation is said to be (a) a red margin to living blister, and (b) fluid containing high concentration of protein if formed during life. In practice, these points may be of little help if death occurred soon after burning.

Electricity. A firm contact electrical mark is usually in the form of a blister, due to the heating effect of the current passing through the high resistance of the skin at the entry point. There is usually no fluid in the blister, which collapses. Often a pale surrounding halo, due to blood vessels constricted by the shock. Microscopic examination of the edge of the blister may show alignment or polarisation of the nuclei of the skin cells, celled 'streaming' due to the passage of electricity, but this may also be seen in purely thermal burns.

Post-mortem decomposition causes blisters in the moist stage of putrefaction. Large areas of skin may rise and become filled with clear bloody fluid. When these burst, there is 'skin slippage' of sheets of outer skin layers. The times at which this occurs is variable, but in average temperate conditions is from one week onwards after death.

'Barbiturate' blisters are a misnomer for those seen in any case of coma. The cause is obscure, but is due partly to gravitational accumulation of fluid due to immobility and partly due to oxygen lack in the skin. As well as drugs inducing long coma, like barbiturates, they may be seen in carbon monoxide poisoning, natural cerebral haemorrhage, etc. Often seen on dependent parts such as buttocks, thighs, calves, loins.

Many diseases give rise to blisters, usually from infections, for example, smallpox, chicken-pox, etc. Also in skin diseases, such as pemphigus. The fluid from contagious diseases is often highly infectious.

BLOOD GROUPS

The forensic use of blood groups and other constituents of blood (especially DNA) fall into two sections: (a) the identification and comparison of blood stains on clothing, weapons, etc; and (b) the investigation of disputed paternity issues.

These topics (together with a few less common uses, such as the identification of parts of fragmented bodies or the separation of new-born infants whose identity is confused in maternity hospitals) constitute the science of 'forensic serology', which has now grown to such complexity that it is a discipline in its own right, similar to forensic dentistry or forensic toxicology. The expertise and technology necessary for the proper investigation of legal issues in which serology is involved must come from specialists in the field.

Such expertise is provided in Britain by the Home Office Forensic Science Laboratory Service; several academic departments of forensic medicine and some private laboratories have expert serologists.

The advent of DNA technology in the late 1980s has made blood group and many other blood constituent tests, such as enzymes, largely redundant.

BLOOD PRESSURE

The contractions of the heart produce a head of pressure in the arteries which is necessary to maintain the flow of blood to the small arterioles and hence to the tissues via the final capillary bed, the blood returning to the heart through the veins.

This pressure is produced by the left ventricle as it contracts during 'systole', the relaxed phase being called 'diastole'. The aortic valve between the left ventricle and the aorta (the main blood vessel leaving the heart) ensures that blood does not fall back into the heart during diastole. However, the pressure in the aorta is greater during systole as the blood jet is thrown out, than in diastole when the pressure is static at the valve. There is therefore a range of blood pressure between 'diastolic' end 'systolic'. This leads to a pulsation synchronous with the heart beat, the pulse at the wrist or neck being due to the pressure difference arriving in rhythmic waves from the heart. The normal diastolic pressure is about 70 mm of mercury and the systolic about 120 mm of mercury; these are often written as 'mm Hg' or, in different modern units, as 'kilopascals'. The normal range varies, but is usually between 110/70 and 140/80 mm/Hg. The two pressures are conventionally written as 'systolic over diastolic'.

Anything significantly higher than the upper limit of these values is abnormal, being termed 'high blood pressure' or 'hypertension'. Gross hypertension may reach 240/130 or even more.

The dangers of hypertension are numerous: physical rupture of an artery may lead to 'strokes' (cerebral haemorrhage), nose bleeds or eye damage: formation and rupture of aneurysms, kidney failure, heart failure due to inability of the heart to maintain the extra work and an increased risk of coronary artery disease.

A low blood pressure is usually the result of some acute injury or illness, such as blood loss, shock, etc. If below 80/50 there is danger of death from failure of perfusion of the tissues, especially heart, kidney and brain. Chronically low blood pressure may be seen in debilitating diseases and adrenal failure (Addison's disease). Acute low blood pressure needs urgent treatment with drugs and/or transfusion of blood or fluids.

BLOOD SPLASHES

When free blood flies through the air, the shape of the resulting splash can indicate the direction and hence the original position of the weapon or victim and sometimes the minimum number of blows.

Figure 19:   Direction of blood splashes

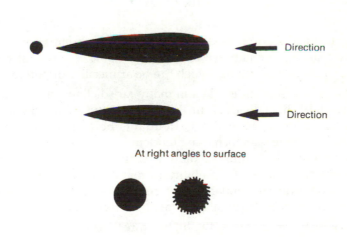

Direction

Direction

At right angles to surface

A blood drop in the air is spherical, but on impact releases a small globule, so that on hitting a surface tangentially, a splash resembling a printed exclamation mark will be formed, with the dot in the leading position. The more glancing the impact, the longer will be the stem of the mark. Conversely, a splash hitting perpendicularly will be circular.

In most cases, such blood splashes will have been thrown off from a weapon which is carrying blood from a wound which has bled profusely, especially the scalp. Usually, the first blow will not carry much blood, as there is often a momentary delay in the escape of blood from ruptured vessels, unless the vessel is a large one. In repeated violence with a weapon, subsequent blows will pick up blood, which will then be flung off on the upswing. This may travel a number of feet, to strike walls, ceiling or furniture, etc, and give a pattern which can indicate the direction. Though there is a considerable and variable scatter from each swing, the general direction can be assessed and any marked variation attributed to a change of direction or point of origin. Over-interpretation must be avoided as, although general patterns are useful, each shower contains spots with a wide variety of trajectories. Bleeding directly from a blood vessel rarely leaves such spots; only arterial blood gushes with any force and this tends to be a jet rather than a shower. Even a large artery will not gush more than a couple of feet from the body. Veins and capillaries only ooze and the blood is never projected from the body, other than by gravitational fall.

BRAIN DEATH

With the advent of modern medical techniques, the brain may die, that is, irreversibly cease functioning, without the inevitable cessation of other vital functions of heart and breathing, which can be artificially supported.

This state of brain death is taken in many jurisdictions to be synonymous with the death of the individual. In Britain, no statutory definition of death exists, the decision of the medical attendants being sufficient, whatever criteria they use. There is an increasing tendency to certify the time of death as that when brain death is unmistakably present. The matter is currently of great importance, because of the ability to maintain brain-dead patients for long periods on artificial ventilation and circulation; and also because of the need to declare death before organs are taken for transplantation.

The brain may die in stages, the higher functions of sentient thought and consciousness being more vulnerable than the basic functions of breathing and heart control. The higher functions are carried out by the cerebral cortex in the upper areas of the brain, whilst the more basic functions are situated in the brain stem and upper spinal cord.

Brain death may be due to the following:

Severe head injury with direct trauma to the brain.

Swelling of the brain (cerebral oedema) following trauma (which includes surgical operation).

Intoxication by a wide range of drugs, such as barbiturates and other depressants.

Deprivation of the blood supply to the brain, either by disease or injury to the main arteries in the neck or by failure of the blood pressure for more than a minimum of three minutes, as in a treated cardiac arrest.

Deprivation of the oxygen content of the blood, even if the circulation is maintained, may lead to brain 'anoxia' or 'hypoxia', a mishap sometimes occurring during anaesthesia or by events such as mechanical obstruction to breathing, as in crowd disasters such as at Hillsborough.

Brain swelling is a common sequel to head injuries, even if there is no fracture of the skull or laceration of the brain. It may lead to brain death because a rise in intracranial pressure may exceed the supplying blood pressure and thus prevent blood from circulating through the brain.

If the brain stem survives and the cerebral cortex dies, there will be permanent coma, but spontaneous breathing may persist and life may continue indefinitely ('persistent vegetative state' – PVS) as in cases such as Karen Quinlan and the Hillsborough victim Tony Bland which had such profound medico-legal consequences; in both these cases, court orders were obtained to allow discontinuation of nourishment to allow death to take place.

Death may eventually supervene due to feeding difficulties, emaciation and infections such as bronchopneumonia. If the brain stem fails, then breathing will cease and conventional death will rapidly follow unless artificial ventilation by machine is instituted. It is this situation which poses such difficulties in the ethical and legal sphere, both from the definition of death and the moral consequences of maintaining a vegetative patient to distress relatives and the monopolisation of scarce and expensive medical resources.

A Code of Practice (*The Removal of Cadaveric Organs for Transplantation,* 1979, London: DHSS) has consolidated and clarified the previous clinical criteria for diagnosing brain death. These are based on the recommendations of the 1976 Conference of Royal Colleges and Faculties of the United Kingdom:

(a) the patient is deeply comatose, this not being due to drugs, hypothermia or metabolic disturbance;

(b) the patient is being maintained on a ventilator because spontaneous respiration had become inadequate or had ceased altogether (relaxant or other drugs having been excluded as a cause);

(c) there should be no doubt that the condition is irreversible and the diagnosed cause has been fully established. Diagnostic tests for brain death include:

- all brain stem reflexes are absent (fixed pupils, no corneal reflex, no vestibulo-occular reflexes, no gag reflex, etc);

- no respiratory movements occur when the patient is disconnected from the ventilator, after ensuring that the arterial carbon dioxide tension rises above the threshold for stimulation of breathing;

(d) testing should be repeated. The interval between tests varies according to the definitions of previous criteria, but may be as long as 24 hours.

(See also 'Transplantation of organs and tissues'.)

BRUISES

Otherwise known as 'contusions', bruises are injuries characterised by leakage of blood from blood vessels under an intact skin. They are often associated with the two other types of wound, the abrasion and the laceration. The colour of a fresh bruise depends on the amount of blood extravasated from the vessels and the depth at which this occurs, as well as upon any pigmentation of the overlying skin. However, they are commonly reddish blue when fresh but varying from a deep purple-blue (almost black in some instances) to a pinkish red.

A deep bruise does not reproduce the shape of the injuring object as faithfully as the surface abrasion, due to the padding effect of the overlying skin, but sometimes such a pattern may be discernible, such as the radiator grille of a vehicle.

Some bruises are in the uppermost layer of the skin immediately under the epidermis and are then called *'intradermal'*. These are often confused with abrasions, but there is no grazing of the outer dead layer of skin cells. Such intradermal bruises may faithfully reproduce the pattern of the impacting object, such as the tread of a shoe or the weave of a coarse cloth.

Small discoid bruises, about half an inch in diameter (sometimes called 'sixpenny' bruises), are typical of finger-tip pressure, especially when multiple and sometimes side by side. These are commonly seen from gripping of the soft upper arm by an assailant and also in child abuse syndrome.

Bruises may not always appear exactly at the site of impact of the injuring object, due to tissue planes diverting the blood. Bruising may be delayed up to some hours after injury (the bruise 'coming out'), as the blood may have to filter up from deeper layers or dense tissue planes.

The intensity of the bruise is generally comparable to the amount of force, except in certain lax areas such as the eyelids – or where there is a propensity to easy bleeding, such as some haemorrhagic diseases or senile states. Old people bruise so easily that the term 'spontaneous bruising' is sometimes used, though there must always be some minimal amount of trauma. Children also bruise easily, due to the softness of their tissues and the transparency of their skin.

Bruising cannot occur where dense tissues surround the blood vessels such as the palm of the hand and sole of the foot. Visible bruising is less apparent in the scalp (partly due to the presence of hair) unless associated with lacerations and abrasions, though deep bruising is commonly seen under the fibrous sheet (aponeurosis) beneath the scalp.

Lax tissues such as the eyelids bruise very easily (see 'Black eye').

Estimating the age of a bruise is fraught with inaccuracies, but a sequence of colour changes can be recognised. The initial purplish red becomes brown in one to three days, then successively develops through greenish brown, greenish yellow, yellowish brown, tan and yellow before vanishing. Photographic studies have claimed that if a greenish hue is visible, the bruise must be at least 18 hours since infliction, but there is great variation in the sequence and timing of colour changes. The colour changes vary from the edge to the centre of a substantial bruise, being more advanced at the margins, a large bruise showing several colours simultaneously.

All but the most florid of these colours may be obscured by racial pigmentation. The above colour changes proceed over a very variable time scale and no accurate calendar can be prepared for dating.

Children and young adults heal their bruises far more quickly than the aged, who may retain their bruises almost permanently.

Complete resolution of a large bruise may take up to three weeks. A yellowish green bruise must have been inflicted at least several days earlier, but no justifiable opinion can be offered to date bruises in a succession of numbered days.

Microscopic examination may assist only slightly in dating bruises, as there is great variation in the date at which the healing process develops, initiated by the appearance of white blood cells, usually many minutes or even hours after infliction. Special stains to reveal iron pigment (haemosiderin) derived from red blood cells can be used – a positive finding of iron granules indicates that the bleeding took place at least 36 hours earlier, as long as the victim survived that long.

Where a number of bruises of the same order of size are present on the same victim, then significant differences in colour indicate that they were inflicted at times separated by at least a few days, even if no absolute dating can be given. This lack of simultaneous production is important in child abuse syndrome, where continued violence may have been taking place.

A bruise may shift after infliction under the influence of gravity. A bruise on the forehead may slide down and pass over the eyebrow ridge to appear in the eyelids as a black eye, and bleeding from a fractured hip can sink to the lower thigh.

Bruises cannot be inflicted after death, but considerable violence may cause a mark in the tissues, such as crushed muscle and an abrasion, which is unlikely to be mistaken for a true bruise.

Bruises formed at or near the time of death cannot be firmly differentiated into ante mortem and post-mortem injuries. Though blood pressure falls to zero when the heart stops, thus removing most of the cause of leakage of blood from vessels, there may be some passive movement of blood from arteries into veins for about 20 minutes after death, due to arterial contraction, and this might allow some slight bruising to occur even after the heart ceases to beat, though the injury will almost always have been suffered before the heart stops.

Bruises usually appear much more prominent as the post-mortem interval increases. Bruises seen soon after death may appear much darker and larger some hours later and even worse in a day or two. Other bruises too feeble to be seen immediately after death may appear next day and this may cause some discrepancies between an initial prosecution autopsy and a subsequent examination carried out for the defence at a later date.

The explanation is that the skin becomes paler in most areas as blood sinks to the back under gravity, causing greater contrast between the bruise and the skin; also a bruise may diffuse from deeper layers towards the surface as the haemoglobin leaks from the red blood cells.

BURIAL

Now the least common method of disposal of the dead, compared with cremation.

After the issue of either a medical certificate of the cause of death by a doctor or a coroner's certificate, the death is registered by the Registrar of Births and Deaths. He issues a certificate of disposal which allows the funeral director and cemetery authorities to bury the body.

After burial, the speed of decomposition varies greatly according to the environment of the grave, the season and the initial condition of the body. However, the rate of decay is greatly reduced compared to a body left on the surface. Animal predators are reduced (rodents, fly maggots, etc). In a conventional coffined burial, the rate of decomposition is much slower than a shallow clandestine internment. Factors such as brick-lined grave or vault, dry conditions, non-acid soil, lack of flooding, all retard decay. In a wet grave, especially in acid-peaty soil with a variable water table, the body may vanish (even bones) within 10–20 years. In dry, sandy conditions, good preservation may be seen after centuries. Some wet graves may produce adipocere formation (qv) which may also preserve the body for many years. The value of exhumation (qv) is very variable and unpredictable due to these inconstant factors, and no accurate forecast can be made of the condition of the body – thus where the indications for exhumation exist, it is always a worthwhile procedure.

BURNS

Injury due to a variety of physical agents, including dry and moist heat corrosive substances, ultra-violet light, X-ray and other radiations and electricity. Usual cause is heat, most often dry. This can lead to burns of varying severity, now classified in three grades after Hebas, each of which incorporates a pair of the six grades of the older classification of Dupuytren.

Grade 1. Burns which heal leaving no skin scar because the full thickness of the epidermis is not killed. Reddening (erythema), swelling and blistering are the hallmarks.

Grade 2. Where full-thickness destruction of skin will lead to scar formation after healing. When fresh, these burns may show shrivelled, coagulated skin surrounded by areas of first degree burns.

Grade 3. Severe destruction of skin and underlying tissues such as muscle and even bone. There may be charring of these tissues. Some classifications of burns incorporate Grade 3 into Grade 2, using epidermal damage as the sole criterion.

The grades are not necessarily related to danger to life, which is more a function of the area involved. Where more than half the body surface is involved, even in superficial first degree burns, recovery is unlikely, except in children, who may survive 60%. In old people, 20% or even 10% surface burns may be fatal. Conversely, charring of a limb may be compatible with recovery, if the initial severe shock stages are survived.

In calculating the approximate area involved, the 'rule of nine' is often used, designating each part of the limbs and trunk as multiples of 9% of the total surface (see Figure 20).

Medico-legal aspects of fatal burns

Were the burns sustained before or after death? The possibility of disposal of a homicide by burning must always be considered.

Burns seen at autopsy may be ante mortem, post-mortem or both. Burns sustained during life show a 'vital reaction' (qv) in that the margins of the burns are reddened and may be blistered. However, where death has supervened rapidly (that is, the burns are 'peri-mortal') this sign is absent. At least several minutes' survival are required for unequivocal vital signs to appear. Where ante mortem blisters are present, it is said that the contained fluid is rich in protein, but that post-mortem blisters contain watery fluid or gas. However, in practice, this method of differentiation is seldom possible or helpful. Microscopic examination for signs of early vital reaction in equivocal cases is less useful than standard textbooks suggest (see 'Vital reaction').

Other significant factors

Apart from the burns, other factors are significant:

Smoke. In most fires, smoke is produced and is inhaled by the living victim. Soot particles are then present in the throat, larynx and air passages, often deep in the lungs. Though passive deposition after death may occur via the open mouth, the presence of soot below the larynx is indicative of breathing having been present during the fire. Similarly, soot particles may be present in the gullet and stomach through swallowing. Rapid flash fires, especially petrol fires in vehicles and aircraft, may not always produce smoke nor carbon monoxide (see below) and death may also be too rapid to allow absorption. Where flames and hot gases are inhaled, the air passages may be burned internally.

Carbon monoxide. Most fires, especially house fires with smouldering fabrics and woodwork, produce large quantities of carbon monoxide (qv). This can only enter the body via breathing and not through the skin, so any raised blood level (above the few per cent seen in smokers and city dwellers) indicates that life was present during the fire. Most victims of house fires have an appreciable level of carbon monoxide in the blood, for example, 20–50% saturation, and this is frequently the cause of death or at least unconsciousness, before the fire reaches the victim. It is important to note that the presence of soot and carbon monoxide confirms life during the fire, but that the converse is not necessarily true. The absence of these signs does not indicate that the person was dead, though the general rule is most helpful.

Heat injuries. A body recovered from a conflagration often shows certain injuries which might arouse suspicion. Second or third degree burns cause 'heat contractures', where the limbs are flexed into the so called 'pugilistic attitude', due to the shortening of the flexor muscles more than the extensors. In addition, shrinkage of the skin may cause extensive splits, especially over large joints such as elbow, knee and shoulder, often precipitated by movements during recovery by firemen, but also spontaneously. These may resemble wounds, but there is no bleeding and structures such as vessels and

Figure 20: **'Rule of nine' for estimating area of burns**

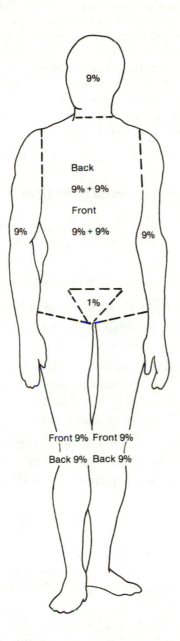

fibres survive in the depths of the splits, which show no vital reaction. They may occur on the scalp, where they may look even more suspicious, especially if associated with a 'heat haematoma' inside the skull. This heat haematoma is a collection of blood, often considerable in amount, which develops between the inside of the skull and the outermost brain membrane, the dura. It is seen where direct heat has impinged on the outside of the head, but the appearance can be confused with a true extradural haematoma (qv), which is always due to mechanical trauma to the head. The blood in a heat haematoma is frothy and chocolate coloured and is due to boiling out of blood from vessels in the membranes and skull, though the precise mechanism is unclear. It has given rise to a number of instances of spurious allegations of homicide concealed by fire.

Causes of death in bodies recovered from fires

Natural causes. Strokes and heart attacks may have preceded the fire and often caused it, for example, when an old person collapses in the act of lighting a fire or gas stove.

Pre-conflagration injuries. Homicidal, suicidal or accidental.

Injuries caused during the fire. Falling masonry and roof beams.

Carbon monoxide poisoning, asphyxia from oxygen lack, and other irrespirable gases such as carbon dioxide.

Poisoning from toxic fumes. Recent research has shown that burning plastics from upholstery and fittings can produce very noxious gases such as cyanide, phosgene and nitrous compounds.

In death from burns, the immediate cause may be:

(a) tissue destruction and/or severe primary shock, pain, etc;

(b) delayed shock and loss of fluid from large areas of burns;

(c) biochemical disturbances from electrolyte disorders in large areas of burning;

(d) kidney failure (delayed several days) due to tissue damage and 'acute tubular nephrosis';

(e) infection and toxaemia from septic burns;

(f) pneumonias, especially after inhalation of flames or hot gas which may also cause rapid death from pulmonary oedema (waterlogging of the lungs); and

(g) gastro-intestinal lesions, such as bleeding or perforation from acute ulceration of the stomach or rarely duodenum (the so called, but uncommon, Curling's ulcer). These are manifestations of stress caused by the burning, similar to adrenal haemorrhage.

'CAFÉ CORONARY'

A colloquial medical term, coined after a series of deaths described in the USA, where supposed coronary deaths were shown to be due to blockage of the throat by recently ingested food, before it has been swallowed into the stomach.

The original series mostly involved men in restaurants, who sat back in their chairs dead whilst eating a meal. Autopsy revealed that the most likely diagnosis of heart attack was incorrect, there being a mass of freshly eaten food impacted in the larynx (the voice box). The deaths were not classically asphyxial, being rapid and usually silent, with no marked congestion of the face or other supposedly classical signs of asphyxia (see 'Air passage obstruction').

Deaths from impaction of a bolus of unswallowed food must be distinguished from inhalation or aspiration of vomit, which is the regurgitation of stomach contents, already completely swallowed. Death from this latter event is much less common than death statistics allege, as it is a frequent agonal and even post-mortem event.

True 'café coronaries' are more common than previously thought and frequently take place in old people's homes and mental institutions, where senile or demented persons bolt their food rapidly, without chewing. It is also seen in mentally deficient children in institutions and in victims of neurological disability, such as motor neurone disease and head injuries.

The rapid and often undramatic mode of death appears due to sudden cardiac arrest, due to the sudden impaction of food in the sensitive larynx, rather than to frank obstruction of the air passages.

CANNABIS

Extract of the Indian hemp plant, Cannabis sativa, the active substances being cannabinol and tetrahydro-cannabinol. The leaves and flowers contain the active principles. The potency varies according to the method of cultivation. Various names for cannabis include marijuana, bhang, hashish, ganga, grass, etc. Absorption is by smoking or eating any part of the plant or the resin extracted from it, which is more potent than the untreated leaves or flowering tops.

There is no evidence that casual indulgence causes any physical harm and cannabis can never cause death from direct toxic action. There is some evidence that long-continued use may lead to physical harm (including possible genetic damage), though the effects of the drug remain a matter of considerable controversy.

The effects of cannabis vary from nil in some persons, to marked mental sensations, though the substance is not 'hallucinogenic' in the true meaning of the word.

Common effects include euphoria, distortion of time, enhancement of colours, sounds and rhythm, a dream-like state, liability of emotions confusion. It is not habit forming in most persons and there are no true withdrawal symptoms. Long usage appears to reduce concentration and efficiency and may have a deleterious effect on any coincident mental illness.

There are effective methods for the analytical detection of the cannabinols in human tissues and body fluids, which persist for some days after using the substance.

CARBON MONOXIDE POISONING

Once one of the most common fatal poisonings in urban and industrial areas, it is far less frequent now that the gas supply no longer contains monoxide, due to replacement by natural gas.

The most common sources of poisoning are now motor exhaust fumes, industrial leakages and defective domestic heating appliances.

Carbon monoxide kills in two ways. First, it has 300 times the affinity for combining with the haemoglobin of the red blood cells than has oxygen. Thus it is a very successful competitor for oxygen, even in low concentrations, and deprives the body tissues of oxygen by occupying oxygen-carrying capacity in the red blood cells. Secondly, it has recently been shown to dissolve in the plasma (liquid part of the blood) and to have a direct toxic effect on the chemistry of the body cells supplied by that blood.

The level of monoxide is usually expressed as a percentage saturation of the haemoglobin. Though the normal level is nil, smokers and city dwellers may have 3–5% saturation.

Symptoms, such as headache and nausea, may begin from 15% according to the individual response. Old persons are usually more susceptible and often are anaemic, so that less haemoglobin is available for oxygen transport. From 40–50% there is incoordination, slurred speech, vomiting and progressive impairment of consciousness and death is likely at any level above 50–60%. Death may occur at 30% in old and debilitated persons, and young children. No strict correlation between levels and expected effects can be made, except in the broadest terms.

Due to the high affinity of carbon monoxide for haemoglobin, minute concentrations can build up to dangerous or fatal levels. One part in 1,000 of air may cause 50–60% saturation within two to three hours. One part in 100 may lead to coma within 15 minutes.

A few breaths of undiluted monoxide, as in industrial or laboratory exposure, may be sufficient to kill.

The middle ranges of saturation may cause symptoms identical with drunkenness, with which this type of poisoning may be confused, especially in transport accidents.

Where a dead body is recovered from a fire, the presence of monoxide in the blood is sure evidence that the victim was alive during the fire, but the opposite is not true, especially in violent flash or petrol fires. No monoxide need be inhaled, even though the victim was alive at the onset of the conflagration. This is of medico-legal importance in allegations of disposal of a dead body by fire (see 'Burns').

Approximate relationship of concentration of monoxide in blood to symptoms and signs:

(a) no effects below about 15%, apart from possible slight headache;

(b) at 15–30%, severe headache, confusion, sickness, visual defects, weakness. May be similar to drunkenness in some victims;

(c) at 30–60%, stupor deepening to coma, vomiting, convulsions. Death in some cases, especially in old people below this level;

(d) above 60%, coma and death in the majority.

This relationship is very variable: two persons who die side by side in the same room may have markedly differing monoxide concentrations when measured at autopsy.

Sources of monoxide poisoning

Motor vehicle exhaust fumes, 4–7% monoxide. A 1.5 litre car engine will generate a fatal level of monoxide in a closed single garage in about five minutes tick-over time.

Faulty heating appliances (gas or solid fuel). Even if fuelled on monoxide-free natural gas, a defect in the burners or choked flue will cause incomplete combustion in absence of sufficient oxygen, so that monoxide is produced in addition to relatively less harmful dioxide. Examples are bathroom water heaters and butane appliances in caravans and boats.

Solid fuel stoves may also generate monoxide if the air supply is restricted.

Blast furnace gas and coal gas (rarely encountered in UK due to use of natural gas) contains 7–10% monoxide.

Lethal levels

Due to the stability of carboxyhaemoglobin in the red blood cells compared with oxyhaemoglobin, fatal levels can build up from very low atmospheric concentrations. One part per 1,000 can cause a lethal concentration of 60% in the blood within 3 hours' exposure. One per cent can cause coma within a few minutes.

After recovery from non-fatal exposure, there may be transient and permanent brain damage, as monoxide causes degeneration in the deeper parts of the brain. Both neurological and psychiatric disturbances may develop and become permanent.

CARDIAC ARREST

Stoppage of the heart, usually sudden and unexpected, is the usual meaning of 'cardiac arrest'. Ultimate cause of death in everyone except where brain death is used as definition.

Numerous causes, but usually related either to intrinsic heart disease or to acute external causes, such as electric shock, over-stimulation of vagus nerve (for example, pressure on neck), anaesthesia, etc.

Sudden cardiac arrest is the only cause for virtually instantaneous death, as seen in a sudden collapse with no signs of life immediately afterwards. Even pulmonary embolism (qv) or cerebral haemorrhage (qv) does not cause such an instantaneous death.

Cardiac arrest is potentially reversible by cardiac massage or electrical stimulation applied to the chest, unless there is severe intrinsic damage to the heart.

Treatment is most likely to succeed when arrest not due to heart diseases, for example, electric shock or vagal inhibition.

Cardiac arrest for more than three minutes may cause irreversible brain damage from deprivation of blood supply, so resuscitation should be avoided if arrest took place more than five minutes earlier, or there may be the risk of restoring heart function to a vegetative patient – though cases are on record where full brain function has been restored after six or even nine minutes of cardiac arrest.

Cardiac arrest strictly means complete stoppage of the contractions of the heart muscle, but 'ventricular fibrillation' and other defects of rhythm may be preliminary stages before arrest. In ventricular fibrillation, the heart muscle twitches instead of pumping in a co-ordinated fashion. This may be corrected by cardiac massage, drugs or electrical defibrillation applied to the chest wall.

External cardiac massage often causes trauma to the chest (fractured ribs or breast bone, bruised muscles and haemorrhage on surface of the heart, etc) which can be mistaken for signs of injury unless the pathologist is aware of the possible artefact.

CARDIOMYOPATHIES

A group of heart diseases of unknown cause, usually found in young adults and which may be a cause of sudden unexpected death in the age group younger than that associated with coronary disease.

Not common, but a forensic pathologist might see one or two per year in a busy coroner's autopsy service.

Sometimes associated with exertion and a number of apparently healthy sportsmen have died during a game and been found to have a cardiomyopathy. It is sometimes familial and where a death occurs, siblings and children may need to be screened for evidence of similar heart abnormality.

The two main types are:

Hypertrophic obstructive cardiomyopathy (HOCM) where there is a large heart with a very thick left ventricle. This thickening is sometimes asymmetrical and a pad of muscle may partly obstruct the outflow tract for blood leaving the left ventricle. Histologically, the muscle fibres of the heart may be arranged in bizarre patterns.

Congestive cardiomyopathy (COCM) where the heart is large and globular, but the chambers are dilated rather than thickened and the main feature is congestive cardiac failure. These are less associated with sudden death than HOCM and run a slower course.

Cardiomyopathy is sometimes confused with myocarditis (qv), which also causes sudden death in the younger age group.

CEREBRAL HAEMORRHAGE

Usually refers to natural disease causing bleeding into substance of brain, as opposed to traumatic bleeding (see 'Extradural haemorrhage', 'Subdural haemorrhage' or natural 'Subarachnoid haemorrhage', all into membranes of brain). Any injury lacerating the brain will cause some intracerebral bleeding, but the usual meaning is bleeding due to spontaneous rupture of an artery within the brain substance.

Often called a 'stroke' if it leads to paralysis or other neurological defect, but this indefinite term can apply to other disorders of the cerebral circulation such as thrombosis. The clinical distinction between haemorrhage and thrombosis may be impossible without ancillary investigations such as CAT scan or magnetic resonance imaging (MRI).

Causes of cerebral haemorrhage

Hypertension (high blood pressure). Most common cause, leading to tearing of small artery, often the 'artery of cerebral haemorrhage' which is one of the lenticulo-striate branches of the middle cerebral artery. This lies near the main nerve tracts which carry the 'motor' (outgoing) nerve fibres and damage is likely to cause a paralysis or weakness of the opposite limbs. If the haemorrhage occurs in the speech area of the left cerebral hemisphere, it may cause speech defect. Large cerebral haemorrhage may cause coma and death, either rapid or delayed any length of time. The normal blood pressure is about 120/70 mm of mercury, but in hypertension, the pressure may rise to over 200/120 (see 'Blood pressure').

Atheroma (arteriosclerosis). Either independently or more often in combination with high blood pressure, atheroma of the cerebral arteries may weaken the vessel wall and lead to cerebral haemorrhage.

Congenital or developmental abnormalities of blood vessels in the brain may lead to bleeding. Most common is the 'berry aneurysm' (qv) of the Circle of Willis (qv), leading to the subarachnoid haemorrhage (qv). Sometimes, this may burst through the brain substance, rather than into membranes. Another cause most common in children and young adults is an 'angioma', an abnormal cluster of blood vessels, sometimes of a tumorous nature. Rupture of this may lead to haemorrhage and severe disability or death. The medico-legal significance of this group is the controversial relationship of any trauma to the rupture and the consequent degree of civil or criminal responsibility.

Another frequent medico-legal problem is the need to distinguish cause from effect in autopsy findings. A large cerebral haemorrhage may be found in a person with a head injury, presumed due to a fall. Did the natural haemorrhage cause the fall or did the haemorrhage occur because of the trauma of the fall? Sometimes, this dilemma cannot be resolved from autopsy appearances alone. Though a large, solitary haemorrhage in the depths of the brain is more likely to be natural than traumatic, there are numerous exceptions. Assistance may be gained from:

(a) the history and circumstances, such as witnessed collapse before striking the head, more likely to be the result of a natural 'stroke';

(b) other evidence of significant intracranial damage and bleeding may tend towards attributing all to injury;

(c) the presence or absence of evidence of high blood pressure (medical history, large heart, etc.) and diseased brain arteries;

(d) investigations such as CAT scan and MRI.

CEREBRAL OEDEMA

Swelling of the brain, most often due to head injury. Fluid may pass from the blood vessels in the brain into the inter-cellular spaces in the substance of the brain, when a diffuse impact force passes through the tissues.

A severe blow or fall may temporarily paralyse the functions of the higher nerve cells (neurones) causing transient unconsciousness (see 'Concussion').

This may be followed by brain swelling, which can occur rapidly, certainly within an hour and probably more quickly. It seems more common amongst children and is a frequent cause of death in child traffic accidents, even when there appears to be no structural damage to the brain, such as bruising or laceration, etc.

Progressive oedema is dangerous and may lead to raised intracranial pressure, as the brain is enclosed within the rigid box of the skull and cannot expand, except to push down against the only exit, the foramen magnum, where the spinal cord emerges. In this area of the skull is the vital midbrain, which carries the control centres for breathing – so oedema may lead to paralysis of breathing, the patient then needing artificial ventilation.

Cerebral oedema may also cause widening of the sutures (seams) between the skull bones in very small infants. It also causes 'papilloedema', blurring of the optic discs in the eyes, due to pressure – this is one of the diagnostic methods for brain swelling, to seek papilloedema by looking in the eyes with an ophthalmoscope, though CAT and MRI scans now add to the diagnostic tools.

The pressure can also cause retinal haemorrhages (qv) in the eye; this may be wrongly ascribed to primary injury such as the shaking, so beloved of paediatricians, when in fact it may be secondary to cerebral oedema.

Cerebral oedema may often co-exist with diffuse axonal injury (qv), both being due to mechanical disruption of the micro-structure of the brain.

CHILD ABUSE SYNDROME

Also known as 'battered baby', 'battered child', or 'non-accidental injury in childhood' (NAI) syndrome.

First described in mid 19th century by Tardieu in Paris, then forgotten until revived by American paediatrician Caffey in 1946, then known as 'Caffey's syndrome'.

Salient features

(a) Repetitive physical (and often sexual and psychological) injury to a child by parent, guardian or temporary custodian.

(b) Main injuries: bruising of skin, fractures of bones, damage to internal organs, especially brain and abdomen.

(c) About 60% recurrence after first injury, 10% mortality if no adequate intervention.

(d) Battering parents were frequently themselves battered children, this behaviour pattern being accepted as the norm.

(e) Parents often young: 'father' frequently a consort, rather than biological parent.

(f) After severe abuse, disparity between clinical findings and the parental explanation, which is evasive and inconstant, often varying between mother and father.

(g) Usually an inexplicable delay between serious injury and the seeking of medical or other assistance, especially in fatal cases. A London series showed an average of 20 hours' delay in seeking a doctor.

(h) Bruises usually on face (around mouth, eyes and ears), arms (especially grip marks above and below elbows), legs, abdomen and chest. Frequently circular 'sixpenny bruises' from adult fingertips. Black eyes, bruised ears and lips common, also tears inside lining of lips.

(i) Internal eye damage common: suspected victims should have expert ophthalmological examination. Retinal and vitreous haemorrhage, detached retina and dislocated lens frequent, from slaps and punches; retinal bleeding usually secondary to brain injury and swelling, though some may be due to shaking.

(j) Fatalities most often due to fractured skull and/or internal brain damage, especially subdural haemorrhage (qv), followed in frequency by abdominal injuries.

(k) Typical fractures common, around elbows, wrist, knees, due to traction and twisting of limbs. Also from squeezing of chest and blows or falls on the head.

Radiology essential to detect multiple fractures and fractures of different ages, indicating intermittent abuse. In small infants, typical pattern of fractured ribs, which break in sequence down the back, parallel to the spine, from side to side squeezing. by adult hands around the chest. After some weeks, these heal with 'callus' formation, presenting a typical 'string of beads' appearance on X-ray.

Front rib fractures rare in infants, almost unknown due to attempts at resuscitation.

Similarly, bruises may be of different colours and thus duration.

(l) Many bizarre injuries, such as cigarette burns, scalds, radiant heat burns. Bites not uncommon, usually from mother. Such cases must have expert dental examination to compare with dentition of adult, as often alleged that other children or even pets caused marks.

(m) Affects all age groups of children, but most common under three years and even more so under 18 months, especially fatal cases. High risk of permanent brain damage with mental impairment, even where death does not occur.

(n) In recent years, a vogue has arisen amongst paediatricians and pathologists to refer to 'shaken baby syndrome' in abused infants with head injury, but doubt has been cast upon the frequency of shaking as opposed to impact.

Because an impact upon the head, especially against a flat surface, need leave no mark on or under the scalp, nor a fractured skull, this absence of overt external injury led many clinicians to think that shaking must have been the cause – though in many instances, this explanation was still accepted even when there was evidence of a scalp impact.

Experimental research has shown that an impact provides energy of the order of 50 times greater than shaking and is far more likely to be the true explanation; some doctors now hedge by calling it 'shaken impact syndrome'.

(o) Much controversy may arise about the force required (especially the distance of a fall) to fracture the skull of an infant and/or cause brain damage.

It must be appreciated that a skull fracture may easily be caused. Weber, in 1985, found that dead infants dropped passively from only 80 cm (32 in) onto a hard floor all suffered skull fractures, and even when dropped onto a variety of soft surfaces, a proportion still fractured.

However, many persons, including infants, may suffer a skull fracture with no resulting disability – it is damage to the skull *contents* which is dangerous.

Any injury of sufficient force to cause a skull fracture has the potential to cause brain damage or haemorrhage into the brain membranes, but this by no means always occurs.

Thus a fall or impact which causes a skull fracture need not be life-threatening if it does not also cause intracranial damage; conversely, fatal brain damage can occur in the absence of a fractured skull.

There is no known quantum of force which will inevitably cause brain damage (which includes subdural haemorrhage). It is conventionally claimed that a fall from adult waist height is the minimum to cause such damage, but there are cases on record of lower falls causing subdural haemorrhage, such as Japanese reports where infants have sustained a subdural haemorrhage when falling over only from a sitting position.

This whole area is one of considerable controversy, especially in the very extensive medical literature and entrenched positions are held by experts on both sides (see also 'Subdural haemorrhage', 'Skull fractures', 'Abdominal injury').

CHILD DESTRUCTION

The deliberate killing of a child capable of being born alive before it has a separate existence. Prior to 1929, this was neither the offence of abortion under the Offences Against the Person Act 1861, nor infanticide, nor murder, as there was no separate existence.

The Infant Life (Preservation) Act 1929 closed the loophole by making it an offence for any person, with intent to destroy the life of a child capable of being born alive, to carry out a wilful act causing the child to die before it had an existence independent of its mother. A statutory defence to this charge, now largely overtaken by the Abortion Act 1967, was that the act was done in good faith for the purpose only of preserving the life of the mother.

This Act required (s 1(2)) evidence that the woman had at any material time been pregnant for a period of 28 weeks or more, as *prima facie* evidence that she was pregnant of a child capable of being born alive. Thus a statutory threshold of 28 weeks' gestation was established for foetal viability, a legal concept that does not necessarily coincide with medical fact, as foetuses less than 28 weeks may survive with modern obstetrical procedures. Conversely, a foetus of more than 28 weeks may not be viable for other medical reasons. Later legislation under the Abortion Act reduced the 28 weeks to 24, to coincide more realistically with modern advances in obstetrics.

The concept of actual live birth does not enter into the definition of child destruction, being important in infanticide. Similarly, 'separate existence' does not have to be proved, only the viability (by maturity) which in theory should allow a separate existence.

The Infant Life (Preservation) Act was the first statute to mention the possibility that destruction of the foetus might not always be unlawful, though in a much more restricted way than the later Abortion Act.

The 1990 amendment to the Abortion Act 1967 (the Human Fertilisation and Embryology Act) means that a registered medical practitioner cannot now be guilty of an offence under the 1929 Act.

CHOKING

Usually refers to internal obstruction of air passages by foreign material. Sometimes used loosely to cover other forms of mechanical obstruction, such as strangulation (qv) (see also 'Air passage obstruction').

Internal obstruction is usually due to the following:

Gagging or obstruction of mouth, for example, watchman tied up during robbery with cloth stuffed in mouth. Initially may be able to breathe through nose until swelling and mucus block this alternative airway.

Food just swallowed – see 'Café coronary'.

Food regurgitated from stomach, but caution needed as this is frequently an agonal or even post-mortem phenomenon (see 'Air passage obstruction').

Inhaled foreign objects, such as toys, bottle teats and household objects in children: dentures, extracted teeth, etc, in adults.

Figure 21:   Choking

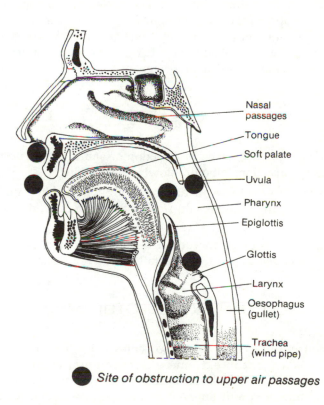

Nasal passages

Tongue

Soft palate

Uvula

Pharynx

Epiglottis

Glottis

Larynx

Oesophagus (gullet)

Trachea (wind pipe)

● *Site of obstruction to upper air passages*

Acute infections, such as diphtheria and Haemophilus influenzae epiglottitis in children; also rupture of pharyngeal abscess.

Choking may give rise to extreme congestive signs in face and neck (see 'Asphyxia') with purple-red coloration and swelling of face, with sometimes blood spots in eyes (petechiae), the latter only if there is forcible coughing and distress. However, many victims die quietly and suddenly from cardiac arrest and show no congestion. These gave rise to misnamed 'café coronary' syndrome.

Treatment must be rapid and consist of removing the obstruction by instrumentation or the Heimlich manoeuvre or making an emergency tracheostomy, that is, an opening in the windpipe below the larynx, which is the usual site of obstruction. Cardiac massage and artificial respiration may be required.

CIRCLE OF WILLIS

A ring or rather pentagon of arteries at the base of the brain, named after Thomas Willis, a 17th century physician. The circle forms a bypass system for the vital blood supply of the brain, supplied by the two vertebral arteries and the two internal carotid arteries, so that if one artery is blocked, blood can be diverted through the ring. Aneurysms (qv) may occur at junctions on this circle and cause subarachnoid haemorrhage (qv).

COCAINE

A common drug of abuse, taken by injection or sniffing. the effects come on within minutes of injection, but more slowly after sniffing.

'Crack' is free-base cocaine, made by heating with baking soda to release the free base from the cocaine salt. Its effects come on and pass off more quickly.

The dangers of cocaine include a rise in blood pressure, sweating, hyperactivity and a risk of sudden heart failure or a brain haemorrhage.

COLD INJURY (HYPOTHERMIA)

Most common in old people, but also seen in children. Less common in younger adults, except in extreme environmental conditions. If body temperature (normally 37°C) drops to 28°C or less, recovery is unlikely. Now a relatively common condition even in European winters, related to low

Figure 22:   Circle of Willis

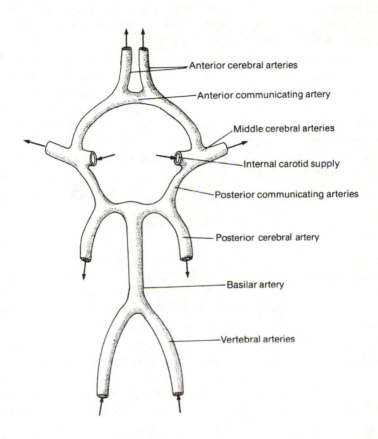

Anterior cerebral arteries

Anterior communicating artery

Middle cerebral arteries

Internal carotid supply

Posterior communicating arteries

Posterior cerebral artery

Basilar artery

Vertebral arteries

environmental temperature. Senility and poor living conditions causes most cases in old people. Poverty, senile dementia, withdrawal into recluse state, poor housing, nutrition, thyroid deficiency (myxoedema) and lack of domestic heating may lead to hypothermia, even in moderately cold weather.

Also seen in unconscious or stuporose persons, from injury, alcohol, drugs or natural disease, if exposed for extended period to cold. Unclothed victims of assault in the open may die of hypothermia rather than their injuries. Exposure on mountains, in cold water, open moorland, etc, may cause hypothermia, especially if exhaustion present.

General signs

Pink or dusky pink colour of skin, especially over large joints like knees, hips and elbows due to pooling of blood in skin, and persistence of oxygenated haemoglobin due to small uptake of oxygen by cold, inactive tissues.

Sometimes skin blistering. In actual 'frostbite', extremities like fingers, toes, nose, cheeks, may become bright red and eventually the tissues die, with later disintegration and separation of the tissues. Internally, signs slight or absent in many cases, but general bright red colour of blood, may be acute haemorrhages in lining of stomach, occasionally haemorrhage into adrenal glands, and haemorrhage or necrosis of pancreas. Diagnosis rests largely on circumstances, temperature during life and absence of other demonstrable cause of death in fatal cases.

CONCUSSION

Unconsciousness following head injury, more accurately 'a transitory period of unconsciousness resulting from a blow on the head, unrelated to any injury to the brain which is apparent to the unaided eye'. Pure concussion, as just defined, lasts for not more than 5–10 minutes. If unconsciousness is longer, then physical brain damage must be presumed.

Post-concussional state of considerable forensic importance. May be automatism, similar to post-epileptic state, in which behaviour is purposeful and possibly criminal, but of which the victim is unaware. False explanations of the circumstances of the injury may be uttered in this state, but which fade and cannot be recollected by the victim when he later returns to normal.

Long term post-concussional symptoms may give rise to civil actions for loss of faculty, etc. These include intractable headaches, loss of memory, irritability, dizziness and vertigo, visual, olfactory and auditory sensory defects, decreased perception and speed of thinking. Where fits supervene, physical damage to the brain should be suspected (see 'Traumatic epilepsy'). It is very unusual for a significant degree of brain damage to occur in absence of some concussion, though length of unconsciousness is not related to severity of damage.

Concussion is an important clinical feature – usually any patient coming to hospital with a history of concussion, however transient, is investigated and admitted for observation, to exclude serious intracranial damage, such as extradural haemorrhage (qv).

Concussion is usually associated with some degree of retrograde amnesia (qv), that is, loss of memory for events immediately preceding the injury. This is due to the normal delay in registering events in the memory, a protective device to avoid recollection of actual injury.

CONSENT TO TREATMENT

All medical care must take place with informed consent of varying degree. The most common type of consent is *implied*, where the actions and demeanour of the patient implicitly provide consent. Thus the presentation of a person at a doctor's surgery, out-patients or clinic implies that the patient is willing to undergo examination and treatment, up to a certain degree of complexity.

This degree covers the usual diagnostic methods of interview, inspection, palpation, percussion and auscultation (with stethoscope). Even here, the usual courtesies of speech on the part of the doctor may reinforce the consent, such as a request to undress or to allow a pulse or blood pressure to be taken.

Beyond these simple matters, consent must be *express*, a specific request being made by the doctor and acquiescence obtained. This extends to intimate examinations, such as rectal or vaginal examinations, to any procedure introducing an instrument or needle into an orifice or beneath the skin, etc. The patient may require some explanation as to why this is necessary, this then becoming *informed* consent.

For complex or potentially hazardous procedures, such as surgical operations, anaesthetics, sophisticated X-ray techniques and many others, *written, informed, express* consent is highly advisable.

Written consent is no better than oral consent in law, but is much more easily proved if later disputes occur. It is usual to have both oral and written consent for any substantial procedure witnessed by an impartial witness. A relative of the patient is less satisfactory, as in any retrospective dispute, they may well not be unbiased.

The concept of informed consent relies upon the right of every patient to be fully cognisant of what is wrong with him and what is to be done about it. However, though in theory every proposed item of treatment should be preceded by a full explanation, this must be modified by a clinical judgment about the effects of such information upon the patient. The two attitudes may well conflict. A full recital of possible risks of an operation may cause the patient to reject what might be a life or health-saving procedure.

Consent is normally obtained from mentally capable adults, that is, over 16 years of age, though this age limit may be lowered if the doctor judges that the younger person can understand and make rational judgments, otherwise consent is given on behalf of minors by the parent, guardian or person *in loco parentis*.

In urgent situations, no consent is needed to save life or ameliorate serious effects of injury or disease. However, the procedure should be limited to the most urgent matters.

In the case of severely mentally incapacitated persons, the consent of relatives is obtained if they live at home, but in an institution, the consent is given by the officers of the hospital, even if relatives are available.

Where a patient is unconscious, then consent may be obtained from relatives, but in urgent situations generally, the prime consideration is what is best for the patient, consent being waived on the principle that a doctor acting in good faith has an ethical duty to carry out all necessary treatment in the expectation that his actions will be upheld in any subsequent litigation.

A similar concept now applies in the case of children of parents holding strict religious views about certain forms of treatment, for example, blood transfusion in Jehovah's Witnesses, though recourse is made to the courts in certain cases.

CONTRE-COUP INJURY

Refers almost entirely to brain damage, though rarely applied to lung bruising.

When a moving head strikes the ground or other fixed surface, the brain damage is frequently sustained diametrically opposite the point of impact, hence the term 'contre-coup'. Conversely, when a weapon strikes a stationary, unsupported head, the brain damage is under the point of impact, the so called 'coup' injury.

Contre-coup injury may be accompanied by a coup injury, but often there is little or no damage at the site of impact. Contre-coup damage is seen when the head strikes either at the side or the back of the head, the injury then being on the opposite side or the front of the brain respectively. The damage need not be exactly 180 degrees from the impact site, often being more diffuse, but still in the general area most distant from the impact.

Occasionally, contre-coup brain damage may be seen on the opposite side of one cerebral hemisphere, rather than on the opposite side of the whole brain.

It is almost unknown for a fall onto the front of the head to cause contre-coup damage at the back of the brain.

The mechanism is obscure and controversial, but shearing stresses, rotational forces and shock waves have all been incriminated.

Medico-legally, contre-coup is most useful in corroborating an unwitnessed claim that a head injury was due to a fall, rather than a blow upon the head, that is, to help differentiate an accident or other fall from a direct assault upon the head. Experimental work in Japan has shown that on impact, there is a momentary vacuum or suction effect within the cranium at the site of contre-coup.

Figure 23: **Coup and contre-coup injuries**

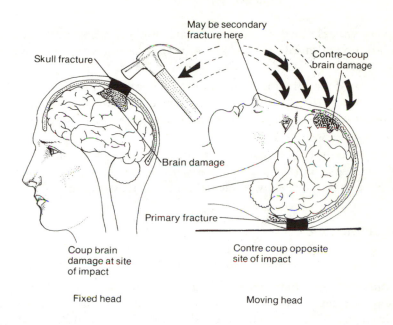

The absence of contre-coup does not rule out a fall, but its presence is almost certain proof of a moving head suddenly being arrested in its motion. There may be a fracture of the skull at the point of impact, but not necessarily so. There is often a laceration or bruise at the site, but many falls onto a flat surface may leave no mark.

There may be contre-coup fractures – where a fall occurs onto the back of the head, the frontal lobes of the brain may be severely damaged, even pulped. Beneath these frontal lobes, the very thin bone that overlies the roof of the eye sockets may be fractured by the same contre-coup forces. This may allow blood from local bleeding to enter the eye sockets (orbits) and appear at the eyelids as deep bruising.

This may be confused with black eyes from direct violence and further complicate the interpretation of an assault (see 'Black eye').

Where a supported head is struck on the opposite side by a weapon, as in a head already lying on the ground or firm surface so that it cannot move away, then contre-coup damage may also be seen.

In the chest, sometimes a heavy fall may produce a type of contre-coup bruising in the lung tissue.

COOLING OF THE BODY
(See also 'Time since death')

A very variable process, used as a basis for estimating time since death. There are considerable inaccuracies in this estimation, even when the optimum data are available, which is often not the case.

The normal mouth temperature of the body at death is 37°C (98.4°F). The armpit temperature is about 2°C less and the commonly used rectal temperature about 1°C higher. The 'normal' temperature may vary by 1°C from one time of the day to another.

The rationale of the test is that, after death, cessation of metabolic processes causes failure of temperature maintenance, so a measurement of the falling temperature will allow a calculation of the time elapsed.

Variable factors

Many variable factors involved, all contributing errors.

Temperature at death may not be 37°C: raised in infections, after vigorous exertion just before death and some brain haemorrhages. Lowered in hypothermia (qv) from environmental causes, but not in haemorrhage as often erroneously stated, nor raised in 'asphyxia', as formerly claimed. The latter error probably arose because many strangulations were associated with violent struggling, which raised the body temperature from muscular exertion.

Rate of cooling is very variable, with no constant linear relationship between temperature and time. There is usually a 'plateau' of normal rectal temperature immediately after death due to lag in cessation of metabolism. This may be half an hour to two hours, or even more, in duration. Then a progressive fall for about the first day until temperature is near environmental – but does not reach environmental unless freezing conditions prevail (or environment is warmer than body, as in tropics, where bodies may never cool, but actually warm up) Thus the only useful part of a temperature graph is during first day, but the angle and regularity of this graph is very variable.

It has long been assumed that during the first few hours, the body temperature drops by about 1°C (1.5°F) per hour, a highly unsafe assumption. Some doctors add an arbitrary 3 hours to this 'rule of thumb' to allow for the plateau, but this is unsatisfactory. The answer cannot be relied upon, and after taking into account other factors to be considered below, can only be used as mid point of a wide range of times, such as 'probably between six and 12 hours'.

Clothing naturally modifies the rate of cooling, the spectrum being from complete nudity to heavy swaddling.

Posture is another factor related to the exposed surface area. A body in a curled up foetal position will cool more slowly than one spread-eagled.

Body shape affects cooling. The mass/surface area ratio is different in a slim person compared with a corpulent one, apart from the fat insulation factor. A child has a greater area/mass ratio and will cool more quickly.

A fat person will retain heat better due to the subcutaneous layer of fat acting as a heat insulator.

Oedema (waterlogging) from heart failure or kidney disease will retain heat longest, due to the high specific heat of water. This has been found to be a more potent factor than fat.

Environmental conditions are all-important. Cold, heat, wind, draughts, rain and humidity all alter the rate of heat loss, but they may not be constant throughout the period since death, that is, temperature changes due to weather, rain, wind, etc, or variation indoors from dying fires to exhausted gas or electricity meters. Thus no calculations can compensate for variation of the cooling rate, especially if the variations are unknown.

Artificial factors may cause gross distortion of the expected cooling rate, for example, hot water bottles, electric blankets, radiant heat from fires.

It is therefore obvious that no meaningful calculations can be made for all possible permutations of these factors. A century of research has failed to improve methods much – for instance, taking two temperatures several hours apart to attempt to gauge the slope of the cooling graph has made no material advance. Accuracy is impossible and errors of 100% are possible.

It is fatuous and misleading for an expert witness to offer a 'time since death' expressed as a single point of time, especially if it is 'accurate' to a few minutes. The best that can be done is offer a 'bracket' which straddles a reasonably wide period and, even then, errors are not infrequent. To attempt unreasonable accuracy is to invite ridicule.

A great deal of research has gone into the heat physics and mathematics of body cooling and numerous formulae exist.

One of the best known is that of Henssge, which is available as a computer program and a nomogram. This is reproduced under 'Time since death', but it must be noted that the smallest range of error, giving 95% confidence, is 5.2 hours.

Other methods of estimating 'time since death', such as potassium in the eye fluid, the residual electrical stimulatability of muscles and a variety of biochemical parameters, are equally uncertain, as most depend ultimately on changes in temperature.

The use of hypostasis (qv), rigor (qv), stomach contents (qv), etc, are even less helpful.

CORONARY ARTERY DISEASE

One of the most common causes of death (especially in men) and the most common cause of sudden death in Western-style society. Due to blockage or narrowing of the coronary arteries by *atherosclerosis* (atheroma) which supply blood to the muscle mass of the heart.

There are two main coronary arteries, both arising from the aorta (qv) just above the aortic valve. The left artery divides into the anterior descending branch and into the circumflex branch; these supply the front and left side of the heart. The right coronary artery has no major branch, but supplies the right side of the heart.

Figure 24:   Coronary artery disease

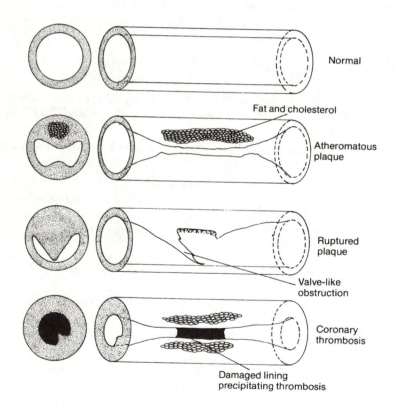

The blockage is a degenerative condition of the arterial wall and lining, which either blocks (occludes) or narrows (stenoses) the channel (lumen). The blockage is due either to thickening of the wall by fibro-fatty masses (atheroma) or to thrombosis on the damaged wall, which blocks the lumen partially or completely. In either event, the heart muscle beyond the point of blockage becomes deprived of blood. If this deprivation leads to death of that zone of muscle (necrosis), this constitutes a myocardial infarct (qv). If the patient survives the infarct, the dead muscle is replaced by a non-functioning fibrous scar.

Where no actual infarct occurs (as in the majority of fatal cases) the long standing starvation of blood may lead to a diffuse replacement by fibrous tissue, or the muscle may survive intact but in an impaired state of vitality. Such a heart is chronically unstable and may suffer a number of sequelae, the severity partly depending upon the area of the heart involved:

(a) *weakening of pumping action* may lead to chronic cardiac failure, with clinical signs of failure;

(b) *electrical instability* of muscle may lead to sudden failure and death;

(c) *irregularities of rhythm*, of any type. May lead to sudden death from ventricular fibrillation (twitching of the muscle instead of regular pumping) or to lesser degrees of rhythm defects.

It is important to appreciate that most fatal cases of coronary artery disease do not have a demonstrable new defect, such as recent thrombosis or infarct. Cases dying in hospital under recent medical care are a 'selected population' due to the onset of symptoms and have a higher proportion of recent new lesions. Sudden, unexpected deaths may reveal nothing new at autopsy apart from their long standing coronary disease. Newer techniques, such as enzyme estimations, may reveal new disease in a proportion of these, but it is often impossible to demonstrate that any fresh event has taken place immediately before a sudden fatal collapse.

Any person with more than 70–80% narrowing of a major branch of a coronary artery is a candidate for sudden death.

Complications

A number of complications of coronary artery disease exist:

Infarction and fibrosis (as described above).

Rupture of the heart through a softened infarct. Common in older people with weak, senile muscle, especially old women. Occurs on the second or third day after onset – leads to filling of the bag around the heart (pericardium) with blood. This is known as a 'cardiac tamponade' or 'haemopericardium' and is rapidly fatal.

Mural thrombosis. Blood clot may settle on the inner surface of the infarct inside the cavity of the heart: fragments may break off and be washed away in the bloodstream, causing embolism (qv) of other organs such as brain or kidneys.

The muscles holding the valve flaps may rupture if infarcted and the septum (partition between the chambers) may rupture, though these are rare.

When healed, a large infarct may produce an extensive sheet of fibrous tissue, which may then bulge under the blood pressure within the heart cavities and form a 'cardiac aneurysm'.

Any person with substantial coronary artery disease is may die at any time, especially if the conducting system of fibres which convey the rhythmic contractions is involved. Such persons are far more vulnerable to sudden shocks, either physical or emotional, and can be precipitated into fatal cardiac arrest or other cardiac abnormalities by assaults, emotional trauma or sudden physical exertion. Thus there is a strong relationship between sudden deaths in these people to a variety of external stimuli, many of which have both criminal and civil relevance in a legal sense (see 'Trauma and disease').

CORONER, DEATHS REPORTABLE TO

According to the Coroner's Rules 1953–80 (Consolidated), deaths should be reported to the coroner:

(a) when no doctor has treated the deceased in his or her last illness;

(b) when the doctor attending the patient did not see him or her within 14 days before the death or after death;

(c) when the death occurred during an operation or before recovery from anaesthetic;

(d) when the death was sudden and unexplained or attended by suspicious circumstances;

(e) when the death might be due to an industrial injury or disease or to accident, violence, neglect or abortion or to any kind of poisoning.

Though not specifically mentioned, other deaths are invariably reported to the coroner, including deaths in legal custody, deaths of persons receiving an industrial disability pension or war pension and any cases in which negligence (medical or otherwise) has been alleged to have contributed to the death.

Though not a statutory provision, it is conventional for the coroner to require deaths to be reported to him where such death has occurred during a surgical operation or under anaesthetic or within 24 hours of recovery from these. Similarly, it is usual for the coroner to request notification of deaths occurring within 24 hours of emergency admission to hospital.

There are local variations in the requirements of individual coroners about the types of death of which they require notification.

In addition, there is a statutory duty upon Registrars of Births and Deaths under reg 51 of the Registration of Births, Deaths and Marriages Regulations 1968 to refer certain deaths to the coroner:

(i) Where a registrar is informed of the death of any person before the expiration of 12 months from the date of the death he shall report the death to the coroner on a form provided by the Registrar General if the death is one:

  (a) in respect of which the deceased was not attended during his last illness by a medical practitioner; or

  (b) in respect of which the registrar has been unable to obtain a duly completed certificate of cause of death; or

  (c) with respect to which it appears to the registrar, from the particulars contained in such a certificate or otherwise, that the deceased was seen by the certifying medical practitioner neither after death nor within 14 days before death; or

  (d) the cause of which appears to be unknown; or

  (e) which the registrar has reason to believe to have been unnatural or to have been caused by violence or neglect, or by abortion, or to have been attended by suspicious circumstances; or

  (f) which appears to the registrar to have occurred during an operation or before recovery from the effect of an anaesthetic; or

  (g) which appears to the registrar from the contents of any medical certificate to have been due to industrial disease or industrial poisoning.

(ii) Where the registrar has reason to believe, with respect to any death of which he is informed or in respect of which a certificate of cause of death has been delivered to him, that the circumstances of the death were such that it is the duty of some person or authority other than himself to report the death to the coroner, he shall satisfy himself that it has been reported.

(iii) The registrar shall not register any death which he has himself reported to the coroner, or which to his knowledge it is the duty of any other person or authority to report to the coroner, or which to his knowledge has been reported to the coroner, until he has received a coroner's certificate or a notification that the coroner does not intend to hold an inquest.

COT DEATH

Colloquial term for Sudden Infant Death Syndrome or SIDS.

Called 'crib death' in North America. Most common single cause of infant mortality after first week of life. At three months of age, more common than all other causes of death combined. Incidence was about one death in every 500 births, but since about 1991, the number in most Western countries has dropped significantly. In UK, the rate is now less than half its former incidence, said to be due to recommendations to sleep infants face up, reduce smoking in the vicinity and to avoid overheating.

SIDS has been known since antiquity (Old Testament) but cause is still uncertain, being a common end result of a number of coincident factors.

There is no single cause, it is a multifactorial event where several predisposing factors come together to cause death.

Culmination is respiratory failure, due to sleep apnoea (cessation of breathing during sleep).

Features

(a) Definite age range, most common at about three to four months, majority between two and eight months, though can occur between two weeks and two years.

(b) Slightly more common in male babies, marked increase in risk for members of twin pair. More common in premature and under-birthweight infants.

(c) Marked social class incidence (more in 'working class') but no social group immune.

(d) Marked seasonal incidence, from October to April in northern hemisphere.

(e) Typical circumstances: child well or has slight illness (a cold, snuffles or diarrhoea) on previous night. Put to bed then found dead in morning, or dies in early part of day; 80% found dead in sleeping place before noon.

Autopsy findings are nil or relatively trivial, insufficient to arrive at definite cause of death.

Numerous theories over the years, but probably a combination of factors, including sleep, a slight infection and a maldevelopment or immaturity of the breathing regulatory mechanism. Respiratory infection may often be 'trigger' that sets off a chain of events leading to oxygen deprivation in blood, enhancing sleep apnoea.

Practical considerations

Cot death is not suffocation from inhalation of vomit (qv) or negligence on part of mother. Such allegations by doctors or coroners reinforce universal guilt of mother, which may lead to anxiety, neurosis or even suicide. Counselling necessary to alleviate family discord from recrimination.

Controversy exists as to the incidence of maternal suffocation amongst the overall numbers of cot deaths. Some paediatric evidence, such as covert television cameras, to indicate that some mothers attempt to smother their infants, even in hospital – called the Munchausen by proxy syndrome.

However, pathologically, there are no positive autopsy signs in either SIDS or suffocation, so no means to differentiate them. Recently, some pathologists allege that finding haemorrhages in the lungs at autopsy (and old iron pigment in the lungs as evidence of previous episodes) is indicative of suffocation; this claim is hard to accept, as it is virtually impossible to obtain test and control samples, as the basis on which the two groups are separated has no other criteria, so the claim is self-fulfilling.

Where two or more SIDS occur in the same family, such a suspicion is strengthened, but impossible to prove in individual cases. Since the dramatic fall in 'true' SIDS since 1991, it is claimed that the proportion of suspicious deaths is thus greater, but the burden of proof of suffocation is usually unattainable, though some illogical bias on the part of some doctors can lead to injustice.

CREMATION (LEGAL REQUIREMENTS)

A clumsy, anachronistic legislation exists, originating in statutes dating back to 1903. Now, cremation is the method of disposal in 75% of deaths, but an outdated system persists, in spite of recommendations of the Brodrick report, entitled *Report of the Committee on Death Certification and Coroners*, Cmnd 4510, 1971, London: HMSO.

Series of documents required for cremation:

Form A: application by family or executors, to be countersigned by person of repute, for example, magistrate or clergyman.

Form B: first medical certificate given by doctor who issues death certificate. Can be any doctor who attended in deceased's last illness, even provisionally registered house officer. He must declare any relationship with and any pecuniary benefit from the will of the deceased. Must view the body, after death.

Form C: confirmatory medical certificate given by a doctor who has been fully registered for at least five years. He must also examine the body and discuss the death with the first doctor. He must also declare any interest and not be a general practice partner of the first doctor. Ideally, he should not be in the same hospital team either (DHSS advice) but this is often disregarded. If an autopsy has been performed, the pathologist usually gives Form C.

Exemption from Form C granted if an autopsy has been carried out by a pathologist qualified for at least five years and the doctor signing Form B knows the result of the autopsy before certifying the cause of death.

Form D: rarely used, but is a request from the medical referee of the crematorium for an autopsy, if he is not satisfied with the two medical certificates. Such cases usually proceed via the coroner's system.

Form E: issued by the coroner, replacing previous forms.

Form F: approving certificate by medical referee of crematorium.

Form G: completion certificate from the crematorium superintendent to certify that cremation has been carried out.

The Brodrick report recommended that this cumbersome system be replaced by a more comprehensive death certificate which will allow any form of disposal. Note that doctors can only give their two certificates if the case has not been reported to the coroner.

CREUTZFELDT-JAKOB DISEASE (CJD)

Several forensic implications exist over this neurological disease. It is infective, but is not due to a bacterium or virus. The cause is a *prion*, an abnormal protein which has the potential to replicate itself in brain tissue.

It is related to *scrapie*, an ancient disease of sheep and to *kuru*, a similar disease transmitted by cannibalism of brain tissue in New Guinea. *BSE (Bovine spongiform encephalopathy)* of cattle is virtually identical to CJD.

Though CJD has occurred rarely and sporadically in humans for many years, a 'new variant CJD' has appeared in the last decade, about 25 cases being reported in Britain to date. It is untreatable and invariably fatal. The presumed incubation period for classical CJD is thought to be many years, though as the source of infection is unknown, this is difficult to establish. The new variant CJD occurs mostly in younger people and seems to have a rapid incubation period.

Medico-legal implications surround the safety of food and also of therapeutic substances. The development of CJD by recipients of growth hormone extracted from pooled human cadaver pituitary glands led to a major negligence action against the Department of Health in 1997.

There is also a potential problem, as with HIV and hepatitis, of the possibility of infection by – and to – health care workers and mortuary staff and pathologists. Special precautions have to be taken in performing autopsies on CJD victims, especially as prions do not seem susceptible to the usual methods of disinfection and sterilisation.

CUT THROAT

Slashing wound(s) on front of neck, most often suicidal, occasionally homicidal. Accidental infliction almost unknown, except from falling through glass window.

Suicidal

Almost always 'tentative cuts', sometimes numerous where hesitant trial incisions are made. This feature is the best distinction from homicidal cut throat. Suicide may be abandoned at this stage in favour of another method, but where successful, a major slash is usually made parallel to the tentative cuts. Many attempts fail, due to throwing back the head, so that the vulnerable great blood vessels slide back behind the shelter of the sternomastoid muscles.

A suicidal slash is usually obliquely across the throat, from high up on the left side (in right handed victims) under the angle of the jaw. The wound tends to be deeper where it begins and tails off to a shallower cut at its termination on the lower part of the opposite side of the throat.

Often, other signs of attempted self-destruction, either contemporary or previous, especially cuts on the inside of the wrist (again, frequently multiple tentative cuts). Wrist cutting is usually not fatal, due to over-extension of the wrist joint allowing the radial artery to slide into a protected position.

Homicidal

No multiple shallow tentative cuts, though there may be several major slashes. These may be in different directions and may involve the face and chest as well. As the head is not thrown back, as in suicides, the skin is not on the stretch, so ragged wounds may be caused through the lax skin. The severity and depth may be extreme, even involving the spinal column. However, undoubted suicides can occasionally cause extreme injury to themselves. Defence injuries (qv) may be seen in murder, but are naturally absent in suicide.

Common features

Whatever the motivation, both types have some common features:

(a) even where the windpipe is slashed open below the larynx, the power of speech may be retained;

(b) considerable physical activity is possible for some time after severe cut throat injuries, unless a carotid artery has been severed leading to rapid exsanguination;

(c) the cause of death is blood loss, especially if a carotid artery is cut. Bleeding from jugular veins may be gross, but is a 'welling up' rather than the active arterial spurting of carotid damage, which may spurt blood a distance of several feet.

Death may also be due to blood blocking the air passages, either through a wound in the larynx or windpipe or through the mouth.

Air embolism (qv) is another rare, but recognised complication if a large neck vein is opened. Damage to the larynx or windpipe may rarely cause an asphyxial type death by the cut tissues blocking the air flow.

DEATH CERTIFICATION

A registered medical practitioner has a statutory duty under the Births and Deaths Registration Acts to give a certificate of the medical cause of death in all cases where he has attended the deceased during life. This attendance is not further defined, but working regulations of Registrars of Births and Deaths indicate that a certificate is not acceptable without notification to the coroner or Procurator Fiscal if more than 14 days has elapsed between the last attendance and the death. However, some years ago, the Registrar General required that a certificate should be issued in all cases where the doctor had been in attendance, whatever the time period, even though he also reports the case to the coroner. This cuts across the long established practice and the matter is not yet clearly resolved.

Whether or not a certificate is issued, the doctor should report the death to the coroner if:

(a) he has not attended the patient for a potentially lethal condition in the last two weeks;

(b) he is not sure of the cause of death;

(c) he is not completely satisfied that the death was due to natural causes.

The present law does not oblige the doctor to see the body after death, though it is most unwise not to do so.

The cause of death is recorded according to international conventions, the sequence being that adopted by the World Health Organisation, modelled on the original devised by the British Registrar General.

Part 1 records the disease or condition leading directly to death, which is subdivided into three antecedent causes (a), (b) and (c). Thus (a) must be due to (b), which must be due to (c). The basic pathological condition is that on the lowermost line and is the one which will be used for statistical purposes.

For example, 1(a) Ruptured myocardial infarction due to (b) coronary thrombosis due to (c) coronary athero-sclerosis.

Often, only one or two lines are used. Modes of death or symptomatology, etc, should not be included in the cause of death, for example, 'Heart failure' or 'Coma', unless qualified on a subsequent line below.

Part 2 records 'any other significant conditions which contributed to death but which were not related to the conditions in Part 1'. This section is frequently misused as a depository for secondary pathological conditions, which usually are not strictly part of the death process.

The standard of death certification is very poor and is worsening Several surveys have revealed that the recorded cause of death, without the benefit of an autopsy, is incorrect in about 50% of cases, of which half are substantial errors.

DEATH, SIGNS OF

No legal definition of death in most countries, other than the conventional medical criteria which vary according to the circumstances, especially in relation to organ donation for transplantation surgery.

Death may be somatic or cellular. The first refers to the permanent cessation of organised life which characterises the individual, that is, breakdown of integrated bodily systems such as breathing, circulation and nervous control. This is the conventional definition of death, but with the availability of modern life support techniques, all three major functions need not now fail together. It is usually the nervous control by the brain which has failed, but respiration and sometimes heart function can be maintained artificially. At this point, it becomes a matter of definitions, semantics and religious and ethical debate as to the presence of life (see 'Brain death').

Cellular death is more straightforward, in that once breathing and circulation have ceased, the body tissues die progressively on a tissue and cellular level. Various tissues survive for different lengths of time: brain cells die in a few minutes, whereas connective tissue cells may last for many hours.

Organs such as cornea, skin or kidneys may be viable for transplantation for hours or even days if preserved under appropriate conditions.

To return to somatic death, the conventional signs (in the absence of artificial support systems) are:

(a) loss of consciousness;

(b) flaccidity of the muscles (though they may react to mechanical and electric stimulation for some hours, until rigor mortis sets in);

(c) cessation of the circulation (no pulse at wrist or neck, no heart beat at chest, no heart sounds through stethoscope);

(d) no respiratory movements or sounds of air entry into lungs;

(e) loss of corneal reflex (sensitivity of front of eye);

(f) loss of tension in eyeball (the pupil of the eye may react to drugs for some hours, but not to light);

(g) special tests such as electroencephalogram (EEG) and electrocardiogram (ECG) reveal a flat tracing of inactivity; and

(h) observing the retina (back of the inside of the eye) with an ophthalmoscope reveals fragmentation of blood column in the vessels.

All these tests may give equivocal results in deep coma, such as barbiturate poisoning.

DECOMPOSITION OF DEAD BODY

Important medico-legally as one of the ways in which time since death can be estimated, though like all methods, there are very wide margins of error. Decomposition (virtually synonymous with putrefaction except where mummification (qv) occurs) is the only incontrovertible sign of cellular death, that is, death of the tissues as opposed to death of the organised functions.

The chronology of decomposition varies greatly with:

(a) *temperature of the environment* (climate, season, interior heating, humidity, clothing, etc);

(b) *nature of the environment* (water, burial, animal predators, etc);

(c) *condition of body* (obesity, dehydration, oedema, infections); and

(d) *refrigerated storage*, either artificial or natural freezing.

General sequence of decomposition in 'average' temperate environment

Green discoloration of abdominal wall, usually over right lower segment where caecum (large intestine) is nearest the surface. The third or fourth day is about average for this, but in heated rooms or tropics may appear in 12–24 hours. Retarded indefinitely in very cold conditions.

Diffuse reddish green discoloration of skin, especially in dependent parts, with 'marbled' appearance of superficial veins five to 10 days, though marked variation.

Swelling of face, abdomen and genitals in male, with moist breakdown of skin, blebs filled with thin bloody fluid and slippage of outer layers of skin, especially in dependent areas of trunk. Tongue and eyes may protrude, hair loosens from scalp, skin of feet and hands may peel in sock and glove fashion in two to three weeks.

Body becomes visually unidentifiable from facial appearance from this time. Bloated appearance, body cavities may break down. Further stages depend upon presence or absence of animal and insect predators, such as maggots, rats and dogs, according to situation of body. Time scale very hard to estimate, being so dependent on season, temperature and predators; likely to be several weeks, but a body can be reduced to a skeleton in three to five weeks in optimum conditions of temperature and predation.

Skeletalisation (qv) progresses, usually complete in two years in temperate countries, but extreme variations possible. Bones with fibrous tissue, cartilage and ligaments still attached, are probably less than five years since death. Dry bones can be anything from two years to many millennia.

As always, environment is more important than time.

DEFENCE INJURIES

Injuries sustained in an attempt to ward off an assailant. Almost always on hands and arms, occasionally on thighs.

Incised wounds seen on fingers, hands and forearms where victim tries to protect himself against attack from a sharp weapon. In knife attacks, the blade may be grasped, causing cuts on the inside aspect of the fingers, often at the creases of the finger joints and on the palm and base of the thumb, especially in the web between thumb and index finger.

They may also occur on the outside (knuckles) from attempts to deflect the blade. Less frequently, they are present on the back of the wrist and forearm. The injuries may vary from small pricks to deep slashes which may sever tendons or blood vessels.

In assault by blunt weapon, the typical defence injuries consist of bruises on the backs of the hands, wrists and forearms, from efforts to ward off heavy blows. Rarely, there may be actual lacerations, depending on the type of weapon used. Such bruises may sometimes be present right up the outer side of the arms to the shoulder, where an arm is thrown across the face and head in an attempt at protection.

In attacks on the genitals, such as kicking, the thighs may be crossed in an attempt at protection and suffer blunt injuries.

DENTAL IDENTIFICATION

A highly specialised field which, in all but the simplest cases, requires the services of a forensic odontologist (dentist with experience of medico-legal dentistry).

Major uses

(a) The identification of the recently dead (and, occasionally, the living).

(b) Identification of skeletal material by means of the jaws.

(c) The examination of bite marks, both on the body and on inanimate objects.

(d) The estimation of age in the living (rarely required in Western countries).

Identification may be needed in individual cases or in mass disasters such as aircraft crashes, where dental identification may be the only means of distinguishing mutilated or burnt victims. The two main approaches in identification from teeth are set out below.

Determination of broad groupings

Determination of broad groupings, such as human origin, age, sex and race. Age can be determined with considerable accuracy in children and young persons from sequence of eruption of milk and permanent teeth. Other techniques used in later age groups, such as attrition (wearing down) and rarefaction (porosity) of roots (modified Gustafson technique).

Recently, a new ageing technique has been developed which depends on the progressive racemisation (conversion of stereo-isomers) of aspartic acid, an amino acid in the teeth.

Sex differences are slight in teeth, but jaw shapes differ. Race may be determined in some instances, such as 'shovel shaped' front teeth of mongoloid races.

Determination of personal identity

Matching of dentition of unknown person with dental records of potential matches. Extractions, dentures, fillings, bridgework and many other reference points can be identified by an expert dentist, either by direct inspection or X-ray. For this matching technique to be successful, dental records must be available. DNA in the pulp of a tooth may also be used for identification, if a matching sample of that person's DNA can be obtained.

Photographic and video superimposition of a skull upon facial photographs of the putative subject are now often used. Also, a face may be built up on an unknown skull, either by anatomical modelling by an expert medical artist or by computer replacement techniques.

Forensic odontology is now a specialised discipline and, for reliable interpretation, an experienced odontologist, rather than just any dentist, must be consulted.

DIATOM TEST IN DROWNING

Diatoms are microscopic water algae with a rigid case composed of silica. There are many thousands of forms of diatoms, which are different in fresh water from salt.

When a body (dead or alive) falls into water, fluid passes down the air passages to the lungs. If life is still present, the heart will be beating and can transport diatoms which penetrate the lung lining to distant parts of the body, but in a corpse this cannot occur.

Therefore, at autopsy, if specimens of bone marrow, blood, liver or kidneys are taken and digested with strong acid or detergents or enzymes, to remove soft tissue, the absorbed diatoms can be seen microscopically in the drowned cases only.

Figure 25:   Principles of the diatom test in drowning

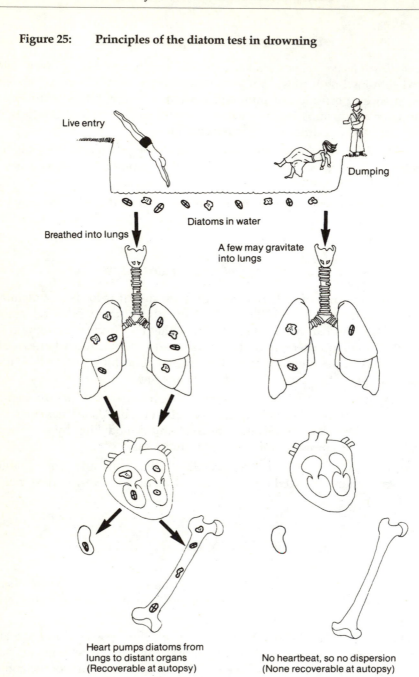

As well as a test for drowning, as opposed to mere immersion, an expert botanical opinion can distinguish sea diatoms from fresh water algae and even identify the likely geographical source in some cases.

Certain factors are needed for successful interpretation, though some authorities discount the reliability of the technique:

(a) there must be diatoms in the water (absent seasonally and in pollution);

(b) there must be strict safeguards at autopsy so as not to contaminate test tissues by surface water on instruments;

(c) the ubiquity of diatoms in environment (even air) must be appreciated, though the number recovered in drowned cases greatly exceeds control numbers of diatoms.

Some experts point to the huge load of diatoms in shellfish, which when eaten, may reach the bloodstream by penetrating the gut wall and thus give a spurious positive result in target organs.

There is considerable controversy as to the practical value of this test for drowning. A negative result certainly never excludes drowning and a positive result is indicative only, never probative.

DIFFUSE AXONAL INJURY (DAI)

An important concept in head injuries. In recent years, microscopic techniques have demonstrated that there is specific injury to nerve cells following severe impact upon the head. Neurones, the essential cells of the nervous system, have a body and many radiating branches, the largest of which is the *axon*, which may be several feet long in some cells which control movement. Where a severe mechanical insult to the brain occurs, many of these axons are damaged and may leak their contents, forming a microscopic globular structure called an axonal bulb or retraction globe. The process is called *diffuse axonal injury* or DAI, which persists for a month or more in survivors.

This may be suspected by gross examination of the brain, when small haemorrhages may be seen in certain parts of the brain, but this must be confirmed by microscopy.

DAI often accompanies cerebral oedema (brain swelling). It is useful, as it may confirm that a substantial impact has occurred to the head, even in the absence of any obvious bruising or laceration of the brain substance.

One problem is that no microscopic changes are visible in conventional staining techniques for a number of hours, usually more than 12 hours after injury, so the victim must survive this long for the microscopic diagnosis to be made at autopsy. Recent research has shortened this period, by using a histochemical method to search for *beta-amyloid precursor protein*, which may reveal DAI within a few hours, perhaps even less than five after injury.

DISSEMINATED INTRAVASCULAR COAGULOPATHY (DIC)

A dangerous blood condition secondary to many causes, some of forensic importance.

The blood develops a tendency to initiate its clotting propensities throughout the body, converting fibrinogen to fibrin, which together with platelets, small cells assisting in the coagulation process, may block small vessels and lead to haemorrhage, infarction and organ failures.

Causes include:

Trauma, causing tissue damage and release of thromobogenic material.

Infections of many types.

Amniotic fluid embolism at childbirth (see 'Embolism').

Hypothermia and hyperthermia.

The dangers are blockage of the microvasculature with fibrin, and haemorrhage due to the failure of the clotting system. It is a highly complex condition, and where an expert is required to evaluate DIC, a haematologist specialising in coagulation disorders would be most appropriate.

DNA

The introduction of DNA technology into forensic science has been the most important advance since earlier this century, when blood groups were first used in identification procedures.

The subject is vast, complex and expanding on a monthly basis; furthermore, in the UK it lies within the discipline of forensic science, rather than forensic medicine or pathology, so no useful explanation can be attempted in a small book such as this.

In summary, DNA is *deoxyribonucleic acid,* the carrier of all genetic information within the cell. It lies within the nucleus and also a different type is in the mitochondria, the organelles embedded in the cell cytoplasm, the DNA of which is transmitted down the maternal line – and which may be more useful in DNA work on ancient material such as bones.

DNA consists of two strands of sugar and phosphate molecules which are twisted into a double helix, the strands being bound together by permutations of four bases, *adenine, guanine, thymine and cytosine,* which form the rungs of a ladder, there being ten such rungs to each twist of the helix. A single DNA molecule may have millions of such links; genetic information is carried on segments of a molecule, called a gene, separated by lengths of DNA which appear to have no function.

In spite of repeated legal challenges, mainly in the USA, no two persons, other than identical twins, have been found to have identical DNA profiles, the possible number of permutations far exceeding the population of the world.

From the forensic aspect, the uses are legion, but all depend upon the comparison of a DNA sample from a person or from trace evidence, with DNA from a control, in order to prove or exclude identity. As with blood groups, merely obtaining a DNA profile in isolation is useless, unless there is something to match it against. Exceptions are the ability to determine the sex of a sample and to determine whether or not it is human.

In paternity testing, DNA now allows positive determination of parenthood, rather than the statistical likelihood or exclusion offered by blood typing in former years.

Sampling for DNA tests

The greatly increased sensitivity of laboratory techniques, such as the polymerase chain reaction (PCR), now allow minute traces to be tested, but larger samples are still preferable where possible. In blood, only the white cells (leucocytes) carry DNA, as the red cells have no nucleus. At least 1 ml and preferably 5 ml should be taken into an EDTA tube.

As with all tissue, live material is better than that from post-mortem, as decomposition can interfere with testing.

Semen and seminal stains, vaginal fluid and swabs, should be air dried and kept at low temperature, if not taken immediately to the laboratory.

From autopsies, spleen, liver, muscle and bone marrow all provide plenty of nuclear material. Hair roots, with nucleated cells attached, were previously required for DNA testing, but now hair shafts themselves are sufficient.

Unless taken straight to the laboratory, deep freezing is the best method of preserving material for DNA analysis.

DROWNING AND IMMERSION

Not synonymous with the cause of death of all dead bodies recovered from water; many corpses from water did not die there and many did not drown.

(a) May be a criminal death, disposed of by throwing body into water – decomposition, passive transportation from the locus of death and delayed recovery may hamper or defeat identification and recognition of true cause of death.

(b) Death from natural causes may have occurred before falling into water, for example, heart attack in a boat or on bank.

(c) Death may have occurred during fall before entering water, from accident or suicide, for example, by striking bridge parapet or other obstruction.

(d) Death may have occurred in water, but not from drowning (natural disease).

(e) Death may have resulted from injuries after entering water – impact with bottom or edge of swimming pool, river or lake: hitting bridge abutment, injuries from propeller of boat, etc.

(f) Death from sudden cardiac arrest (shock) from suddenly entering cold water. More likely in drunken state or emotional tension. May be due to sudden cooling of skin especially if flushed from alcohol, or from a jet of cold water impinging on the sensitive lining of nose or throat – the so called 'vagal inhibition' (qv).

(g) True drowning may be demonstrable.

Drowning

Not merely asphyxia as formerly thought; a much more complex mechanism, different in salt water from fresh.

In fresh water drowning, there is massive absorption of water through lungs, due to osmotic pressure effects. Blood volume may increase by 50% within one minute. This causes sudden strain on heart pumping function: also

Figure 26:   Mechanism of fresh water drowning

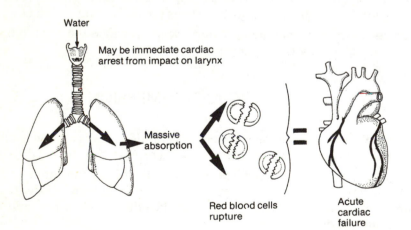

dilution of plasma causes red cells to rupture, releasing potassium, which is heart muscle poison. These factors combine to cause death from heart failure before lack of oxygen takes effect.

Note that the great increase in blood volume may give a falsely reduced value for post-mortem analyses, such as alcohol or drugs, which may be 50% less than the true concentration immediately before death.

In salt water drowning, osmotic pressure differences prevent absorption of water and in fact withdraws water from the blood into the lungs, causing severe pulmonary oedema, the source of the froth frequently seen at the nostrils in any type of drowning. However, heart failure is less rapid than in fresh water drowning and survival is longer.

Signs of drowning

Variable, may be minimal or absent, especially if delay since death. So called 'dry lung drowning' not infrequent and presents none of the so called classical signs.

Dry lung drowning means either that death was rapid due to cardiac arrest and is not drowning at all; or that all the water in the lungs has been absorbed into the bloodstream, leaving no post-mortem waterlogging.

Autopsy diagnosis is then difficult, often by exclusion of other causes in conjunction with knowledge of circumstances.

Note that signs of immersion are not necessarily the signs of drowning – wrinkled skin, gooseflesh (cutis anserina), mud staining, sodden clothing.

Positive signs of drowning (often absent) are fine froth exuding from nostrils and mouth or present in air passages. A delay of a few hours or more after recovery may allow froth to dissipate.

Over-distended lungs filling the chest cavity due to plugging of small air passages by mucoid froth; sometimes large quantity of swallowed water in the stomach, though this can occur post-mortem. Similarly, foreign material such as weed or sand in the air passages may be a post or ante mortem sign.

Chemical tests, such as Gettler's chloride test on the blood, have been discarded and are useless, even in freshly recovered bodies.

Diatom test (qv).

Time since immersion. Great variation, as in all timing of death. Depends on temperature and contamination of water and on stagnant or fast flowing water. On average, cooling is twice as fast in water as in air at the same temperature. Whitening and wrinkling of skin of palms and feet occurs within one or two hours, but a few minutes in a hot bath.

Later putrefactive changes slower than in air, but within two weeks, skin slippage and loosening of hair, with detachment of skin of hands and feet slightly later, though environment may cause variation in time of several hundred per cent.

Adipocere (qv) may form, being most common in immersed bodies due to the need for water to convert fat to soapy and waxy compounds. Minimum time usually several weeks to a few months.

Injuries. May be ante mortem or inflicted after death from trauma in water. Marine or fresh water predators include crabs, fish, rats, etc. Injuries may be from rough river bottom, rocks, piers, bridges, etc, or from propellers of high-speed outboard motors, which leave characteristic injuries of regularly spaced slashes.

Due to the washing action of water, no haemorrhage remains around external injuries and it is very difficult to distinguish the two groups. Internal injuries should present no problems.

Former claims about time of surfacing of body, posture of male and female corpses, etc, are now discounted as useless speculation, as so many variables exist.

DRUGS AND MEDICINES

See 'Misuse of Drugs Act 1971'

ECSTASY
(see also 'Amphetamine')

A so-called 'recreational drug' of abuse, a derivative of amphetamine, chemically being 3:4-methylene dioxymethamphetamine (MDMA), also called 'XTC'.

Although there have been a number of well publicised deaths, considering the widespread usage of the substance amongst young people, its toxicity is relatively low.

A moderate dose of 75–100 mg produces effects within 20–60 minutes.

Its actions are similar to that of amphetamine ('speed') with sometimes spasm of jaw muscles and grinding of teeth, and the hyperactivity of the users, especially at prolonged 'raves', can lead to dehydration, high temperature, loss of sodium and exhaustion and muscle damage.

The deaths are likely to be due to some personal hypersensitivity, rather than the usual slower complications.

ELECTROCUTION

For electrocution, fatal or otherwise, to occur there must be a passage of electricity through the body from an entry to an exit point. Without this passage there are no ill-effects, as in birds perched on overhead cables. The entry is usually a live conductor and the exit either an earthed object or another conductor at zero potential, such as the neutral line of the supply.

The biological damage depends on the amount, that is, both the time and the amperage of current flowing through the body, but the pressure, that is, the voltage, is related to this as per Ohm's Law (current = voltage/resistance). Fifty milliamperes flowing across the heart for a few seconds is very likely to be fatal. To achieve this current flow, the voltage is usually in excess of 100 v, though death has been recorded at 50 v and even 24 v, though the time of flow was long. Most electrocutions occur from domestic supply voltage of 240 v.

The resistance of the thick dry skin of the palm of the hand is of the order of one million ohms, but when damp, from sweat or wetness, it is reduced to a few hundred ohms, thus greatly increasing the current flow.

Most electrocutions (about 80–100 fatalities a year in the UK) occur from passage of a current from a hand, either to earth via the feet or via the opposite hand. Death is usually due to fibrillation and arrest of the heart muscle. Less often, death is asphyxial from paralysis of the breathing muscles of chest and diaphragm. Much less often, current enters the head, as in workers on overhead wires and electrified railways. Here, direct brain damage may occur, including paralysis of the breathing centres in the brain stem.

Figure 27: **Clinical effects of electrocution**

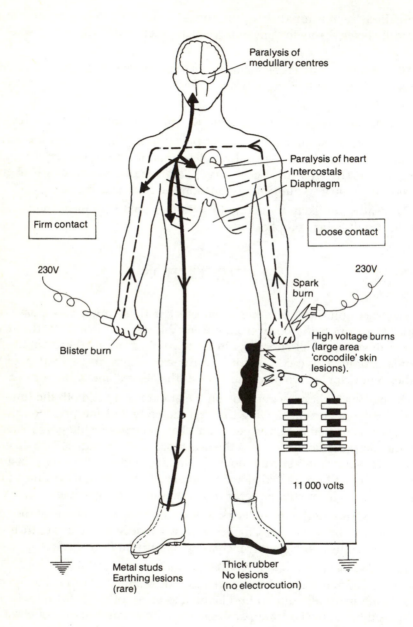

Fatality likely if a good earth; as in wet ground, damp concrete, metal pipes, etc. Exit on feet may be marked by electrical burns corresponding with metal boot studs.

Signs

Electrical burn (more accurately 'mark') on skin, usually of hands. Difficult to see in clenched fist of rigor mortis. May be tiny and insignificant. Firm contact mark is a collapsed blister. An intermittent or 'jump' spark burn shows a central yellow core of melted skin, with a pale surrounding zone. No other specific changes: said to be 'streaming' of nuclei of skin cells due to electrical polarisation, but this may be seen in thermal burns as well.

Other signs such as 'fragmentation of heart muscle' are spurious.

Rigor mortis is known to supervene much more quickly after electrocution. Cardiac arrest from electricity is the condition *par excellence* which may respond to prolonged cardiac massage and artificial respiration.

EMBOLISM

The movement of an abnormal substance through the blood vessels, with subsequent impaction at the first junction where the larger vessel divides into branches. Embolism may occur in either arteries or veins, but its harmful effects are almost always in arteries, especially the pulmonary artery.

The abnormal substance may be any of the following, which are further described under the first three headings:

Thrombo-embolism, where blood clot is washed along the vessels. This is by far the most common type, most important medico-legally (see 'Pulmonary embolism').

Air embolism, where air or other gas gains entry through a defect in a vein (see 'Air embolism').

Fat embolism, usually following a bone fracture, where the marrow fat leaks into ruptured blood vessels. It may also be seen as a post-mortem artefact in severe burns. Almost all fractures – and many soft tissue injuries involving fatty areas such as the buttocks – result in minor fat embolism, but almost all is filtered out by the lung capillary bed. Only if so much is released that it penetrates the lungs, can it reach the arterial circulation and cause problems or even death by impacting in small vessels in the brain, heart and kidneys (see 'Fat embolism').

Amniotic fluid embolism, from the contents of the pregnancy sac; the fluid around the foetus may be forced into the circulation during or following childbirth, especially when complications such as ruptured uterus occur.

The fluid contains skin squames of keratin from the baby, which may be identified at post-mortem by microscopic examination of the lungs. Death is presumed to occur from some 'allergic' response to the protein in the fluid, causing profound shock and collapse. A frequent complication is disseminated intravascular coagulopathy (DIC) (qv).

Bone marrow embolism in fractures. The blood-forming tissue in the marrow cavities of bones often becomes dislodged into the circulation when fractures occur. This may be helpful in distinguishing ante mortem from post-mortem fractures, when investigating, for instance, air crashes. For embolism of distant organs to occur, the circulation must naturally have been in operation at the time of fracture, that is, the victim was still alive.

Foreign body embolism: rare, but shotgun pellets have embolised into vital blood vessels such as a coronary artery.

ENTOMOLOGY

The study of insect infestation on bodies (see 'post-mortem entomology').

EPILEPSY

A common neurological disease with frequent medico-legal aspects. There are two main types of epilepsy:

(a) grand mal, where fits involving physical movement occur;

(b) petit mal, where the episodes consist of transient unconsciousness without fits.

There is also psychomotor epilepsy, characterised by a disorder of behaviour which may manifest itself as antisocial or criminal acts. Epilepsy may be thought of as a sporadic disturbance of brain activity leading either to loss of function (unconsciousness) or active movement (fits). Everyone is a potential epileptic, but the normal threshold is too high for stimuli to be effective, except in extreme conditions such as electric shock, high fevers and some poisons. The threshold is much lower in children, for example, the common convulsions of high temperature.

A certain proportion of people retain a low threshold and are actual or potential epileptics, this potential usually being diagnosable by electro-encephalography (EEG). There is a definite familial tendency to epilepsy. In both grand mal and petit mal, a premonitory 'aura' is common, which may take many forms, including sensory abnormalities of sight, hearing or smell. After the fit, a post-epileptic state is common, again pleomorphic, but commonly deep sleep, disordered behaviour or 'post-epileptic automatism', where a certain pattern of actions is irresistible. During this state, antisocial, dangerous or criminal acts may be carried out.

Petit mal consists of sudden loss of senses and consciousness – the 'falling sickness'. There may be danger to the patient or to those in his care. In the grand mal attack, a preliminary 'tonic' state occurs where the muscles are tensed, followed by a 'clonic' state where rhythmical muscle contractions constitute the classical fit. The tongue may be bitten, respiration is prevented and physical injuries may occur.

Where fits are continuous or repeated with little interval, the condition of 'status epilepticus' exists. This may cause death from exhaustion or injury, but epileptics can suddenly die for no discernible reason, even when not in status or even in a fit. There is modern evidence that many epileptics have damage to their heart muscle from repeated attacks of oxygen lack during previous fits. Death may also occur from asphyxia when an unsupervised epileptic has a fit with his face in a pillow – or drowns in a bath. Epileptics usually have amnesia for a variable period before, during and after a fit, which again may have profound legal connotations in regard to criminal responsibility.

Applications for motor vehicle driving licences must reveal any propensity to fits and usually an epileptic will not be allowed to drive. However, this is a matter for determination in each case, dependent upon medical opinion as to the complete suppression of fits by appropriate drugs, such as Epanutin (phenytoin) and similar and more modern medicaments. The use of the electro-encephalograph (EEG) is not always reliable, as a much larger proportion of the population have an epileptiform EEG than those who actually show any signs of fits.

Most epilepsy is 'idiopathic', that is, there is no morphological abnormality visible on examination of the brain. A small proportion is 'traumatic epilepsy', which may arise from old brain injury, such as a previous fracture of the skull, which causes pressure on the brain or some abnormality which can be recognised at autopsy. This variety has particular legal aspects due to the compensation issues relating to the original causative injury.

EXPECTATION OF LIFE

The years of life expected to remain to a man or woman at any given age have been statistically assessed in actuarial tables. This is a blanket calculation for the whole population, not taking into account the state of health of any individual.

The expected longevity of a particular person may assume considerable legal importance where life has been prematurely terminated by an unnatural event, predominantly transport or occupational accidents. Where a civil action in negligence succeeds, the potentially large damages may be significantly reduced if it is shown that the expectation of life of the deceased would have been shortened by some natural disease, even if the accident had not occurred.

Medical opinion is usually sought to affirm or deny such a reduction of expectation of life. This is based on a study of the medical records during life and the post-mortem findings after death.

The main diseases likely to reduce expectation of life are cardiovascular, and coronary artery disease is easily the most frequent problem. It must be said that medical opinion on this matter is fraught with uncertainty and speculation, especially where heart disease is concerned. Where a cancer is involved, opinions may be firmer, though even there, the natural history of the disease and the alternative modes of treatment make prognosis far from accurate.

In degenerative arterial disease, though some clinicians will give opinions with considerable confidence, the truth is that huge variations in prognosis exist, with no means of anticipating what would have been the actual outcome. There are some statistical surveys of the prognosis of various grades of coronary artery disease (qv) but the individual multiple variations of the state of the vessels and of the heart muscle make it impossible to apply these with confidence to any given person.

A person found at autopsy to have, say, 80% narrowing of the main left coronary artery, but no signs of current or past damage in the heart muscle, may have dropped dead next day – or may have lived for 20 years.

Where the heart muscle shows fibrosis from previous infarction, the prognosis is much worse, but again he may have lived for ten years, whereas the first man may have died next week. There is no way to be accurate about this matter and medical experts have to 'pick a figure from the air', based loosely on the grade of disease found at autopsy or recorded in the medical history.

All that can usefully be offered is to suggest, on the balance of probabilities, that a person with potentially lethal disease would probably not survive until the actuarial date for average life span – and to hazard a reasonable guess as to the proportionate reduction of that period, which can only be speculative.

EXHUMATION

The raising of a body after burial is most often carried out for administrative reasons, such as the removal of a burial site or the re-burial of the person in some other grave. In the medico-legal context, exhumation is performed to allow a post-mortem examination of the corpse, either for the first time or as a re-examination. The length of time for which exhumation is worthwhile varies according to the nature of the examination required and the likely environmental conditions of the burial. In peaty, waterlogged ground, a body may vanish, including the bones, within 10–20 years; whereas in dry, well drained soil, soft tissues may survive for many years in a recognisable state. Previous embalming also retards decomposition.

Where poisons are being sought, the physical state of the body is less important and drugs such as barbiturates may be found after at least 8–10 years: heavy metallic poisons such as arsenic, antimony and lead may be recovered after many more years, again depending upon the local conditions.

Where anatomical and morphological evidence is being sought, the prospects of success are less, but if the conditions of preservation are good, then exhumation may be worthwhile up to 5–10 years after burial, depending upon the nature of the disease or injuries suspected.

If examination of the bones is required, as for identification purposes, then this period may be extended almost indefinitely.

Where poisons are being sought, it is vital to obtain control material from the coffin, its internal lining and from the adjacent soil above, below and at the sides of the casket.

The law concerning exhumation varies from country to country, but where crime or some important civil claim rests upon the outcome, it is usual for permission to be sought from a judicial or executive authority.

In England and Wales, exhumations are only lawful if authorised by a coroner, the Home Secretary or a faculty of the Ordinary (that is, a bishop).

The coroner for the district in which the deceased died theoretically has the power to order exhumation in cases in which he did not hold an inquest when the death took place, so that he can subsequently hold such an inquest If he had held an inquest, then his jurisdiction has ceased. In practice, it seems now that the procedure in all cases is to make application to the Home Secretary for an exhumation. Good cause has to be shown why such a procedure is necessary.

The procedure adopted at an exhumation mainly concerns identification of the body and the avoidance of public offence. It is now rare for the actual examination to be carried out in some inadequate shed at the edge of a cemetery. The churchwarden, sexton, superintendent of the burial ground or a surveyor must definitely identify the grave plot with reference to plans and records. Where the coffin is recovered (usually behind screens at an early hour of the day) a funeral director should identify the name plate and coffin as that which he buried. The coffin lid is loosened at the graveside to allow the escape of noxious fumes and then the coffin removed to a properly equipped mortuary for examination by a pathologist well experienced in forensic autopsies. Again, the grave clothes and coffin furniture should be identified by the undertaker, where possible.

When the examination is complete, the body is usually reburied in the same grave, either in the same coffin or another if the original was in a bad condition.

The value of the examination is naturally very variable (as stated) but, where the issues are serious, the information gained may often be more useful than might be expected, certainly within the first few years after burial.

EXPLOSION INJURIES

The rise in terrorist activity in many parts of the world has caused the incidence of explosion trauma to increase markedly.

Formerly seen only in the military or industrial accident situation, the detonation of explosive devices causes a wide spectrum of injuries. In general, the destructive power of 'home made' devices, even when quite sophisticated in terms of the arming and firing components, is far less than military bombs, mines and shells, due to the less powerful explosive compounds used and also to a less massive confining container around the charge. This difference is reflected in the nature of the injuries, as pure blast damage is uncommon in terrorist devices except at very close range and is most often seen when a premature detonation kills or injures the terrorist himself (so called 'own goal').

Types of injury

Penetration, laceration and abrasions by bomb fragments. The casing of the device, adjacent loose objects, and sometimes metal missiles deliberately incorporated, fly away from the focus of the detonation and impinge upon any body in their path. At relatively close range, this produces a typical picture of multiple, stippled wounds of varying size and depth, the skin sometimes being 'peppered' as in shotgun blasts, though the marks are usually of very uneven size. Death may occur from larger fragments penetrating vital structure and this may occur up to many yards away from the explosion.

Gross injuries and disruption of the body. Complete dismemberment and evisceration is not a common feature of terrorist bombs except at minimum range, usually when the victim is holding or carrying the device or standing directly over it. Even in the latter situation, the damage tends to be polarised to the nearest part of the body and can give good evidence for reconstructing the position of the victim, for example, destroyed legs suggest a bomb on the ground with the victim standing next to it or frontal abdominal and thigh injuries suggest the device was held on the lap. In all types of close range explosion, the skin is often darkened and discoloured from the effects of the chemicals and products of explosion, as well as from burns and dirt blasted into the skin by the explosion.

Injuries and fatalities may often occur not from the direct effects of the device, but from secondary damage such as falling masonry or roof beams when a building collapses or burns from fires started by the bomb. Crushing, internal injuries, traumatic asphyxia (qv) and direct fractures and trauma present the same features as similar injuries in other circumstances.

Burns from the direct effect of the explosion may occur if the victim is near the device, but other effects from direct trauma are more likely to be fatal if the range is small enough to allow heat effects.

Blast injuries in the true sense are not common in the terrorist situation, as mentioned earlier, unless military devices have been obtained. However, they may be seen in confined spaces and industrial fatalities. Blasting in mining and quarrying or massive explosions in munitions or chemical factories may produce severe blast effects. This effect is due to a wave of high pressure air travelling away from the focus of explosion at about the speed of sound. The high pressure front is followed by a zone of negative pressure. A pressure of over 100 lb/sq in is necessary to produce significant damage to a person and this can be generated by the adjacent detonation of a 70lb charge. However, the effects diminish by the inverse square law with distance, so that this charge would produce only 15 lb/sq in at 30 ft distance. The shock wave injures by direct transmission through the body surface. Organs with a relatively uniform composition, such as liver and muscle, suffer little damage, but where an organ has a variable composition, especially with junctions between air and solid components (such as lung), then severe damage may occur. Disruption and haemorrhage are common due to the shock wave acting with differing intensity on different tissues. The ear is also often damaged in blast injuries.

Where injury is severe, identification becomes a problem and even the estimation of how many victims were involved may present difficulties. A careful post-mortem examination is essential in order to reconstruct the events as fully as possible.

EXTRADURAL HAEMORRHAGE (OR HAEMATOMA)

Accumulation of blood and blood clot between the inner aspect of the skull and the outermost layer of the brain membranes (the dura mater). Sometimes called 'epidural' haemorrhage.

Invariably the result of a head injury, usually with a fracture of the skull, but between 9% and 19% of cases occur without skull fracture, mostly in young people with a more elastic skull. The middle meningeal artery is usually the source of bleeding, as it runs in a groove or tunnel up the inside of the skull above the ear. The middle meningeal is involved in 54% and the posterior meningeal in 21%.

Rupture of one of these vessels, usually due to a fracture line crossing the vessel, allows blood to escape into the potential space between skull and dura.

The blood and clot slowly accumulates over hours or up to a day, during which there may be no or slight symptoms after recovery from the probable transient concussion (qv). This 'latent' or 'lucid interval' is typical of extradural haemorrhage. Eventually, the haemorrhage reaches a size sufficient to press on the brain. This leads to unconsciousness, often neurological signs of weakness of the opposite side, and other symptoms and signs detectable by a neurological examination. These may progress to a fatal result if surgical intervention to open the skull and evacuate the blood clot is not undertaken. It was formerly held that this was the type of head injury that responded best to surgery, but more recent opinion suggests that the mortality rate remains high even after operation.

The progressive enlargement of the extradural haemorrhage (EDH) will indent the underlying brain and sometimes push that hemisphere of the brain across the midline. The brain stem becomes compressed into the base of the skull by the swelling of the rest of the cranial contents above it.

Death is due to raised intracranial pressure leading to failure of the vital centres in the brain stem which control breathing and heart function. Failure of a doctor to diagnose or anticipate the risk of an extradural haemorrhage has led to many allegations of negligence, both in general practitioners and in A and E doctors. Many patients have attended and been discharged home, only to be re-admitted to die in a coma the following day.

Figure 28:   Extradural haemorrhage

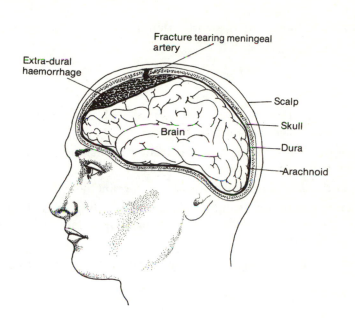

FABRICATED INJURIES (SELF-INFLICTED INJURIES)

Superficial self-inflicted injuries with often a characteristic pattern, but not suicidal in intent.

Motives

(a) To cover some criminal activity, for example, robbery or fraud, by alleging robbery with violence against themselves.

(b) To feign injury for insurance, compensation or malingering reasons or to elicit sympathy for some personal reason.

(c) To support a false allegation of assault against another person.

(d) Psychiatric origin, for example, woman fabricating sexually orientated attack. Also gross mutilation, often genital, by paranoid schizophrenic, often with religious basis.

Apart from the last type, injuries are usually trivial and present no threat to life.

Features

(a) Usually multiple, parallel scratches of uniform, slight depth.

(b) They avoid vital and sensitive areas such as eyes, nose, mouth.

(c) Often confined to, or more marked on left side in right handed persons.

(d) Usual sites are face, forehead, sides of neck, front of chest, backs of hands (especially left) and back of shoulders.

(e) Are absent in inaccessible sites such as the lower back.

Often do not correspond with fabricated damage to overlying clothing. Gross injuries due to severe self-mutilation in psychiatric patients usually involve amputation of genital organs, cut throat and sometimes self-blinding.

FAT EMBOLISM

Blockage of small arteries by globules of fat (see also 'Embolism'). Common condition after fractures, but rarely of fatal degree.

After fractures or extensive injury to fatty tissues such as buttocks, fat escapes into the bloodstream through torn veins. May also occur in surgical operations on bones, joints or breast. Origin is the fat stores in bone marrow or adipose tissue under skin.

Globules are carried to lungs, where most are held up by the tiny capillaries, but if the volume of fat exceeds a certain (variable) threshold, it escapes from the further end of the lung circulation and enters the left side of the heart and hence the arterial system.

Globules can then block small branches of vital arteries, especially in the brain and coronary vessels and cause small haemorrhages at the impaction site. Most frequent action is to damage the nerve centres in the brain stem, leading to coma and death from heart and lung failure. Often a latent interval of a day or two between fractures and onset of coma – causes difficulty in differentiation of head injury (especially extradural haemorrhage) from cerebral fat embolism.

Fat may be recognised in body fluids, such as sputum or urine, but this occurs quite often when no fatal cerebral embolism occurs.

Small haemorrhage in skin often a sign of fat emboli. post-mortem finding of fat globules in lungs is of no particular significance, as it is so common. After death from burning, spurious post-mortem fat embolism may be found, due to melting and boiling of fat after death.

Some academic controversy exists as to true source of fat – whether directly from fat stores in bones and tissues, or by chemico-physical alteration of normal emulsified fat in blood into larger globules.

FEMUR, FRACTURE OF

The most common domestic accident, very frequent in old people, especially women, due to increasing rarefaction of bone and subsequent brittleness. Death rate is relatively high, though greatly improved in recent years due to surgical repair by hip replacement and other metal prostheses. The bones of old people become more fragile due to 'osteoporosis' of skeleton as whole, where the calcium content is reduced. The neck of the femur, just below the hip joint, bears most stress and easily fractures due to any fall or serious twist.

Dangers of fractured femur

Rapid death from pain, shock and blood loss. The latter might be considerable into surrounding tissues and muscles and in old people, often anaemic, the loss is more serious. In healthy, younger persons fractured femur due to serious accidents, such as traffic injuries, may be fatal from gross shock and haemorrhage. The fracture is then usually of the shaft, rather than the neck.

Bronchopneumonia may supervene within days or weeks. Sometimes called 'hypostatic', because immobility in bed, shallow breathing due to pain and accumulation of lung fluids and secretions due to flat posture, encourage the growth of infective bacteria.

Pulmonary embolism (qv) is common, due to tissue damage, immobility in bed and pressure on calves of legs.

The so called 'spontaneous fracture' of the femur is a misnomer, and really means a fracture with minimal trauma, even turning over in bed, due to the presence of some disease process such as a tumour or severe brittleness (see 'Fractures').

FINGER-NAIL MARKS

Superficial abrasions or shallow lacerations on skin. Seen most often in strangulation and in child abuse syndrome.

In strangulation, they are most commonly inflicted by the victim, who struggles to tear the hands of the assailant or a ligature from the neck. Scratches are often vertical, running up and down the front and sides of the neck beneath the chin, but may be along the line of a ligature. Even in self-hanging, nailmarks may be seen alongside the rope, from reflex scrabbling.

Other nail marks may be from the assailant, but usually shorter, crescentic marks due to static pressure, often associated with disc-shaped bruises from finger-tip pressure.

In still-born infants and suspected infanticides, spurious signs of strangulation may be due to finger-nails imprinted or dragged along infant's neck in frantic effort at self-delivery by lone, often inexperienced young mother.

Finger-nail scratches may be linear, due to dragging along skin surface, or semi-lunar, due to static digging in. In the latter, care is needed in interpretation of direction of hand when inflicted, as it has been shown that the concavity of the mark may in fact be caused by convexity of nail, due to elastic rebound of skin under tension.

Skin and blood may be trapped under the finger-nails of a scratching hand; scrapings or trimmings of such nails may allow the forensic laboratory to confirm the presence of skin and blood, to confirm its human origin, to determine its sex and to determine the individual, by DNA technology, all of which can differentiate the victim from the assailant.

FIREARM WOUNDS

Two main types, according to weapon: (a) from smooth bore shotguns; and (b) from rifled weapons – revolver, automatic pistol, rifle, machine gun, etc.

Smooth bore weapon wounds

The shotgun emits numerous small projectiles in a narrow extended cone, thus the size of wound increases with distance from muzzle. There are two main types of shotgun – 12-bore (larger) and 410 (smaller). Cartridges contain shot, propellant powder or granules, and plastic, felt or cardboard discs, cups and wads, all of which may contribute to the wound.

Entrance wound. Features of entry wound vary, according to distance of discharge:

(a) *contact:* circular, but often split due to entry of gases, especially over bony areas such as skull. May be a muzzle mark on skin, but not common. Burning of margins, hairs. Bruising around hole, with soot and powder soiling. Great internal disruption, especially when fired into head. Pink coloration of tissues from carbon monoxide in gases. Wads and discs in wound as well as shot. Single large hole, no spread of shot;

(b) *near-contact:* circular, unless very near when split to admit gases. Burnt margins, soot and powder tattooing, though less with modern propellants. Wads and cups in wound;

(c) *mid-range:* up to two metres. Some burning and powder tattooing at lower end of range, depending on weapon and ammunition. Large single hole, maybe irregular margins. A few stray satellite pellet holes may begin at a few feet range;

(d) *distant discharge:* over two metres. Progressive enlargement of pellet pattern with diminution of central hole until latter vanishes at about seven to 10 yards. Diameter of pellet spread in inches roughly equals range in yards, but this varies greatly with weapon and ammunition. No burning or powder tattooing. Wads, plastic cups and discs travel two to four yards, but occasionally up to six yards. Distant 'peppering' rarely fatal unless associated heart disease or shot through eye, etc.

Shotgun wounds rarely exit through trunk but may traverse limb or neck, especially when fired into mouth in suicides.

Figure 29:   12-bore shotgun injuries

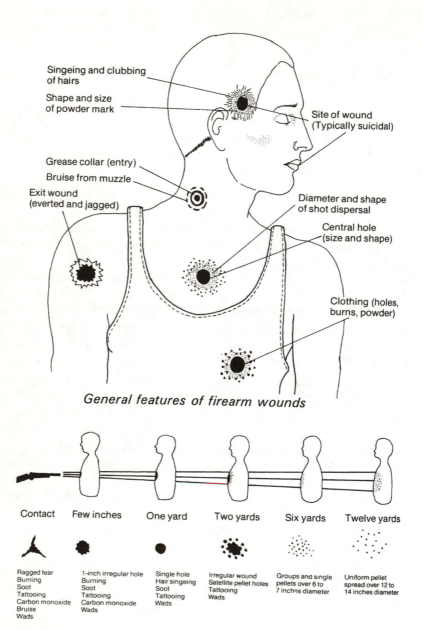

Singeing and clubbing of hairs

Shape and size of powder mark

Site of wound (Typically suicidal)

Grease collar (entry)

Bruise from muzzle

Exit wound (everted and jagged)

Diameter and shape of shot dispersal

Central hole (size and shape)

Clothing (holes, burns, powder)

General features of firearm wounds

Contact	Few inches	One yard	Two yards	Six yards	Twelve yards
Ragged tear Burning Soot Tattooing Carbon monoxide Bruise Wads	1-inch irregular hole Burning Soot Tattooing Carbon monoxide Wads	Single hole Hair singeing Soot Tattooing Wads	Irregular wound Satellite pellet holes Tattooing Wads	Groups and single pellets over 6 to 7 inches diameter	Uniform pellet spread over 12 to 14 inches diameter

Rifled weapon wounds

Much higher muzzle velocity than shotgun (up to 3,000 ft/second). Also the single projectile is heavier, so energy ($\frac{1}{2}$ mv^2) much greater than with shotgun pellet. Thus, both entrance and exit wounds frequently occur, though modern military weapons may have very high velocity and small bullet, designed to fragment in the body and thus deliver all their kinetic energy without loss from exiting.

Entrance wound. Features of entry wound vary, according to distance of discharge:

(a) if *contact*, may be ragged or stellate tear due to entry of gas. Bruising and mark from muzzle (not due to recoil as often stated in textbooks, as recoil takes the muzzle away – it is due to gas pressure forcing tissues against muzzle);

(b) *near discharge:* soot immediately around hole, though modern propellant relatively 'clean'. May be unburnt propellant flakes on skin. At short range, same features, though round hole, with inverted edges. May be soiled if lead or lubricated bullet. Abrasion ring or friction from passage of bullet through outer skin layer. General appearance like lead pencil thrust through skin, with inverted margins;

(c) *distant shot* cannot be gauged as to range, once distance too far. Hole small due to steady gyro trajectory of bullet: at extreme range (may be over a mile with a rifle) the bullet may begin to oscillate or even tumble and cause a bigger wound;

(d) size of hole need not correspond to calibre of bullet, due to elastic recoil of skin – hole usually smaller unless very close discharge or a tumbling bullet.

Exit wounds

Usually larger, more irregular (stellate or cruciate) with everted margins. However, some exit wounds hard to differentiate from entry. If solid object struck within body, then tumbling or fragmentation of bullet or bony structures may cause larger, ragged or even multiple exit wounds. If skin at exit site supported, for example, by trouser or brassière band or pressure against wooden door, then the exit wound may not be everted and may look like entry.

Direction of shot

This is better estimated with rifled weapon by projecting a line from entry and exit wounds, though deviation may occur from striking internal structures, especially bone. Interpretation of direction must take into account the posture of the body at time of impact – this may not be known and may be unexpected.

Direction is more difficult in shotgun wound due to diffuse nature of pellet spread – X-ray may assist. Skin wound is helpful – circular pellet spread in frontal discharge, becomes progressively more elliptical as shot comes from side.

In rifle wound, direction affects circular or elliptical shape to lesser extent: undercutting of wound edges in oblique impact. Smoke blackening in near discharge may assist in assessing direction, especially with shotgun: elliptical in oblique discharge.

FOETUS (FETUS)

Foetal state exists between conception until birth (or in law, until separate existence). 'Embryo' is usually taken to mean the very early stages of gestation before the detailed human shape is attained.

Though in law, a foetus attains 'viability' at the age of 24 weeks' gestation, modern obstetrical care allows some younger infants to survive. At 36 weeks the foetus attains 'maturity', though birth is usually several weeks later than this, around the 40th week.

Length of gestation – see 'Pregnancy'

Foetal development

At full term of about 40 weeks, the foetus shows:

(a) a weight of 2,550–3,500 g;

(b) a crown–heel length of 48–52 cm, crown–rump length 28–32 cm, head circumference of 33–38 cm;

(c) the finger and toe-nails have grown beyond the tips of the digits (not reliable);

(d) the head hair is more than 2 cm in length;

(e) the male's testes are present in the scrotum and the female's labia close the vaginal opening; and

(f) ossification centres are present in the lower end of the femur (thigh) – about 6 mm diameter – and upper end of the tibia (shin) in 80% of infants, as well as in the cuboid of the heel.

At 36 weeks, the length is about 45 cm and the weight around 2,200 g. At 28 weeks, the length is about 35 cm and the weight 900–1,100 g.

The Haase Rule for length of gestation is that, up to the 20th week, the length in centimetres is equal to the square of the age in lunar months.

Beyond the 20th week, the length in centimetres, divided by five, is the age in months.

FOREIGN BODIES

Intrusive deposition of foreign matter into tissues or body cavities. Usually refers to solid, inorganic (often metallic) objects, rather than to bacteria or living organisms.

Foreign bodies can be introduced into the body as follows:

(a) From *trauma*, such as firearm or explosive injury, traffic or transport accidents or any penetrating injury carrying foreign material into wound. Industrial accidents another common cause, as well as DIY accidents at home with power tools, hammers and chisels, etc.

Foreign bodies may enter through skin wound, into eye, mouth or air passages, etc. Food bones may penetrate stomach or intestine.

(b) During *surgical operations*: foreign bodies such as surgical instruments, swabs, needles, etc, retained after surgical procedure completed.

(c) *Children and mental patients*, more so than normal adults, may introduce foreign bodies into throat, stomach, larynx, windpipe, anus, vagina, etc. In some forms of sexual aberration, foreign bodies may be introduced into bladder via the urinary passages or into the rectum via the anus.

Surgical exploration or visual detection via gastroscope or bronchoscope may be needed.

X-rays almost always used to detect and localise internal foreign bodies, especially if object is radio-opaque. Glass fragments, common in motor accidents, are almost always visible on X-ray.

Foreign bodies have particular relevance in medical malpractice actions, either because of retention after operation or because of failure of doctors to search adequately for foreign body on attendance at an Accident and Emergency department.

FRACTURES

Physical discontinuity of a bone due to mechanical stress. Amount of stress required to exceed fracture threshold related to condition of bone, for example, osteoporosis or rarefaction of bone in senility and in some kidney or endocrine diseases which have abnormal calcium metabolism.

Certain diseases with abnormal fragility of bones, such as some varieties of *osteogenesis imperfecta*, are often invoked in defence against child abuse.

Where a localised focus of disease exists in a bone, such as a secondary tumour from a distant cancer, then the so called 'pathological fracture' may occur. This is often termed 'spontaneous', but still requires some trauma, albeit minimal.

If fracture associated with breach of skin, called 'compound', with risk of infection.

Fracture at a joint termed 'fracture dislocation', common in spine. In children, bones are more pliable and less brittle, so fractures are often incomplete, called 'greenstick', with angulation but no complete loss of continuity.

Dangers of fractures

Immediate pain, shock and haemorrhage. Bleeding can be severe, either externally in a compound fracture or internally around bone. This bleeding itself may contribute substantially to death, especially in anaemic old people. Pre-existing heart disease may be exacerbated to cause sudden or rapid death.

Infection of tissues, especially in compound fracture.

Kidney failure due to crushing of muscles or low blood pressure from shock and haemorrhage.

Bronchopneumonia, especially in the aged, due to enforced immobility allowing stagnation and infection of lung secretions.

Fat embolism (qv) within a day or two.

Pulmonary embolism (qv) usually within a week or two, due to deep vein thrombosis in legs, following tissue trauma and immobility.

Failure or long delay in healing and subsequent deformity.

Complication of treatment, for example, anaesthesia, tight plasters, need for extensive surgical repair, etc.

FRONTAL SINUS IDENTIFICATION

The frontal sinuses are convoluted air spaces within the bone of the skull, in the centre of the forehead, extending outwards above the eyes. Their pattern as seen on X-ray is unique to every individual, as characteristic as fingerprints: this applies especially to the scalloped upper border of the sinuses, as well as to their general size and shape.

Used in identification, even of badly decomposed or burned body, especially in mass disasters such as air crashes. The sinuses are protected from even severe charring by fire. Must have a pre-existing X-ray available for comparison, obtained from hospital or other records. Complete reliability in matching if this is compared with post-mortem X-rays of skull.

Chronic infection, such as sinusitis, may blur or even distort the radiographic individuality, but this is a relatively uncommon source of difficulty in matching sinuses.

GANGRENE

Death of tissues, usually an extremity such as fingers, toes, arm or leg, usually due to failure of adequate circulation. Tissues surrounding wounds can also become gangrenous, as well as internal organs such as appendix. Gangrene of limbs may be dry desiccation or moist putrefaction: the tissues usually discolour and go through spectrum of red, purple, black or green.

A particularly virulent form of gangrene is known as 'fasciitis', due to rapid spread of an infection through the tissues of a limb or trunk.

Causes

Loss of blood supply, such as arterial degeneration in diabetes or arterio-sclerosis. Also when artery is blocked by embolism (qv) and in frostbite, where blood supply ceases.

Infection, which may be primary or follow an injury to the affected part. May also supervene in tissues dying from lack of blood supply. Great danger of death from septicaemia or local toxaemia.

Gas gangrene

This is a particular type of infective gangrene due to anaerobic bacteria (which shun oxygen), usually *B perfringens* (formerly known as *Clostridium welchii*). Putrid smell and puffy tissues due to gas formation. Used to be almost invariably fatal without amputation, but antibiotics now effective in earlier stages.

GENERAL MEDICAL COUNCIL (GMC)

Originally established by the Medical Act (1858) to allow the public to distinguish between qualified doctors and quacks.

Primary duties are to:

(a) maintain the Medical Register;

(b) supervise medical education;

(c) exercise disciplinary function over medical profession;

(d) establish standards of medical ethics and professional conduct; and

(e) investigate defects in physical and mental health of doctors relating their fitness to practice.

The GMC is directly responsible to the Privy Council and consists of members elected by registered medical practitioners every five years, members nominated by university medical schools and Royal Colleges, and lay members nominated by the Privy Council.

Medical Register

British doctors may be fully or provisionally registered. The latter are new graduates who must spend at least 12 months in approved house officer appointments and show proof of satisfactory progress before being admitted to full registration.

Overseas doctors may be granted either full or limited registration depending upon complex arrangements relating to their previous medical education and fluency in English. Most will have to sit the PLAB (Professional and Linguistics Assessment Board) examinations to gain admission to the Register.

The Register now also give indications as to the speciality of fully trained registrants. UK registration must be granted to EEA nationals qualifying in their own country.

Disciplinary functions of the GMC

Complaints about the professional behaviour of doctors reach the GMC:
(a) from all convictions of doctors in criminal courts via the police;
(b) from official bodies such as NHS trusts and health authorities;
(c) on sworn statements from members of the public; and
(d) from divorce cases, now only if the aggrieved party alleges a breach of professional behaviour.

All complaints are examined by a member of the GMC, the *Preliminary Screener*. Trivial, obviously unfounded or fatuous complaints are eliminated, the remainder go to the Preliminary Proceedings Committee for consideration (similar to committal proceedings). The doctor may be invited at this stage to answer the complaint. If a *prima facie* case is considered to exist, the case goes to the Professional Conduct Committee, where a full hearing is held with witnesses on oath and legal representation on both sides.

The Committee decides whether there has been 'serious professional misconduct' and may:
(a) dismiss the complaint;
(b) admonish the doctor;

(c) postpone judgment – in effect, a probationary period of any length, during which the doctor must obtain proof of good behaviour in order to avoid an adverse judgment;

(d) suspend the doctor's registration for a period not exceeding one year; or

(e) direct the Registrar to erase the doctor's name from the Register. In this case, an appeal may be made to the Judicial Committee of the Privy Council. If the appeal is not upheld, the doctor may apply at 10 month intervals for restoration of his name to the Register.

A doctor erased or suspended from the Register loses all privileges as a registered medical practitioner.

A Health Committee investigates doctors whose fitness to practice may be impaired by any physical or mental disability.

A more recent development is the establishment of professional performance machinery as, formerly, complaints about a poorly performing doctor, who was not committing professional misconduct, could not be dealt with. Now such doctors are investigated, monitored and may be required to undergo re-training. If they fail to improve or refuse to co-operate, they may be removed from the Register.

GLASS INJURIES

In general, similar to incised wounds by knives and razors, but may be even more cleanly cut due to the exquisitely sharp edge. The wound lacks any marginal bruising, which may be seen on some knife injuries where the weapon is not very sharp. There may be slicing of the skin in an undercut fashion, so that an oblique cut is made into the thickness of the skin by the very sharp edge – this may cut through hair roots in hairy parts, revealing a stippled appearance.

Where the glass fragment is irregular, the wound may also be misshapen, even bizarre. A sharp spicule may cause a stab wound. Fragments of glass may detach and can be seen on X-ray, as almost all glass is radio-opaque, contrary to popular belief.

The damage caused by shattered windscreen glass is highly characteristic due to the nature of the uniform fragments of pre-toughened glass used in motor vehicles. The face is the usual site of injury and may be covered by multiple small V- or Y-shaped abrasions and shallow lacerations.

Other glass injuries are often seen in bar brawls where a shattered drinking glass is used as a weapon. Severe facial injuries are common, due to projections and spicules of glass smashing or penetrating the skin.

It may be difficult or impossible to tell from the wounds whether a glass was used intact and smashed on the victim's face, or whether the glass was pre-smashed to be used as a weapon. Substantial glasses may not break on impact and then the features are naturally that of blunt injury only.

Glass-type cuts can be caused by broken pottery, such as a coffee mug, if the glaze is exposed as a sharp cutting edge by an oblique fracture of the pottery.

Glass injuries, sometimes fatal, can also occur from persons falling or being pushed through a window or glass door.

GLUE SNIFFING (SOLVENT ABUSE)

A common form of drug abuse, mostly amongst children and teenagers, though no age is exempt. Many organic compounds, especially halogenated hydrocarbons, may be used, such as the solvents used in proprietary glues. These have potent effects on the brain when inhaled, similar to chloroform or trichloethylene, though in fact the most common solvent of glues such as 'Evo-stik' is toluene, which is not a halogenated compound. Many other substances, such as typewriter correcting fluid (for example, Tippex), gasoline, paint strippers, fire extinguisher fluid, cellulose solvent, etc, are misused in a similar fashion. Another form of inhalation abuse is from aerosol cans of various substances, including that used to treat sprained muscles. Lighter fuel and hydrocarbon gases, such as butane and propane, may also be inhaled.

A particular danger of inhaled pressurised gases is the possibility of sudden death from a vagal inhibition (qv) type reaction when the refrigerating effect of released gas impinges on the back of the throat. This has been seen a number of times with the use of small cylinders of butane intended for cigarette lighters.

Solvents are easily available and cheap, often shoplifted; users inhale the fumes from glue extruded from the tubes and pass into a presumably pleasant state of disorientation and even coma.

The substance is often squeezed into a plastic bag, which is placed over the face or head. This in itself is dangerous, even without the presence of solvent, as it can cause asphyxia very rapidly. Though most solvent sniffing has no permanent ill effects, there is a danger of sudden death from an effect on the heart, which can fibrillate or arrest. The mechanism is thought to be a sensitisation by the solvent of the heart muscle to catecholamines, adrenaline-like compounds generated by the body. These can send the heart into a state of abnormal rhythm.

Vomiting and choking are also possible and in a small proportion of long term users, the toxic solvents can cause irreversible liver disease.

HAEMORRHAGE

Loss of blood from body surface or into body cavities or tissues. Danger to life is related to (a) volume lost, (b) speed of loss, and (c) fitness and age of person.

Total volume of blood in body is about six litres (10 pints). Rapid loss of two pints is dangerous to life, but much more can be lost over a longer period (days) if volume is made up from other body fluids.

Persons with anaemia (thin blood) or any other systemic disease are at greater risk from the effects of haemorrhage.

Internal haemorrhages

Bleeding into alimentary canal may appear in vomit (haematemesis), often brown due to alteration by stomach acid, or may appear in stools (melaena), usually black unless massive or bleeding low down in canal, when it may remain red. Many causes, including peptic ulcers (of stomach or duodenum), cancer of stomach or intestines, or internal injuries.

Bleeding into air passages and lungs is usually bright red due to oxygenation and is frothy from mixture with air (haemoptysis). Causes include tuberculosis, cancer and chest injuries.

Bleeding into heart bag (pericardium) rapidly fatal due to embarrassment of heart's filling capacity – 'cardiac tamponade'. Usual causes are a ruptured aortic aneurysm (qv) or a ruptured myocardial infarct (qv).

Bleeding into abdominal cavity (haemoperitoneum) usually occurs from trauma such as ruptured liver or spleen or bruised intestines.

Bleeding into chest cavities (pleura) from wounds of lung or leakage from large blood vessels, such as aorta. Common in chest stab wounds. Uterine and vaginal bleeding from abortions, menstruation and disease.

Small pin-head haemorrhages in eyes and skin, called petechiae (qv). When larger, called ecchymoses.

Haemorrhage inside skull (see 'Extradural haemorrhage', 'Subarachnoid haemorrhage' and 'Subdural haemorrhage').

A relatively small volume of blood spilt upon a flat surface may give a false impression of a large amount lost.

HAIR

Modified skin composed of keratin, the same protein as the epidermis (outer layer of skin). Extruded from small follicle or 'silo' embedded in skin. Grows at about half a millimetre per day on head and face.

Hairs can be identified as to species and sometimes to race. Since the advent of DNA techniques, the sex and personal identity can be obtained from the root cells and even the shaft.

Characteristics of hair displayed by thickness, external skull pattern, cross-sectioned shape, relative size of cortex and medulla (inner and outer layers), colour, etc.

Apart from DNA, no way of matching individual hairs to any one person, but marked dissimilarity in colour, shape and texture may exclude matching. Pubic and armpit hair different in texture from head hair.

Other characteristics of hair include the presence of artificial colour or bleach; whether the hair has been cut or has a natural end; whether it has been plucked out with the root or shed naturally in the cycle of 'moulting'.

Some racial characteristics may also be present in hair, the negroid type being elliptical in cross-section, the mongoloid being circular, with caucasian intermediate. The whole subject is complex and requires the assistance of a forensic biologist.

HANGING

Death due to suspension by the neck: usually not truly 'asphyxial' in nature (see 'Asphyxia').

Almost always accidental or self-inflicted. Homicidal hanging virtually impossible, unless victim shows signs of restraint (bruises, etc) or is incapacitated by drink, drugs, fear, etc. Accidental hangings seen in children entangled in cot harness and in young male adults as a result of masochistic practices (qv).

Mechanisms

Death is often rapid, virtually instantaneous, due to jerk on carotid arteries, producing reflex cardiac arrest (qv). This is the most common single mechanism, even in the short drop employed by suicides. The face is usually pale, with no congestion or petechial haemorrhages in eyelids or lips. The latter is seen in a proportion of cases, especially where the hanging is 'incomplete', that is, where the body is not fully suspended clear of the floor, but slumped with partial support.

Few post-mortem signs internally. Hyoid bone (qv) usually not fractured.

In the slower deaths, constriction of neck veins and airway obstruction, due to raising of tongue against the palate at the back of the throat. Obstruction of jugular veins causes dark congestion and purple cyanosis of face and neck above ligature. Pin-point petechial haemorrhages may appear in face, eyelids, whites of eyes, etc (see 'Asphyxia'). Less common than sudden death hangings.

There may be terminal convulsions which can kick over stool or chair, etc. May be reflex scrabbling at rope, leaving fingermarks.

The rope or cord commonly becomes imprinted onto the skin of the neck, causing a groove. The pattern of the weave frequently remains. After death, the hanging mark usually becomes parchment-like or leathery due to drying.

Soft fabrics can be used for hanging, even folded towels, scarves, etc. They may leave a narrow groove like a rope, due to pressure from tension bands in the fabric.

Even shoe laces, string and belts may be used, especially in deaths in custody, where ingenuity leads to improvisation of available material.

Except sometimes when a slip knot is used, the partly circumferential mark will show a defect at the point of suspension, where the vertical tension on the knot carries the ligature away from the skin. This is usually at the back of the neck or under one ear, but may rarely be in front of the chin.

There need be no high suspension point, hanging being quite possible from doorknobs and bedposts, the slumped weight of the body being sufficient.

The post-mortem hypostasis (qv) should be in the legs and hands.

In hanging with a long rope (as in judicial hanging), the vertebrae of the neck may become fractured or dislocated, with damage to the spinal cord and spinal shock. Complete disruption of the spine may occur with stretching of the neck, or even decapitation.

HEAD INJURY

Many varieties, with varying classifications. External damage is not necessarily related to intracranial damage, which is the serious consequence.

Types of head injury

Scalp damage. Lacerations bleed copiously due to profuse blood supply, but rarely fatal unless extensive scalping as in some traffic accidents. Blunt injuries to scalp may cause wounds which closely resemble knife, axe or cleaver wounds, because of splitting over firm support of skull. Differentiation from incised wounds:

(a) edges show rim of bruising;

(b) hairs often bridge the gash;

(c) strands of fibrous tissue may survive in depths of wound.

Where the scalp injury (laceration or bruise) is on the front of the head, if victim survives more than a few hours, may get a black eye due to blood tracking down under the scalp and accumulating in the eye socket (see 'Black eye'). Scalp injuries may continue to bleed profusely after death, especially from dependent wounds.

Skull fractures (qv) may or may not be associated with either scalp damage or underlying brain damage; 25% of head injuries with fatal brain damage do not have a skull fracture.

Many skull fractures, including those in infants, may cause no disability at all and may remain undiagnosed in life. It is the damage to the cranial contents which is dangerous.

Intracranial damage is the major danger to life in head injuries, the scalp and skull lesions usually being only a concomitant indicator of substantial trauma. Brain damage may be superficial and/or deep and meningeal haemorrhage (see 'Extradural haemorrhage', 'Subdural haemorrhage' and 'Subarachnoid haemorrhage') very common.

The brain itself may suffer:

(a) *contusions* (that is, bruised either on the surface of the cortex or deep inside);

(b) *lacerations* on the surface;

(c) *deep haemorrhages* (which must be carefully differentiated from natural haemorrhages, which may have caused an accidental injury, rather than be the result of an injury);

(d) *occult damage* to brain substance, causing *cerebral oedema* (qv) and *diffuse axonal injury* (DAI) (qv). Common in closed head injuries and in children. Examination of brain needs special techniques to demonstrate microscopic damage of DAI, but this cannot be seen unless victim survives for at least a number of hours;

(e) where a moving object strikes a stationary head, usually a 'coup' brain injury occurs under the point of impact. Where a moving head strikes a fixed surface (as in falls or projection from a vehicle), then if the back or side of the head is the site of impact, 'contre-coup' damage (qv) occurs to the diametrically opposite part of the brain.

HEART

The heart is about the size of a fist, varying in weight between 280–380 g in normal adults. Marked variation in size, related to body weight and build. The estimates given in many anatomical textbooks are smaller than usually seen in contemporary British subjects at autopsy. New tables are at variance with older estimates.

A large, athletic young man may have a heart of 420 g but this is the upper limit of normal unless the subject is of very large build. Above this, there is usually disease present, most often high blood pressure, which enlarges the heart due to the extra work required to pump against hypertension.

A small heart is seen in old age, unless disease keeps it large. A senile heart may be only 200 g or even less.

The heart lies inside a thin bag, the pericardium, which normally has only a moistening of fluid for lubrication. Increase of this fluid is an 'effusion' and inflammation of the bag is 'pericarditis'.

The main bulk of the heart mass is formed from the left ventricle which overlaps the right ventricle and forms the apex or bottom point, which is often vulnerable to knife wounds.

The heart lies obliquely in the chest, the apex being five to seven cm to the left of the midline in the fifth intercostal space (gap between fifth and sixth ribs). It thus lies inside and slightly below the left male nipple, though there is appreciable variation (see Part I, Figures 7 and 8).

The surface of the heart lies about three to four cm below the surface of the skin in the apex region, though this naturally varies with the amount of fat and muscle on the person.

Much of the heart is protected by the breast bone, but part of the left ventricle and a narrow band of the right ventricle are accessible each side, and vulnerable to knife stabs. The aorta (qv) is also vulnerable in the second intercostal space, where it lies superficially.

Wounds of the heart from knives usually puncture a ventricle allowing blood to escape into the pericardium, where death occurs from blood loss and/or 'cardiac tamponade', that is, prevention of the heart's action by stopping filling due to the constricting action of the tensed pericardial bag. Paradoxically, wounds of the right ventricle may be more lethal than those of the higher pressure left ventricle, due to the lack of the self-sealing property of the thick-walled left chamber.

Figure 30:   Section through the heart

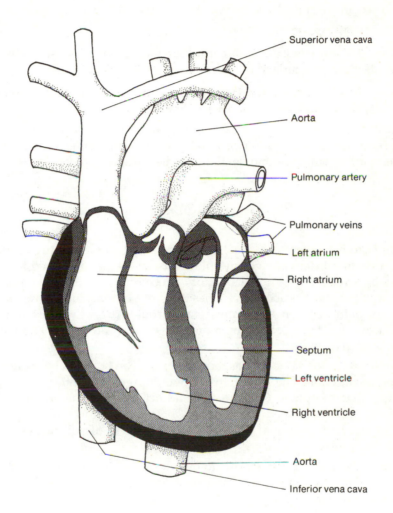

Superior vena cava

Aorta

Pulmonary artery

Pulmonary veins

Left atrium

Right atrium

Septum

Left ventricle

Right ventricle

Aorta

Inferior vena cava

HEPATITIS

Inflammation of the liver, usually due to viruses, though other micro-organisms can affect the liver, mainly through the bile ducts (cholangitis).

Viral hepatitis is of three main types:

Hepatitis A, contracted through eating infected food. It is usually benign, though deaths can occur and the liver damage may be progressive.

Hepatitis B and C, contracted through virus entering the body direct, via injections, blood transfusions, and sexual intercourse.

Shared unsterile syringes used by drug abusers, hetero and homosexual carriers, contaminated blood products and possibly infected health care workers such as surgeons and dentists may be the agent of infection.

HEROIN

Heroin is both a potent medicinal substance and a common drug of misuse, being a chemical derivative of morphine. It can be manufactured legally or illicitly by a relatively simple laboratory procedure. It is di-acetyl-morphine (diamorphine) and has about five times the effect of morphine, dose for dose. A potent pain killer, it is the most dangerous drug of addiction and its manufacture has been banned by a number of countries, as other analgesics can be used in its place.

It is active in the same way as morphine, and can be taken by swallowing, sniffing or injection. The symptoms of overdosage are similar to, but more profound than morphine. Overdosage in addicts is often due to a new source of the drug being obtained which has not been 'cut' as much as the previous supply, that is, not diluted so much with a variety of substances such as glucose or lactose.

Although many deaths are due to overdosage of heroin, rapid death may also occur from hypersensitivity on lower dosage – this may occur with first time users or habituated takers.

Stupor, coma and especially depression of breathing are the hallmarks of heroin and morphine poisoning. Waterlogging of the lungs (pulmonary oedema) is a specific feature of heroin intoxication or hypersensitivity. Infections from the use of shared, dirty and unsterile injection equipment are common, as in morphine addicts, and death from septicaemia is a well known complication of addiction, as is infection by HIV and hepatitis.

HISTOLOGY

The study of tissues under the microscope; when abnormalities are sought, it is *histopathology*.

Clinical histopathologists study tissue from operations for disease, especially cancer; tissues are (or should be) taken routinely from post-mortems to seek occult disease not visible at the gross dissection.

Tissue is placed in 10% formalin (formaldehyde in water or saline) and processed in the laboratory, this taking a few days, though there is a rapid frozen method. The tissue is embedded in paraffin wax blocks and thin sections cut and stained on glass slides, usually by the haematoxylin and eosin method (H and E), though there are hundreds of special stains.

Modern advances include histochemistry, where certain substances, especially enzymes, are rendered visible, and immunocytochemistry, where antigens and antibodies are labelled to become visible.

Histology may occasionally provide vital medico-legal evidence and slides may need to be re-examined by experts for the defence where the issues indicate.

HUMAN TISSUE ACT 1961

The statute governing the donation of organs and tissues, the obtaining of permission for post-mortem examination and, less importantly, the substitution of cremation for burial of bodies used for anatomical dissection.

The major provision of the Act is to regularise the obtaining of human tissues and organs for transplantation, therapeutic use, medical research and teaching, though there are some deficiencies in the drafting of the Act which have given rise to ambiguities in interpretation. Tissues may be taken from a deceased person by the person lawfully in possession of the body, for the above purposes, if:

(a) the deceased during life expressed a request in writing (or orally in the presence of two witnesses) that he desired any or specified tissues to be used for such purposes; or

(b) after having made reasonable inquiries, the person in possession of the body has no reason to believe that neither the deceased nor the surviving spouse or any surviving relative had any objection.

The person lawfully in possession of the body is almost invariably an administrator of a hospital or institution, or a deputy.

The removal of tissue must be carried out by a fully registered medical practitioner who must satisfy himself that life is extinct (for definition of death, see 'Death, signs of'). No such removal may be performed without the consent of the coroner (or Procurator Fiscal in Scotland) in deaths which may be the subject of an inquest. Authority for removal of tissues cannot be given by a person entrusted with the body only for the purposes of interment or cremation.

A defect in the wording of this Act is that 'reasonable inquiries' are subject to wide interpretation end 'any surviving relative' can also give rise to difficulties. In actual practice, instead of the person in possession of the body 'making reasonable inquiries as may be practicable to exclude objections', a positive act of permission for post-mortem examination is sought from the nearest available relative in the shape of a signed and witnessed form of consent. For transplantation, written permission is not usually obtained, but a note confirming the relatives' lack of objection is recorded in the clinical notes.

Though in law the pre-mortal consent of the deceased is sufficient authority for donation of organs, it is unlikely for this to be done in the face of adamant post-mortem objection from near relatives. However, with the increasing use of the kidney donor card, now being extended to other organs, it is usual for the spouse or other near relative to be the witness signatory, so later objection in these cases would be very uncommon.

Following medical scandals relating to commercial exploitation of donors, which ended in disciplining of some doctors by the General Medical Council, the Human Organ Transplants Act 1989 limited the scope of donation by living donors by restricting transplantation between persons who were not genetically related and created a regulatory authority to police such activities.

Post-mortem examinations

Similar provisions extend under the Human Tissue Act 1961 to the performance of post-mortem examinations (but only so called 'clinical autopsies' not under the direction of the coroner or Procurator Fiscal, where no permission is required). As before, authority for post-mortem examination may be granted if the person lawfully in possession of the body is satisfied that the deceased left written or witnessed oral permission (a rare event) or is satisfied after such reasonable inquiries as may be practicable that the deceased had not objected and that the surviving spouse or any other relative do not object.

The lack of objection is invariably confirmed by positive written witnessed permission. The standard Health Service form of consent has now two clauses: (a) in relation to the post-mortem examination itself, and (b) permission to remove 'limited amounts of tissue for therapeutic purposes, teaching and research'. This latter clause may be deleted by a relative if so desired.

The Human Tissue Act 1961 does not extend to Northern Ireland, which has a similar Act dated 1962.

HYMEN

Membrane at the lower end of the vagina. Various forms when intact, which must be distinguished from damage due to first intercourse. An intact hymen may be completely imperforate, a condition which requires surgical treatment, as the products of menstruation are unable to escape. The aperture may be very small, insufficient to allow normal intercourse, though this is not necessarily a bar to pregnancy, which can occur from semen being deposited upon the vulva or even between the thighs.

The usual form of intact hymen is a wavy-edged fold of mucous membrane with smooth margins. This may or may not allow penile penetration. After intercourse, the membrane is usually damaged, tearing in one or more places. This rapidly heals up within a few days, leaving a smooth edge, but can usually be distinguished from an intact hymen by the presence of indentations which extend back to the level of the vaginal wall.

After repeated intercourse or childbirth, the hymen virtually disappears, a few remnants being called 'carunculae myrtiformes'.

Soon after rupture of the hymen, whether by penile penetration, or by masturbation, the edges of the torn hymen will show slight bleeding, swelling and perhaps bruising.

Hymenal damage is not synonymous with rape or forcible intercourse, such damage often being present after any full penetration. Other injuries above or below the hymen must be sought to corroborate a charge of rape. The hymen is sometimes examined for damage by inserting a glass globe on a stem into the vagina and partly withdrawing it so that the hymenal margins are spread over the globe. An inflatable balloon, containing a light for trans-illumination, has also been developed for this purpose, but a careful conventional gynaecological examination will give satisfactory evidence when carried out by an experienced practitioner.

HYOID BONE

A small horseshoe-shaped bone in the upper part of the larynx or voice box, of considerable forensic significance because of its use as an indicator of violence applied to the neck. (See also 'Larynx'.)

Figure 31:   The hyoid bone

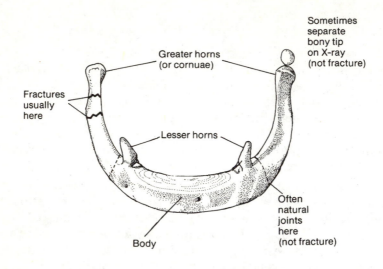

In fact, though the hyoid has gained most attention as an indicator of strangulation, it is the *superior horns of the thyroid cartilage*, which lie below the hyoid, which are much more vulnerable and are better indicators of neck pressure.

The hyoid bone is about three to four cm in size, both from side to side and front to back. It consists of a firm bar of bone in front (the body), from which two horns curve backwards to form the greater horns or cornuae. There is usually another pair of small spurs arising from the base of the greater horns, but these have no medico-legal significance.

When the neck is squeezed from side to side, as in manual strangulation (and much less often in ligature or hanging compression), the hyoid may fracture, usually on one side, but very occasionally on both sides. The fracture itself is clinically inconsequential, being unassociated with any dangerous sequelae, but it is an index of substantial trauma to the neck – though certain criteria must be strictly applied to ensure that an apparent hyoid fracture is genuine.

The following points are relevant:

(a) fractures only occur when the hyoid is calcified, that is, where the structure is bony rather than cartilaginous or gristly. Such calcification, sufficient to allow fracturing, is almost never seen in young people below the age of about 20. Calcification is progressive with age and most fractured hyoids are seen in middle-aged and elderly victims;

(b) a large proportion of hyoids have natural joints between the body and the horns, which are mobile and can give the impression of a fracture, especially to a pathologist insufficiently experienced in medico-legal work. The joints may be on one or both sides and a unilateral joint may be mistaken for a fracture. X-ray assists in recognising a joint, but also the position of the joint is different from the usual site of fracture. Joints are usually at the junction of body with horn, whereas a true fracture is almost always towards the tip of the greater horn, often within a cm of the tip. However, recent work has shown that the tips are often naturally mobile due to extra joints or separate calcification of the extremity;

(c) a fracture must be shown to have occurred during life to have any significance. Though not as common as sometimes stated in forensic medicine textbooks, the accidental fracture of a hyoid may occur during removal of the neck structures at autopsy. Ideally, a fracture caused during life should reveal a small haemorrhage surrounding the fracture site, due to blood being extravasated while the circulation is still functioning. A post-mortem fracture will theoretically reveal no such bleeding. Unfortunately, in a small number of cases, this sign is unreliable, as even a post-mortem fracture can allow slight passive bleeding to stain the adjacent tissues and be visible in microscopic sections. Conversely, definite ante mortem fractures proven on other grounds, such as associated laryngeal damage, may have no discernible haemorrhage. However, the presence of bleeding at the fracture site is usually a valuable corroborative indicator of injury during life;

(d) it is common for X-rays to be taken of the larynx in strangulation cases and the X-ray film to be produced in evidence. The demonstration of a fracture by this means does not form incontestable proof of strangulation – it merely confirms that the hyoid is fractured, but cannot assist in differentiating ante mortem from post-mortem infliction. Other criteria of laryngeal damage, such as haemorrhage into the overlying 'strap' muscles of the neck, other laryngeal fractures and possibly haemorrhage into the lining membrane of the larynx, are more helpful in establishing trauma.

An X-ray may be valuable in demonstrating a joint rather than a fracture and in detecting separate ossification of the tips of the horns. Such a joint has been missed both on dissection and on X-ray by pathologists, and where X-rays are available, a defence opinion should be sought as to the genuine nature of an alleged fracture;

(e) more often, the superior horns of the thyroid cartilage, which are below and parallel to the hyoid horns, are fractured in pressure on the neck – though it must be emphasised that many deaths from such strangulation reveal neither fractures of the hyoid nor thryoid, especially in young victims;

(f) significant, though not great, pressure has to be applied to the neck to fracture a horn, and there is great variation in the fragility of the bone. In many old people, the calcified, almost chalky bone is extremely brittle and will break easily;

(g) it is possible to fracture the hyoid by a blow or a fall onto the neck, rather than by manual pressure, but this is exceedingly rare. It is also possible to crack other cartilages in the larynx, such as the larger thyroid plate or the cricoid cartilage; this may be caused by strangling or by a direct blow to the neck and rarely to a fall on some projection.

The significance of hyoid fractures is always dependent upon other findings in strangulation, such as finger-tip bruises in the skin, bruising of the muscles in the neck and other signs in the larynx such as mucosal haemorrhages. The solitary finding of a fractured hyoid with no corroborative injuries can never be accepted as proof of strangulation;

(h) ligature strangulation causes hyoid fracture far less often than manual strangulation, though it can occur. Hanging seldom fractures the hyoid bone.

HYPERPYREXIA OR HYPERTHERMIA

Condition of raised body temperature, sometimes fatal. Normal mouth temperature is 37°C (98.4°F); rectal temperature about 1°C higher.

Causes

Heat exhaustion, due to salt depletion and dehydration from environmental causes, such as climate or boiler rooms, etc.

Heat hyperpyrexia, due to a failure of body temperature-regulating mechanisms, again from environmental conditions.

Severe infections, the true 'fever' caused by micro-organisms, viruses and their toxins disturbing the heat regulatory centres.

Certain brain lesions, especially pontine haemorrhage, affecting the heat regulatory centres in the pons of the brain stem.

Malignant hyperthermia (qv), a condition usually following anaesthesia with halothane or suxamenthonium drugs, though it can arise with simple nitrous oxide anaesthesia. The temperature may rise to 42°C in this condition.

HYPOSTASIS (POST-MORTEM LIVIDITY)

Gravitational settling of the blood after death. Hypostasis is more descriptive, 'lividity' being an older and inaccurate term.

When the circulation ceases at death, the veins and the partly contracted small arteries relax and allow blood to flood passively into the smaller vessels. Gravity causes most of it to sink to the most dependent parts, though there is usually an earlier stage of blotchiness, even on upper skin surface, due to local variation in degree of vessel dilatation. This early stage may commence within an hour after death or may be delayed or absent. The main hypostasis may also begin within an hour or two and is well marked within four to five hours in the average case. *However, the timing is quite unreliable as an index of the time since death.* Hypostasis may be minimal or even undetectable in some cases, especially anaemic old persons and some infants. Hypostasis persists until overtaken by decomposition, usually several days later. In deeply pigmented bodies, especially racial coloration, hypostasis may be difficult or impossible to detect.

The usual pattern is of hypostasis on the back of the body, neck and back of arms and legs in persons lying face-up after death. There are white patches over the shoulder blades and buttocks where pressure against the supporting surface has excluded the blood. When the body has lain in some other position, the hypostasis will be situated appropriately, unless the body has been moved since death.

It was formerly believed that hypostasis became fixed some hours after death and therefore could not move again if the body was disturbed. This is most unreliable, as hypostasis may move, either totally or partially, at any time after death. Tests such as trying to blanch rigor by finger pressure, to derive information about time since death, are used by some continental pathologists, but are quite unreliable.

The colour of the hypostasis is of more forensic use than its totally unpredictable timing. A cherry red hue is diagnostic of carbon monoxide poisoning. A darker red is suggestive of cyanide and brownish colours may be due to methaemoglobin or sulphaemoglobin, usually due to industrial exposure. In death from hypothermia (qv) the skin may be bright pink or brownish pink, due to unreduced oxy-haemoglobin in the tissues. This may even be seen as a post-mortem phenomenon in bodies from cold water and also after refrigeration.

Many corpses have a dark blue or purple hypostasis due to a congestive death with de-oxygenated blood in the tissues. Caution must be observed in not associating this with an asphyxial process, unless other criteria are present (see 'Asphyxia'). Skin haemorrhages within areas of dependent hypostasis are common as a post-mortem phenomenon some hours or even days after death, especially over the shoulders and back – they have no significance and must not be confused with true petechiae.

Hypostasis occurs in the organs as well as the skin and produces discoloration in the heart and intestines, etc, which have been misinterpreted as disease or injury by inexperienced pathologists.

The blotchy stage of hypostasis may be mistaken for bruises, but on cutting into the areas, the blood will be seen to be within the vessels if the appearance is due to hypostasis. If the tissues are stained with blood, then a bruise is present: microscopical examination may be required to confirm the extravasation of blood in doubtful cases.

IDENTIFICATION

The establishment of the individuality of a living or dead person. Forensic medical evidence is required when from unconsciousness, debility, mental abnormality or, rarely, deliberate refusal, identity cannot be provided directly by a living person; or when, in the case of the dead, lack of witnesses or the state of the body present direct identification.

The problem resolves itself into the following questions:

(a) What is the sex?

(b) What is the age?

(c) What are the height and weight?

(d) What is the race?

(e) What is the personal identity?

In the case of fragmented, scanty or bony remains, an additional question might be: are the remains human? This requires expert anatomical and perhaps laboratory serological investigation to differentiate between human and animal origin.

In the living

The sex, approximate age, stature and race may be self-evident in most cases, though an accurate estimate of age (especially in young persons) may be required (see 'Age estimation'). Personal identity is usually the prime question in the living and the following are the usual paths of investigation:

(a) facial recognition, directly or by photography, by means of witnesses. A number of remarkable errors have been reported in respect of photographic recognition;

(b) finger, palm and sole prints are unique if undamaged, but there must be matching prints on record for comparison;

(c) lip prints, vein patterns on the back of the hand and the configuration of the ear have been claimed as unique criteria, but they are hardly likely to be on record ante mortem as a means of comparison;

(d) teeth and dentures may provide definite matching (from structure, number, extractions, fillings and other dental work) if dental records are available (see 'Dental identification');

(e) height and weight may exclude identity, but can never confirm it. Errors in previous estimation and changes in weight can complicate the issue;

(f) congenital defects (moles, birthmarks, limb deformities, etc), scars of injuries or surgical operations, tattoos, asymmetries, etc, may be specific enough to assist in identity;

(g) blood typing, these days almost exclusively through DNA;

(h) occupational stigmata (for example, coal miner's blue scars) may assist, but are far less numerous and specific than in former years.

In the dead

The same criteria as above can be used in the intact body but, where decomposition or skeletalisation has occurred, or where only fragments are available, additional help may be obtained from:

(a) radiography of certain bones and teeth, for example, frontal sinuses which are unique to every person. However, previous X-rays must be available for matching;

(b) direct measurement of bones for estimation of height, sex and race (see 'Skeletal identification');

(c) photo or video superimposition and computerised or anatomical facial reconstruction.

Identification of the dead may be required (a) in single instances, to investigate a crime or the cause of death and to restore the body to relatives for disposal, or (b) in mass disasters such as air crashes, where large numbers of bodies, often fragmented and perhaps burnt, need to be identified for investigative, compensatory and ethical reasons. This process requires a highly organised operation, with skilled experts such as pathologists and dentists on the scene.

IMMERSION

See 'Drowning and immersion'.

INCISED WOUNDS

Wounds made by sharp cutting weapon (knife, razor, cleaver, etc) or broken glass, pottery glaze, etc.

Subdivided into *cuts* or *slashes*, where the length is greater than the depth, and *stabs*, where the depth is greater than the width.

The word 'cut' is unsatisfactory and ambiguous in medico-legal terminology, as it can mean either a laceration or an incised wound.

An incised wound shows clean-cut edges with no crushing or bruising. On the scalp, it can be confused with a laceration unless closely examined (see 'Scalp').

Incised wounds can bleed copiously, especially on the head; they can bleed more than blunt lacerations, as blood vessels are not crushed, but slit. Deep stab wounds have danger of profuse internal haemorrhage from penetrated large vessels, but any slash may lead to fatal bleeding if major artery involved.

As with stab wounds, the severity of the wound depends mostly on the weapon. Sharp points and edges will produce long, deep cuts with little physical effort. Factors such as strength and sex of assailant, toughness of skin and age of victim of little importance compared with efficiency of cutting edge.

Incised wound usually gapes, with eversion of centre of wound, the total length of which may shorten due to elasticity of skin and contraction of underlying muscles. Appearances depend on anatomical area wounded. Gaping is not a reliable index of infliction during life, when wounds are found on corpse.

Post-mortem bleeding is often profuse (especially on head), especially if wound is dependent after death, allowing blood to escape by gravity. If wound made some time before death (many minutes or hours), then vital reaction (qv) may be seen in edges. This is the only definite proof of ante mortem infliction, unless bleeding is torrential and arterial, spurting in nature, indicating active heart beat. Potentially fatal complications of incised wounds are haemorrhage, infection and air embolism.

A long knife wound where the skin is loose (for example, the abdomen) may cause a zig-zag incision, due to the skin being pushed in front of the blade in an irregular fashion.

INFANTICIDE

Until 1922, the unlawful killing of any infant was murder. In that year, the not infrequent occurrence of mental stress in the mother leading to such killing was legally recognised by the Infanticide Act, which was repealed and re-enacted with certain amendments in 1938.

This created an alternative charge to murder with lesser penalties, if a woman by any wilful act of commission or omission causes the death of her child being under the age of 12 months, it being shown that the balance of her mind was disturbed by reason of her not having fully recovered from the effect of giving birth or from lactation consequent upon the birth.

Several medical points are of importance:

(a) only the mother can plead this lesser charge;

(b) although the Act allows a 12 month period, most killings occur within the first few hours or even minutes after birth;

(c) only the clearest evidence of deliberate killing by an act of commission or omission is proceeded upon;

(d) the law presumes a still-birth and the onus is upon the prosecution to prove a separate existence (not just a live birth);

(e) indictments are relatively few, because (1) identifying the mother of a concealed, often decomposed, infant is difficult; (2) pathological proof of live birth is difficult and evidence of separate existence even more difficult; and (3) proof of a wilful act causing death is difficult, especially if by omission;

(f) in many cases, insufficient medical evidence leads to an alternative charge of concealment of birth.

See also 'Live birth'.

INTESTINE

Lower part of alimentary canal or gastro-intestinal tract. Reaches from exit of stomach (pylorus) to anus. Entirely within the abdomen. Divided into:

(a) the duodenum, about 25 cm long, into which the bile and pancreatic ducts open;

(b) the small intestine about 5 m long, the first part of which is the jejunum and the lower part the ileum;

(c) the large intestine or colon, subdivided into caecum (which carries the appendix), the ascending, transverse, descending and finally sigmoid colon;

(d) the rectum passing down through the pelvis to the anus.

Medico-legal significance

Intestine sometimes ruptured by blows on the front of the abdomen, as in child abuse or kicking in the adult. External marks on the skin need not be present even with gross internal injury. In infants, the duodenum may be severed by a blow compressing it across the unyielding bone of the spinal column, which lies at the back of the abdominal cavity.

Intestine is tethered by a membrane called the mesentery. This may be ruptured or perforated by blows on the abdomen. Where the intestine is penetrated by injury, death may be due to shock and haemorrhage or to a peritonitis caused by leakage of contents into the peritoneal cavity.

Lining of the intestine may be damaged by many poisons: for example, arsenic, antimony and other heavy metals may cause diffuse damage, with diarrhoea.

Figure 32: **Alimentary canal and intestines**

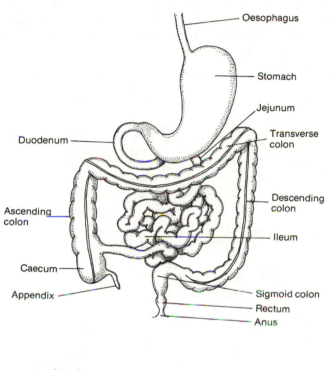

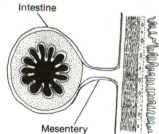

Natural perforation of intestine is a relatively common occurrence, frequently fatal:

(a) perforated duodenal ulcer (a chronic peptic ulcer) floods the peritoneal cavity with digestive juices and food, causing acute chemical peritonitis or infective peritonitis if prolonged;

(b) perforated diverticulitis (small pouches on the large intestine) may cause a faecal peritonitis and rapid death, usually in old people. Cancer of the large intestine may also perforate.

JAW, INJURIES TO

The lower jaw, or *mandible,* is a horseshoe-shaped bone which turns up at the free ends into flat plates ('rami') which run in a back to front plane. At the tops of these plates are the 'condyles', two rollers which fit into grooves on the under-surface of the base of the skull, forming simple hinge joints.

The upper jaw is the *maxilla,* the lower part of the face, continuous with the rest of the skull. It may suffer extensive fractures in facial injuries, especially kicking.

Blows on the point of the jaw may cause a violent impact to be transmitted upwards via these joints, which may lead to concussion or even brain damage, though it is unusual for the floor of the skull to be fractured in this way.

A violent blow to the jaw may cause it to be fractured, the site varying according to the point of impact. A blow on the point of the jaw may crack the jaw in the front midline, through the 'symphysis' or front seam. A blow on the side may split the jaw either through the tooth-bearing region or through an ascending ramus either at the rear angle of the jaw or higher towards the joint. It is possible for a blow on the side to fracture the opposite side, either solely or in addition to a fracture on the same side. Dislocation of the joints may occur from a side blow.

A fractured jaw can be a relatively serious injury, needing expert and urgent treatment, sometimes with wiring together of the fragments. The lining of the mouth or gums may be ripped, when the fracture is said to be 'compound', with the broken bone exposed. Detachment of teeth and severe bleeding may pose a risk to life from blockage of the mouth and air passages, but most simple fractures are unlikely to be lethal.

A relatively common combination of injuries, sometimes fatal, is a blow on the jaw which causes the victim to fall backwards (especially if drunk) from a standing position onto the back of the head, with the likely sequel of lacerated scalp, and possibly fractured skull and brain damage. In this type of injury, there would probably be 'contre-coup' brain damage (qv).

KICKING

Kicking is a common method of inflicting serious, sometimes fatal injury. The shod foot, especially the heavy boot currently in fashion amongst aggressive youths, forms a potentially lethal weapon which runs no risk of contravening legislation restricting the carrying of more obvious weapons.

Injuries may be caused by the foot delivering a direct swinging blow. Here, the force delivered is greater than that from a fist, due to the larger musculature of the leg and the added weight of foot and footwear. Another mechanism is stamping downwards, usually on a victim already on the floor. The heel may be used and there may be a backward component to the action, causing shearing stresses in the tissues.

Another very injurious method is to stamp with the heel or sole, then twist, which can cause tearing of the skin and tissues. Occasionally, a female shoe with a sharp, narrow heel may be involved, when actual stab wounds can be inflicted.

Where a kick glances tangentially across the skin surface, severe shearing stresses may be inflicted, with tearing of the surface. Direct kicks can cause severe internal damage. Where clothing is interposed, there may be no external damage, but rupture of the liver, intestine, spleen or lung can occur from extreme violence. Kicks in the male genitals may cause death from pain or may raise a very large blood-filled swelling in the scrotum. The urethra (urine passage) may be ruptured.

Kicks in the neck are especially dangerous: the windpipe or larynx may be ruptured and death occur from blockage of the airway or reflex cardiac arrest (qv). The muscles of the neck may be ruptured and extensive bruising may occur, especially under the angle of the jaw, which may be fractured, sometimes in several places.

One recently recognised danger of kicking in the neck region is that of subarachnoid haemorrhage (qv) due to rupture of a vertebral artery or other vessel in the base of the skull. Kicks high in the neck, below the ear, are especially prone to cause this injury.

Kicks on the head may lacerate the scalp and fracture the skull and cause any type of internal head injury.

The differentiation of kicks from punches may be difficult or impossible, but certain pointers exist. Kicks are rarely seen in the centre of the chin or forehead. The degree of surface damage is often greater in kicking and scuff marks and even patterned abrasions from the sole or heel may be visible. Bony injury beneath surface bruising is more common in kicking, due to the greater force employed. Kicks are often delivered into concavities of the body, such as under the jaw, the loin, the armpit area of the exposed side and the groin. The prominence of the cheek and eyebrow may be kicked, especially with a glancing blow, and the face may be ground under a stamping heel, causing fracture of the nose. In general, the best method of differentiating kicks from punches lies in the greater degree of damage inflicted and also the presence of patterned marks from toe-caps, sole or heel.

KIDNEYS

Paired organs in the back of the abdominal cavity, which filter waste products and excess fluid from the blood.

Kidney (renal) failure

This may be due to many causes, some of medico-legal importance:

(a) intrinsic kidney disease, such as nephritis;

(b) failure of blood supply, including low blood pressure in shock after injury or surgical operations;

(c) crush syndrome, due partly to (b) and also to blockage by muscle haemoglobin from damaged limbs;

(d) acute tubular necrosis – a manifestation of shock, partly synonymous with (b) where low blood pressure and sometimes toxic substances cause damage to the kidney tubules;

(e) poisoning by a wide variety of substances, including infections.

Temporary kidney failure

This can be treated by dialysis, which eliminates the waste products until the kidney recovers – this is most successful in causes such as shock and poisoning. Where the kidneys are irreversibly damaged, either dialysis must continue for life or a kidney transplant must be performed.

Dialysis may be either via the bloodstream (haemodialysis), where the bloodstream is diverted through an external filter system, or by peritoneal dialysis, where large volumes of fluid are washed through the abdominal cavity, removing the waste products through the thin membranes of the peritoneum which cover the intestines.

LACERATIONS

The third class of wounds, being more serious than bruises or abrasions (qv). A laceration is defined as a wound which penetrates the full thickness of the skin and, of necessity, severs blood vessels and leads to bleeding. Beneath the skin is the subcutaneous layer of loose fibrous tissue containing many arteries, veins and nerves. The laceration may extend more deeply and involve muscle and 'fascia', the thin sheets of fibrous tissue which separate the various muscle compartments.

Lacerations may be ragged, where due to blunt or tearing impact, or clean-cut, where caused by a cutting instrument (see 'Incised wounds'). However, where a blunt injury occurs over a firm base, especially the head, a clean split may be inflicted (see 'Head injury', 'Scalp wounds').

The edges of a blunt laceration tend to be inverted and bruised, though the latter may be confined to a narrow rim. The danger to life depends upon the site and extent of the injury. If large blood vessels underlie the wound, such as the neck, armpit or groin, then fatal haemorrhage may occur. If the skin loss is profound, such as with a 'flaying' laceration of a limb due to the rotating impact of a vehicle wheel, then gross shock, haemorrhage and infection may prove fatal. Bleeding may be more profuse from an irregular laceration than from a clean knife slash, as in the latter, complete transection of blood vessels may allow elastic retraction and reduced bleeding, whereas tearing and partial rupture in a blunt injury may keep the vessel open.

LARYNX

The voice box or 'Adam's apple', more prominent in males. Consists of a complex cartilaginous box at the upper end of the windpipe, with its entrance protected by a flap (epiglottis) which prevents food from entering from the adjacent pharynx (back of the throat).

Immediately above the main part of the larynx (thyroid cartilage) is a horseshoe-shaped bone, the hyoid (qv).

The upper end of the thyroid cartilage also has two slim horns (cornuae or *superior horns*) which lie parallel to the horns of the hyoid bone and are joined to them by a membrane. This is of importance in fracture of the horns during strangulation (see 'Hyoid bone', 'Strangulation').

At the lower end of the larynx is a single ring of cartilage, shaped like a signet ring, which is the cricoid; this may be fractured in the front from severe pressure or a blow. The main plates of the thyroid cartilage may also be cracked from severe strangling pressure or a direct blow, either from a kick or vehicle accident, or a Karate-type chop.

Figure 33: **Larynx and hyoid bone**

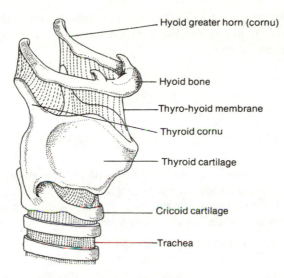

Hyoid greater horn (cornu)

Hyoid bone

Thyro-hyoid membrane

Thyroid cornu

Thyroid cartilage

Cricoid cartilage

Trachea

Anatomy of the larynx

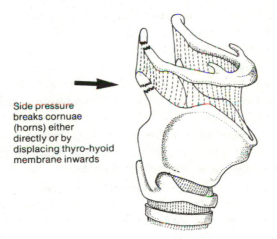

Side pressure
breaks cornuae
(horns) either
directly or by
displacing thyro-hyoid
membrane inwards

Mechanism of hyoid fracture in strangulation

The interior of the larynx may become blocked and cause death from sudden cardiac arrest or asphyxia. The entrance or glottis may be blocked by food just swallowed (see 'Choking') or swelling of the membranous margins. This is called 'glottal oedema' and may occur from allergy, such as stings or specific food; from infection such as Haemophilus influenzae in children; or from inhalation of irritant fumes.

Blockage from dentures, small toys or any foreign inhaled object may also cause sudden unexpected death (see 'Choking').

The urgent treatment of a blocked larynx is tracheotomy, the making of a hole in the windpipe just below the larynx, unless an endo-tracheal tube can be inserted through the mouth.

LIGATURE

Surgically, a tight constricting thread applied to a blood vessel to staunch bleeding.

Forensically, a strangling band applied around the neck; all manner of materials may be used, from thin wires to flat bands of fabric. The ligature usually leaves a characteristic mark, red during life, but becomes brown, leathery and parchment-like from drying after death.

The pattern of the ligature, such as spiral rope or woven cord, may be clearly imprinted. The same features are seen in hanging (qv) but the position on the neck is different. In homicidal strangling, the mark will run more or less horizontally and a cross-over point is often visible. In suicidal strangling, there may be several loops of ligature and a knot or other means of maintaining the pressure. The latter features by no means preclude self-application before unconsciousness and death supervene.

A ligature fractures the laryngeal structures less often than manual strangulation, but hyoid and thyroid cartilage damage sometimes occur. Congestive changes and petechiae are often seen, more frequently than in manual strangulation, as there is less likelihood of sudden cardiac arrest from pressure on the carotid sinuses, which finger pressure may provoke.

As in manual strangulation, there may well be bruising of the neck, less often from the assailant, but vertical scratches are frequent from the victim scrabbling at the ligature in an attempt to remove it.

Bruising may occur in the tissues under the ligature, but generally there is less trauma than in manual strangulation. Where the ligature has been applied over clothing, the skin mark may be minimal or absent, but the weave of the fabric may be imprinted on the skin, as in manual strangulation, where hand pressure is applied over a collar.

A wide band of fabric can be used as a ligature, but on bare skin, this often leaves a narrow mark due to tension lines in the stretched fabric. Also, where a wide band has been used, it is possible to kill by constriction without leaving any mark on the neck, especially in children.

In post-mortems on infants or, sometimes, on fat people, skin creases on the neck have been mistaken for ligature marks. These are pale areas contrasting with the more reddened area of hypostasis.

The signs that a ligature was applied during life include the obvious congestion and petechial haemorrhages above the mark, with often some tissue swelling; and, sometimes, a line of small dotted haemorrhages along the line of the ligature.

LIVE BIRTH

Not synonymous with 'separate existence', though the latter must include live birth. As defined by the Births and Deaths Registration Act, a still-birth is one where the child has issued forth from its mother after the 24th week of pregnancy and which did not at any time after being completely expelled from its mother, breathe or show any other signs of life; thus, a live birth is defined by implication from this description.

These legal definitions do not coincide completely with medical interpretation – for instance, to a doctor, a baby might be obviously alive when half-born, but if those signs of life fade before the feet are expelled from the maternal passages, then legally, there was no separate existence. This theoretical discrepancy led to the Infant Life (Preservation) Act (1929) to cover child destruction.

Again, with modern obstetrical expertise, foetuses under 24 weeks can be live-born (even at 18 weeks, though they are unlikely to survive) and may survive from about 22 weeks.

Separate existence requires the extrusion of the whole infant from the body of the mother, but this does not include the umbilical cord or placenta (afterbirth).

Proof of live birth

For a charge of murder or infanticide to lie, evidence of separate existence must be offered. This, as stated above, is not medically synonymous with live birth, but unless live birth can be proved, then legally, a separate existence cannot have occurred.

Witnessed observation at the time of delivery is the best and only absolute proof of live birth, but in most forensic situations this is lacking due to the circumstances. The debate then revolves around the retrospective examination of a dead infant.

Establishment of breathing is usually the only helpful criterion. When a child is being born, a point is reached where its head is first exposed to the air and it is then able to breathe. At or about the same time, the placenta becomes functionally detached from the lining of the womb and can no longer deliver maternal oxygen. This provides a stimulus for the initiation of air breathing.

Such breathing may begin whilst most of the baby's body is still within the maternal birth canal, so a separate existence has not yet been legally established. Where a pathologist examines a dead new-born child, it can be very difficult or impossible to give a firm opinion on whether breathing did begin. Lungs which have not breathed are solid, dark red, collapsed and airless, whilst those where breathing has become established for a few minutes become spongy, pink, crepitant (crinkly to the touch) and light in texture.

However, there is a whole spectrum between these two obvious states and where there are any signs of post-mortem decomposition (as so often happens in concealed births or delayed examinations), no reliable opinion can be offered.

For many years, the so called 'hydrostatic test' was employed to distinguish lungs that had breathed, but this has now been completely discredited by most experienced medico-legists, though some still erroneously cling to its fallacious results. The rationale was to drop the lungs and/or pieces of lung into water, to see if they would float. Sinking meant no breathing, floating meant that breathing had occurred. However, even with later enforced modifications, such as the complete exclusion of lungs with any trace of decomposition (which produces gas from putrefactive processes) and various mystical manoeuvres such as compressing and treading lung fragments in cloths, the test is quite fallacious. The best description of the hydrostatic test was given by Professor Polson, who said, many years ago, 'the test was suspect even in 1900 and requires no detailed discussion, because it is now known to have no value'.

In spite of this and other authoritative opinions, such as Shapiro and Gordon, reliance is still placed in the test in some quarters, without scientific foundation. The best that can be said for it is that floating lungs have no evidential value; if they sink, then they were likely to have come from a still-birth. Of course, any attempts at resuscitation completely negate any assessment of the condition of the lungs.

Other pathologists rely upon the microscopic appearance of the lungs, but this also is fraught with uncertainty in the frequently marginal cases where respiration may only have lasted for a short period. The argument that the height of the cells lining the air passages is an index of breathing (high columnar cells – no breathing; low flattened cells – breathing) has been shown to be related to maturity of the infant, not a function of respiration.

The most reliable test is the naked-eye examination by an experienced pathologist of the fresh lungs at autopsy. Where definite pinkness, sponginess and crepitation are apparent, then respiration probably occurred. Anything less than these definite signs is unacceptable and the benefit of the doubt must be given.

The umbilical cord progressively shrivels after birth and drops off some days later. This is a late sign and is not helpful in the majority of cases where a still-birth has to be distinguished from death very shortly after delivery. In the first day the cord becomes shrivelled, but this may also happen in a still-birth. In a live baby, a reddened zone of separation is seen at the umbilicus in 36–48 hours and the cord is usually cast off before the end of the first week.

Food in the stomach is naturally a sign of live birth.

If the baby has been washed and tended (with removal of the cheesy vernix from the skin), it is likely to have been a live birth, but not necessarily so.

Air in the stomach is not a reliable sign, as both post-mortem changes and artificial respiration can produce this appearance, apart from the active swallowing of air.

Maceration. Where a new-born baby is macerated, that is, decomposed in a certain way which indicates death *in utero*, then still-birth is established. Similarly, very gross congenital deformities, sufficient to make the child a monster, may usually (but not invariably) be taken to be incompatible with a separate existence.

The whole problem is fraught with uncertainties and the invariable rule for the pathologist must be to assume still-birth unless there is incontrovertible evidence of live birth. As this is usually based on evidence of breathing, the pathologist is unable to say that this is also definite evidence of a separate existence, as breathing can and does occur whilst the baby is still not fully extruded from the mother.

Evidence of feeding, and separation of the cord, must be demonstrative of a separate existence.

LIVER

The largest organ of the body, situated in the upper abdomen, almost entirely protected under the edge of the rib cage. The usual weight is about 1,500 g: in disease states, such as alcoholic fatty degeneration, this may increase to twice normal size, but after prolonged disease, such as cirrhosis, it may shrink below the normal weight.

The liver performs most of the chemical processes connected with metabolism and the processing of digested food, but has many other functions, such as producing bile – a substance which both provides an alkalising medium for digestion in the intestines and removes the waste produced by the breakdown of old blood cells.

Many diseases afflict the liver. One of the most common is a virus infection called 'infective hepatitis' or 'yellow jaundice', of which there are three main types, Hepatitis A, B and C. The first – and least dangerous – is usually spread via the gastro-intestinal tract, the other two by virus gaining direct access to the body, as in injections, including drug abuse, transfusions, or by sexual intercourse.

Jaundice, which is an accumulation of bile products in the blood, can be caused by any process which either prevents the outflow of bile ('obstructive jaundice'), for example, gallstones or cancer of the pancreas or liver, or from liver failure, in which damage to the liver cells fails to clear the bile pigment ('bilirubin') from the blood.

Alcohol is the most common liver poison. Taken over a considerable period (at least a couple of years) even moderate excess of alcohol may lead to fatty degeneration and enlargement of the liver – partly due to a direct toxic effect and partly due to poor nutrition, especially proteins and vitamins, which is common in heavy drinkers.

If the fatty degeneration persists for a long time, then the liver cells may die and the organ may contract and become nodular and fibrotic, the condition known as cirrhosis.

The liver is vulnerable to heavy impact upon the abdomen and lower chest, such as may be suffered in traffic accidents or kicking. The organ may rupture or tear, allowing blood to escape into the abdominal cavity. It has remarkable powers of repair and regeneration.

LONGEVITY

See 'Expectation of life'.

LSD (LYSERGIC ACID DIETHYLAMIDE)

The initials are derived from the German *Lyserge Saure Diethylamid*.

One of the group of psychoactive drugs, often termed 'psychedelic' or 'hallucinogenic', though this description is not strictly accurate. Other drugs with a broadly similar action include mescaline and extracts from certain fungi, such as psilocybin from the Liberty Cap, a European magic mushroom.

Minute amounts of these drugs can cause gross distortions of perception, with visual and auditory fantasies. Though not physically dangerous in a toxicological sense, mechanical injury and even death may occur from rash acts undertaken whilst this abnormal state persists, such as falling from heights under the impression that the subject can fly, or attempting to stop moving trucks with one hand. Occasionally, the sensual distortions are so gross as to lead to acute psychic disturbances. True dependence and withdrawal symptoms do not occur with these drugs.

MALIGNANT HYPERTHERMIA

A condition of high body temperature almost exclusively associated with anaesthesia, where the use of some anaesthetic agents and muscle relaxants trigger a metabolic change in the muscles, with great heat production, sometimes reaching 43°C, the normal being 37°C.

Succinylcholine relaxant and halogenated anaesthetics, especially halothan, are the most frequent initiators of hyperthermia.

It occurs about once in every 10,000 anaesthetics, estimates ranging from one in 5,000 to one in 70,000.

It is familial and other relatives should be tested in case they are exposed to the same danger.

MASOCHISTIC (SEXUAL) ASPHYXIA

A common form of sexual deviation, almost totally confined to men, usually adolescent to middle-aged. Very few female instances quoted in world literature.

Fatal cases encountered because of failure of equipment, but this is obviously only the tip of the iceberg of successful deviants. Sexual pleasure, presumably orgasmal, is obtained by achieving transient deprivation of blood to the brain, usually by pressure on the neck or blockage of the breathing passages.

A running noose tightened by extending the legs or by a counterweight is most frequent, though enveloping the head in plastic or pressing the face against some occluding fabric is sometimes encountered. The syndrome is usually signposted by other evidence of deviation, especially transvestism, bondage, masks, pornography, mirrors, etc. Some are bizarre in the extreme and may involve solvent inhalation, the use of anaesthetic gases, etc.

The vast majority of deaths are accidental and represent a failed episode in a long established habit. A proportion seem to have some intrinsic 'death wish' element, as the mechanics of the procedure would appear to admit of no prospect of survival. However, there still may be no definite intent to commit suicide and most cases are undoubtedly non-suicidal, as can be seen by attempts to pad the neck to avoid a mark from the noose and other evidence of a repetitive trait.

Lack of awareness of this relatively common accident leads some uninformed coroners to label them as 'suicides', which may have undesirable legal and social consequences for the family. Not infrequently, a young boy, even down to the age of 12, may be found hanged. There is usually a sexual element in these deaths, albeit occult or obscure, even though they may be wrongly attributed to 'experimenting with ropes after seeing television Westerns'!

METHADONE

An opiate pharmaceutical which is a powerful analgesic, but also intended for the replacement treatment of heroin and morphine addicts. It has become a drug of abuse in itself, deaths in Scotland in 1995 exceeding those from heroin.

It is usually prescribed as a syrup, widely available on the illicit drug market. Overdose is common, whether as a prescribed replacement for heroin or used as the sole drug of abuse.

MISUSE OF DRUGS ACT 1971

In 1973, this Act came into force to sweep away the previous legislation of the Dangerous Drugs Acts and the Drugs (Prevention of Misuse) Act 1964.

A drug is defined by the World Health Organisation as 'any substance, other than those required for the maintenance of normal health, that when taken into the living organism may modify one or more of its functions'.

The WHO definition of drug dependence is 'a state, psychic and sometimes also physical, resulting from the interaction between a living organism and a drug, characterised by behavioural and other responses that always include a compulsion to take the drug on a continuous or periodic basis in order to experience the psychic effects and sometimes to avoid discomfort of its absence. Tolerance may or may not be present.'

The current Act was designed to control the misuse of drugs of many kinds, but especially narcotics and other drugs of dependence. It categorises drugs of dependence into various degrees of harmfulness and grades the penalties for misuse. It also brings UK law into line with international agreements on drugs.

It controls unlawful possession and trafficking, prescribing and supply, trading and production of such drugs, and affords means of constant surveillance of drug dependence in the UK. It also has provisions for notification of addicts and the fostering of education and research in relation to drug dependence. The Act applies to Northern Ireland as well as to England, Wales and Scotland. It contains 23 sections and 5 Schedules.

Some major provisions

Section 1 established a statutory body called the 'Advisory Council on the Misuse of Drugs', which advises the government on all aspects of the drug problem, with particular emphasis on the social aspects. This Council has at least 20 members, drawn from the medical, dental, veterinary, pharmaceutical and chemical industries.

Section 2 deals with the categorisation of drugs of dependence, classing them into three groups, Class A, Class B and Class C, graded for penalty purposes:

Class A lists the most dangerous drugs of dependence such as morphine, heroin, cocaine, pethidine, LSD, methadone, cannabinol and injectable amphetamines.

Class B contains addictive drugs of intermediate potency including oral amphetamines, cannabis plant material and resin, codeine, dihydrocodeine, methylamphetamine, and a number of other synthetic substances including certain barbiturates.

Class C drugs are rarely involved in dependence but are included for the sake of completeness. These include substances such as certain benzodiazapines, chlorophentermine, meprobamate, pipradrol, etc.

The classification into the three groups above is mainly for the purposes of categorising the maximum penalties which may be applied for offences, on the basis of the drug's potential harmfulness when misused.

A totally different classification is used for the purposes of the controls to be applied to their use for legitimate purposes. This is the classification which mainly concerns the pharmacist and is set out not in the actual Act, but in the Regulations.

This second classification is broken down into four schedules:

Sched 1: Prohibited drugs, except with Home Office authority, for example, cannabis, LSD, raw opium, ecstasy.

Sched 2: Full controlled drug requirements in relation to prescribing, safe custody, keeping of registers, for example, diamorphine, pethidine, cocaine.

Sched 3: Barbiturates, meprobamate, pentazocine, etc.

Sched 4: Benzodiazapines, etc.

Sched 5: Preparations containing small amounts of controlled drugs.

Further legislation under the Act is the reconfirmation in 1973 of the Notification of and Supply to Addicts Regulations. A person is regarded as being addicted to a drug if (and only if) he has, as a result of repeated administration, become so dependent on a drug that he has an overpowering desire for the administration of it to be continued. Under the regulations, any doctor who attends a person whom he considers is addicted to any drug in the following list, must within seven days furnish certain particulars to the Chief Medical Officer of the Home Office.

No doctor may administer or authorise the supply of cocaine or diamorphine or their salts to an addicted person except for the purpose organic disease or injury, unless he is licensed to do so by the Secretary of State.

Sections 3, 4 and 5 concern the import or export of controlled drugs, the production, supply or an offer to supply such drugs and the possession of drugs of dependence. Apart from exempted persons, such as doctors, dentists, veterinary surgeons, etc, it is an offence to possess or to attempt to possess a controlled drug unless to prevent an offence or to hand the drug to some suitable person.

Section 6 makes it an illegal act under any circumstances to cultivate the cannabis plant.

Section 7 contains the exemptions granted by the Home Secretary to certain drugs or to persons from the foregoing sections. This is naturally intended to allow those persons properly entitled to handle such drugs to obtain the legal possession of such substances. A number of other sections control the use of premises for the preparation and smoking of opium, cannabis, etc, and a number of other matters mainly of concern to the police.

Sections 10 and 11 control the packaging, labelling, transport and disposal of control drugs and the documentation of possession and transactions. This section particularly concerns doctors and pharmacists. It also includes the notification of addicts to the proper authority by doctors, as brought into force by the previous legislation. This notification of addicts was reconfirmed in the Notification of and Supply to Addicts Regulations 1973.

Section 13 concerns prohibitions for failure to notify addicts and authorising prescribing to addicts. Though neither of these matters is an offence under the Act, they would lead to an investigation and to possible prohibition of prescribing in the case of an individual practitioner who flouts the regulations.

Section 15 provides that if the Home Secretary considers that a doctor is prescribing in an irresponsible manner in respect of drugs of dependence, he can refer the matter to a professional panel for quick action and depending on their advice, the doctor may be prohibited from further prescribing of such drugs. Other sections provide for safeguards relating to withdrawal of the right to prescribing and describe tribunals and advisory bodies with nominated members from such bodies as the GMC, the Royal Colleges and the BMA.

Section 17 states that the Home Secretary may require any doctor or pharmacist to provide information about prescriptions if it appears that there is a social problem arising in a certain area.

MOBILITY AND ACTIVITY AFTER INJURY

Except in gross destructive injury of the brain, heart or large blood vessels, it is unsafe to be dogmatic about the ability or inability of an injured person to move and to perform certain acts. Especially in brain injuries, the ability to walk, speak and perform co-ordinated movements may be retained even where there has been gross cerebral damage, especially if confined to the frontal areas. Similarly, it is possible for suicides repeatedly to shoot or stab themselves in the head, neck or chest, even where some or all of the wounds would, individually, appear to be rapidly fatal.

Though most gross injuries are indeed associated with sudden and immediate loss of consciousness and function, this is by no means a uniform response. In head injuries, unless the damage involves vital areas of the brain, it is unsafe to deduce the ability, or lack of it, from purely post-mortem findings.

Neither can an autopsy prove or exclude the presence of a period of concussion after a head injury, though a strong probability might be expressed if evidence of a forceful impact is obtained.

More confident assumption of instant incapability may be made if:

(a) heart function must have ceased abruptly, such as in cardiac arrest (provable by witnesses, not autopsy), large penetrating injuries of the heart or gross rupture of the aorta, where sudden catastrophic loss of blood pressure must have led to immediate deprivation of blood supply to the brain;

(b) where extensive brain damage has affected the brain stem and upper spinal cord, involving the control centres for heart and breathing.

In cases of severe chest injury, such a 'flail chest' from multiple rib fractures or severe external or internal bleeding, a clinical opinion may be more valuable that that of an autopsy pathologist, though even experienced clinical advice must be viewed with the acceptance of very wide physiological variation.

MORPHINE

The unripe seed capsules of the poppy *Papaver somniferum* provide crude opium, which contains a mixture of natural narcotic alkaloids. These include morphine, codeine, thebaine, papaverine, etc. From morphine, several derivatives can be made including heroin (qv), which has about five times the narcotic power of morphine.

Morphine can be taken by mouth, smoked or be injected. The fatal dose is impossible to estimate, due to personal variation and the great tolerance which addicts develop: in the latter, many times a therapeutic dose has to be taken in order to attain any narcotic effects.

The therapeutic dose is of the order of eight to 20 mg. In a non-habituated adult, a likely fatal dose might be about 180 mg . Much lower doses have killed and anything over 60–100 mg is potentially dangerous, 250 mg usually causing death.

Addicts can tolerate far higher levels, equal to fatal amounts in non-habituated persons.

Liver and lung disease form dangerous conditions for morphine takers, as the liver is responsible for detoxifying the drug and the depressant effect on breathing makes it unwise to administer morphine to those with chest diseases.

The effects of morphine appear within half an hour of swallowing and within minutes of injection (usually into an arm or leg vein, as with heroin). Fatal overdoses usually kill within six to 12 hours, though deaths have occurred within the hour. Preliminary euphoria is followed by drowsiness, weakness, headache, giddiness, deepening into stupor and then coma if the dose is large enough. The pupils of the eye are contracted, until just before death, when they often become large. Death occurs from depression of respiration, with eventual cessation of breathing.

Post-mortem signs are limited to non-specific appearances of a congestive death, but there may be marks of injection on the limbs, especially at the bend of the elbow, the forearm or thigh. These may be scarred and infected, due to the unhygienic methods of 'mainlining' with unsterile syringes and medicine droppers, as with heroin.

Addicts who share needles with each other run a substantial risk of contracting viral hepatitis, a frequently fatal infective jaundice, as well as HIV.

Toxicological analysis may recover morphine from the blood, urine or skin around an injection site and also from the bile on the gall bladder. However, even fatal poisoning cases may give disappointing results on autopsy analysis, especially on blood levels, which may be extremely low or even negative in undoubted morphine deaths.

MUMMIFICATION

A relatively uncommon type of post-mortem change in temperate climates, in which the body undergoes drying and partial preservation instead of putrefying. It requires a dry environment, warmth and a current of air assisting the process. Most commonly seen in the bodies of new-born infants, sometimes in infanticide or concealment of birth, who are hidden in a dry place, such as an attic, cupboard or chimney. The lack of bacteria in the baby recently delivered from a sterile womb discourages putrefaction and the body may become dry, hard and shrivelled.

Adults dying in hay lofts or attics may undergo the same change, the skin becoming brown, hard and tightly stretched, though the features may remain recognisable for long periods.

The leathery tissues may persist for many years, eventually being destroyed by moths, beetles, mice and other predators. The body may escape detection because of the absence of the smell of putrefaction. The gaunt features may become covered with moulds or fungus.

Mummification is much more common in dry desert climates where the process of artificial mummification was first suggested by the frequency of natural conversion (Egypt and South America).

MUTILATION

The deliberate disfigurement or dismemberment of the living or dead body. May be from sadistic or sado-sexual motives, where horrific injuries can be inflicted: or may be self-inflicted (see 'Fabricated injuries').

Additionally, mutilation of murdered bodies may be to facilitate concealment or transport and to hinder identification.

Types of mutilation

Sadistic mutilation is almost invariably inflicted upon a woman by a man and typical patterns exist, the damage usually having a sexual orientation. Knife wounds are by far the most common – slashes and stabs involving breast, genitals, abdomen, buttocks and thighs are typical. Stabs into the breast may be multiple and sometimes are patterned, for example, radial or circular. Injuries may be confined to the nipple, including complete amputation or bites far more severe than those seen in amorous excitement. Sometimes, the whole breast may be removed, usually as part of fatal injuries or post-mortem mutilation.

The abdomen and pubic region are also targets for sado-sexual attack – the pubic eminence or the vulva may be slashed. The abdomen may be opened and in extreme cases of the 'Jack the Ripper' type, intestines and other organs, including the womb, may be removed and may be displayed in ritual fashion.

Penetration of the abdomen, either directly through the front wall or *per vaginam* by a variety of instruments and weapons, is also a well known 'Ripper' perversion, sometimes associated with bizarre bondage and patterned wounds. Slashes and stabs on the buttocks and injuries to the anal region also have sado-sexual connotations. Less clearly defined sexual motives may lead to decapitation, again sometimes associated with ritual acts (the *Byrne* case).

Post-mortem mutilation may be a variant of the above injuries, but a totally different motive exists as an attempt to dispose of a dead body, usually the victim of homicide. The object is to divide the body both to make the disposal of smaller fragments easier, and also to make identification impossible. Clandestine cremation may be attempted or even passing the body through a waste disposer (*Lofrumento*, USA). More often, disposal by burial or in water is employed.

The possibility of surgical experience is often discussed, but in practice such expertise is rarely present (for example, Fred West), though several cases in recent years have involved butchers. The instruments used need not be particularly specialised nor sharp, as the *Byrne* (Birmingham) decapitation, which was performed with a blunt table knife. The forensic science aspects resolve around the recovery of blood and tissue traces from the scene, including drains and pipes and the possibility of DNA matching.

Forensic medical aspects include the anatomical proof of human remains and the determination of sex, age and other identity (qv).

MYOCARDIAL INFARCTION

Death of part of the heart muscle due to blockage of a coronary artery.

One of the forms of 'heart attack', but all such attacks certainly need not be infarcts. Death may ensue at any time after the onset of the infarct, from immediate sudden death to survival for many years, but an infarct always leaves the residual danger of a subsequent infarct or death from one of the other sequelae of coronary artery disease (qv).

The most common cause of a myocardial infarct is a coronary thrombosis, though this again is not invariable. The features classically consist of pain in the chest passing down one or both arms or to the back, sweating, sickness, pallor, breathlessness and collapse, but there is a wide spectrum of symptoms and indeed, many infarcts are 'silent' or are mistaken for 'indigestion', being demonstrable only as a retrospective finding at post-mortem examination.

At the moment of blockage of a coronary artery, usually by a thrombus, the dramatic signs of infarction do not commence. There is a latent period which may be hours or even a day or so until a threshold point is reached when the symptoms begin. This makes the diagnosis of an infarct difficult at post-mortem, if death has occurred soon after the blockage, and makes the interpretation of some accidents equally difficult. For instance, a man may collapse at the wheel of his car or the pilot of an aircraft may become incapacitated at the controls. Though long standing coronary artery disease can be seen at post-mortem, there may be no fresh abnormality to explain the accident and insufficient time may have elapsed for an infarct to be visible to the naked eye (up to 24 hours) or even to standard microscopical examination (8–12 hours). There are newer methods available using enzymes and fluorescence microscopy which can reveal infarction within 3–6 hours, but specialist techniques are needed. This has profound medico-legal importance in accident investigation and even in criminal cases, where death following an assault can be shown to be due to, or contributed to, by a heart attack.

Where a myocardial infarct is not fatal (the majority of cases), healing of the muscle occurs and a fibrous scar develops, taking about three months to attain its permanent appearance.

Any person with such scarring is always vulnerable to heart disorders and the risk of sudden death from instability of the heart muscle function (arrhthymias, ventricular fibrillation and cardiac arrest).

It is now statistically proven that sudden severe exertion can precipitate sudden death in persons with coronary artery disease, but these are rarely acute myocardial infarcts.

MYOCARDITIS

An inflammation of the heart muscle, often fatal. Many general infections may include the heart, such as diphtheria, but the term is usually reserved for inflammatory conditions of obscure cause, sometimes viral.

A type which has been blamed for many sudden unexpected deaths in young adults is called *isolated myocarditis* or sometimes *Fiedler's* or *Saphir's* myocarditis.

For a firm diagnosis, post-mortem microscopic evidence of an inflammatory cell reaction and areas of heart muscle necrosis (qv) must be obtained.

Criteria have sometimes been relaxed and a few scattered inflammatory cells seen in the heart muscle are insufficient for a firm diagnosis. A survey of fatal transport accidents in the RAF and in Australia, where natural disease could have played no part, showed that an appreciable number of victims had minimal signs in the heart that might in other circumstances have been called myocarditis.

NECK-HOLD DEATHS

Deaths usually in police custody, though some occur during other altercations.

Like positional or postural asphyxia (qv), this was first reported in the USA, when a standard police restraint method, using an arm around the offender's neck, led to a series of deaths. The police arm-lock was of two types, one where the forearm was used as a bar across the front of the subject's throat and another, soon proscribed, used the crook of the elbow centred on the throat. The latter is more dangerous, as the forearm and upper arm form the limbs of a 'V' which can impinge on the carotid sinuses and cause cardiac arrest (see 'Vagal inhibition'). The forearm bar was thought to be safe, but it can also cause death, either by blocking the airway by pressing the larynx upwards and backwards, or by cardiac arrest from general pressure on the neck, especially in adrenaline-mediated circumstances of a violent struggle.

In Britain, arm-locks are now excluded from police procedures, because of a series of fatalities.

NECROSIS

Death of living tissue, usually from deprivation of blood supply (called infarction), physical damage (mechanical injury, heat, cold, electricity, chemicals, radiation, etc) or infection.

Medico-legally, more important types include necrosis of heart muscle (see 'Myocardial infarction'), or periphery of limbs from embolism (qv) of main arteries or cold injury, and necrosis of brain, often called softening, which leads to strokes.

OBSCURE OR NEGATIVE AUTOPSY

Though the autopsy is vastly superior to clinical examination in determining the cause of death, between 5–10% of autopsies provide no satisfactory answer, even when the most extensive investigations are made. These are most frequent in children and young adults. The 'cot death' (qv) or Sudden Infant Death Syndrome accounts for some, where by definition, no morphological findings are apparent.

In young adults, sudden unexpected death remains unexplained in a small but significant proportion, sometimes associated with extreme exertion on the sports field. When all ancillary investigations, such as microscopic examination of tissues, microbiology, toxicology and virology, prove negative then the cause must remain 'unascertainable'. Occasionally seen in older persons, these examinations may be termed an 'obscure' or 'negative' autopsy. The mechanism of death is due to some occult malfunction which leaves no morphological or chemical signs.

The death is presumed to be due to natural causes, usually a sudden cardiac arrest or other form of heart failure, though this cannot be objectively demonstrated.

The reason that more cases appear to occur in young persons may largely be explained by the fact that they do not have the overlay of arterial degenerative disease that is so common after middle age. Where a man of 60 drops dead, for instance, the true cause of death may in reality be just as occult as that of the 20 year old football player on the next mortuary table. But because the older man is likely to have some degree of coronary artery disease, or thickened left ventricle due to high blood pressure, there is a natural and understandable tendency for the pathologist to ascribe the death to that, even though the extent of the disease may be only marginally sufficient.

Another cause of apparently negative autopsy findings is an insufficiently thorough post-mortem examination. In reviewing such cases, a very detailed examination of the coronary system may reveal a blocked vessel that was previously overlooked. Microscopic (histological) examination may reveal disease unapparent to the naked eye (a myocarditis – inflammation of the heart muscle – for instance). Less often, bacteriological or virological investigations may reveal a pathogenic infection. More often, analysis of body fluids and organs may show some toxic substance, including a high level of alcohol, which might not have been suggested by the circumstances.

Where a thorough examination still provides no satisfactory explanation, the pathologist must resist the temptation to offer a speculative cause of death based on minimal findings, which he would not accept in other circumstances. To the younger pathologist especially, such a temptation is increased by the fear of censure for failing to provide an answer. All pathologists are naturally influenced to some degree by the need to satisfy the coroner or other law officer, as well as the family, by providing some explanation. However, it is well known and accepted that a small proportion of autopsies remain obscure, and truth should not yield to expediency.

PATTERNED INJURIES

Abrasions give the most detail of the nature of an inflicting object. Bruises show a more blurred pattern, but sometimes are useful, especially some time after infliction when surrounding swelling subsides. Intra-dermal bruising, in the uppermost layer of the skin, may provide a good reproduction of the impacting object and is often mistaken for an abrasion. After death, the intensity of abrasion damage is usually enhanced due to drying of the bared skin surface and bruises usually become more visible, albeit progressively blurring over time. Lacerations rarely give an accurate imprint of an inflicting object, unless the outline is particularly distinctive, such as a large wrench, etc. (See, also, 'Abrasions', 'Bruises', 'Lacerations').

Types of patterned injury

A geometric pattern, often in vehicle accidents, may occur when the grid of a radiator, headlamp rim, mascot or tyre tread is imprinted on the skin. Hard fabric, such as the cord weave of a driving glove, may mark the skin, as in heavy slaps on a cheek. Woven or plaited cords or thongs, as in ligatures or whips, may leave a clear pattern.

Pressure through woven fabric, such as strangulation through a polo-necked jumper, may leave a clear imprint, as may a neck chain.

Recognisable patterns can form from blows from distinctive weapons, such as a hammer-head, spanner, etc. The exact size need not be matched by the skin mark, as both the elasticity of the skin and tissue swelling may distort the mark. Also, the impact may be glancing and a sliding mark of larger size may be inflicted.

The clearest patterns arise from a perpendicular impact without any tangential movement. Where deep injury exists under the skin, as in a depressed fracture of the skull, the size of the internal injury may be larger than the causative weapon, due to spreading of the force of impact and the intervention of the overlying soft tissues.

A bar or rod commonly leaves a distinctive pattern of two parallel lines of bruising, with undamaged tissue between. This is due to the direct pressure expelling blood from the central zone, but the skin edges being forced inwards, causing shearing damage and bleeding from small vessels in these marginal zones.

A 'target' bruise is due to the impact of a spherical object, such as a hard sphere (for example, a squash ball) or even a round hammer-head, and may cause a 'target' bruise, with a central pale area surrounded by a zone of haemorrhage.

Figure 34: **Mechanism of bruising from a rod or bar**

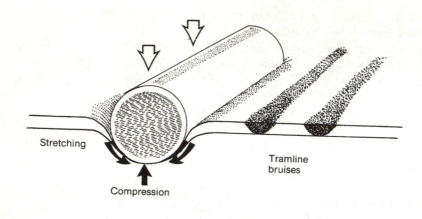

Finger-tip bruises are disc-shaped and about 1–2 cm in diameter, often in groups, sometimes suggesting or indicating a row of finger-tips. Commonly seen in child abuse, where they are situated above and below large joints such as elbow or knee, or the chest or abdomen, on the neck or on the sides of the trunk from gripping by adult fingers. Also seen in adults on the upper and lower arms, from gripping during an altercation. Common on the neck in manual strangulation.

Finger-nail marks may be linear (scratches) due to moving friction of the nails along the skin. These may be multiple and parallel; scrapings of the nails of the assailant (or victim where scratches are defensive) may reveal blood and skin remnants which can be identified by DNA.

Static finger-nail marks are usually crescentic. If deep and bleeding, they usually mean a rapid impact rather than steady pressure. Note that the curvature of the crescent may be in the opposite direction to that of the inflicting nail, due to elastic recoil of the skin when the nails are removed.

A contact wound from a firearm (qv) sometimes shows an abrasion or bruise from the rim of the muzzle, sometimes with a characteristic impression of the foresight or other shaped part of the muzzle. This is often erroneously called a 'recoil imprint', but is not due to the recoil of the weapon, which always moves the gun away from the skin. It is due to gas entering the wound and ballooning the skin against the muzzle.

'Brush' abrasions or grazes are linear scratches due to tangential impact, commonly seen from skidding across a road surface ('gravel rash'), but may occur from a glancing blow, especially a kick.

PETECHIAL HAEMORRHAGES

Tiny pin-head sized haemorrhages, found in the skin, eyelids, eyes and internal membranes such as the pleura (covering of the lungs) and pericardium (membrane around the heart).

Petechial haemorrhages, especially on the lungs or heart, were formerly thought to be diagnostic of asphyxia (qv), but this is quite incorrect. They certainly can appear in asphyxia, but are often absent: conversely, they are commonly present in non-asphyxial conditions, and can even appear post-mortem.

True petechiae are caused by a sharp rise in pressure in the veins, so many types of congestive death, from heart disease and other natural causes as well as trauma, may cause damming back of the blood in the veins as the heart fails terminally. Such congestive changes in the organs may be accompanied by petechiae, but rarely in the skin.

In the forensic context, where the veins are mechanically blocked, as in pressure on the neck from strangulation, then the rise in venous blood pressure may cause marked congestion and produce petechiae above the level of obstruction. However, if death ensues rapidly, from cardiac arrest (see 'Strangulation'), then insufficient time elapses for the congestion and petechiae to develop. This time is very variable, but is probably longer than 30 seconds.

Petechiae from pressure on the neck are seen in the loose skin of the upper eyelids, in the skin of the cheeks, forehead, chin and neck, in the inside of the eyelids and on the whites of the eyes.

In the chest, they may occur under the pleural membranes (subpleural petechiae or 'Tardieu spots'). These were once thought to be proof of asphyxia, but are commonly seen in all types of death, especially in the fissures and near the root of the lung, where a few petechiae may usually be found. However, if numerous and taken in conjunction with facial haemorrhages and evidence of pressure on the neck or obstruction of breathing, they are useful confirmatory findings if interpreted cautiously.

Petechiae may also be seen on the surface of the heart and on the thymus gland in infants – this gland lying above the heart. It has been shown by trial photographic studies (Gordon and Shapiro) that petechiae can actually develop on the surface of the heart in the course of a post-mortem; also, petechiae commonly appear in areas of dependent hypostasis after death (see 'Hypostasis') so there is no doubt that they can be a post-mortem phenomenon. However, petechiae in the eyes or facial skin are usually evidence of a congestive process, though this is by no means synonymous with asphyxia (qv). It should be noted that petechiae in the eyes can occur after violent sneezing or in whooping cough, again due to a sudden rise in venous blood pressure.

The most gross congestion and petechiae are seen in the so called 'traumatic asphyxia' (qv), due to damming back of blood from fixation of the chest.

The whole topic of 'asphyxial petechiae' is undergoing very critical review in forensic medical circles and the old classical interpretations should be accepted with great caution, as it is now clear that the appearances are highly non-specific.

PNEUMOCONIOSES

Industrial lung diseases due to inhalation of dust; now all scheduled diseases under the Industrial Injuries Act, such as coal workers' anthraco-silicosis, asbestosis, slate workers' and quarry workers' silicosis, baggasosis, byssinosis, etc.

It must be appreciated that the mere inhalation and retention of dust in the lungs does not constitute a disease. There must be some response ('host reaction') by the body, which leads to pathological changes which cause an impairment of function of the lungs, or to some other abnormality, for example, tumour formation in asbestos exposure. An analogy may be drawn with the hands of a mechanic, which, though dirty, are no less efficient. This distinction is sometimes not appreciated by those engaged in compensation procedures.

Coal workers' pneumoconiosis

Medically, 'anthraco-silicosis'. Coal is carbon, mixed with various amounts of other rocks. It is the silica which is dangerous, not the carbon. The coal dust reaches the furthest parts of the lung (small bronchi or air passages and the air cells or 'alveoli') and may remain there inert, causing nothing more than 'dust retention', which is not a disease state. Commonly, the body reacts to the silica in the dust and forms small nodules of fibrous tissue. This is simple pneumoconiosis and is graded in life according to the X-ray appearances, in accordance with the 1971 International Labour Office Classification of Radiographs of Pneumoconiosis.

Category 1:   few small, rounded opacities.

Category 2:   numerous small, rounded opacities, normal lung marking still visible.

Category 3:   numerous small, rounded opacities, obscuring the normal lung markings.

The size of the X-ray opacities or shadows are measured in an ascending scale as 'p', 'q' and 'r'.

A more serious condition is complicated pneumoconiosis or progressive massive fibrosis (PMF), where infection, either septic or tuberculous, appears as a progression from simple pneumoconiosis. The opacities are more than 1 cm in size and may reach 10 or 15 times that size in advanced cases. It is the complicated disease, or PMF, that forms a danger to life and causes severe disability. The role of simple pneumoconiosis in causing symptoms is disputed and it never leads to death.

Large opacities on X-ray (PMF) are classified as Categories 'A', 'B' and 'C', according to the size of the shadow.

According to many authorities, simple pneumoconiosis is symptomless. Any symptoms experienced by men without complicated disease is attributed to coincidental lung disease, the most common being chronic bronchitis and emphysema, which is now itself accepted as occupational, contrary to former medical opinion.

Category 'A' PMF is also held officially to be without symptoms, disabling disease being due to Category 'B' and 'C' masses.

Miners with either rheumatoid arthritis or an occult tendency to rheumatic disease may get a special type of lung opacity, called the Caplan lesion. It is not necessarily related to the degree of lung function disability. Extensive PMF leads to obstruction of the lung circulation and to loss of lung function, as well as to congestive heart failure. It is the only cause of death in coal workers' pneumoconiosis, leading to 'cor pulmonale', heart failure due to restricted circulation through the lungs, though concomitant chronic bronchitis and emphysema have their own mortality, again partly from congestive cardiac failure and partly from impaired oxygen exchange in the lungs.

Coal miners do not get any increased risk of lung cancer; in fact the rate is slightly lower than in the general population. Though PMF is often associated with tuberculosis, there is no increased risk of contracting the disease as a result of occupation, only a variation in the nature of the infection as a result of dust in the lungs. This is not true of silicosis, seen in gold miners and quarry workers, which predisposes to tuberculous infection.

Silicosis

A pneumoconiosis contracted in many industries including quarrying, gold mining, slate work, stone dressing, ceramics, etc. Like coal workers' disease, it may be simple or complicated, but there is a greater degree of fibrosis. Tuberculosis is a frequent complication, silica appearing to facilitate infection, unlike the situation with anthraco-silicosis.

Asbestosis

Asbestos is ubiquitous in the urban environment and almost everyone has a small number of asbestos fibres in their lungs. Like other pneumoconioses, damage occurs only when there is a host reaction to the substance. The number of mineral fibres in a lung can be assessed after post-mortem by ashing a sample of lung and counting the resistant fibres.

Three types of dangerous sequelae to substantial asbestos exposure exist:

Asbestosis is a pneumoconiosis due to fibrosis of the lungs and is comparable to the previous conditions, though the fibrosis is more diffuse and usually involves the pleura, the coverings of the lungs.

An increased risk of lung cancer, indistinguishable from the cancers which arise spontaneously or as a result of smoking. Such cancers occur in a third to a half of cases of asbestosis, smokers with asbestosis being much more at risk, of the order of a 20 fold increase. It should be noted that increased lung cancer only occurs in the victims of actual asbestosis, not in persons merely exposed to asbestos dust.

Mesothelioma: there is a well substantiated connection between asbestos exposure (not necessarily asbestosis) and the type of tumour called 'mesothelioma' which usually affects the pleura and, less often, the lining of the abdominal cavity. The condition is accepted (where related to an industrial history of asbestos exposure) as a compensatable scheduled disease under the Industrial Injuries Acts. The disease is invariably fatal, but may take up to 15–20 years after exposure to become manifest. A substantial exposure to asbestosis is usually necessary for mesothelioma to develop. It must be appreciated, however that in about 15% of cases of this tumour, no exposure to asbestosis can ever be proved, the condition arising spontaneously.

The various types of asbestos have widely different and dangerous effects There are six varieties, but only three (white, blue and brown) are used extensively in industry. Blue asbestos (crocidolite) has a particular danger of mesothelioma production and is now banned from import into the UK. White asbestos (chrysolite) now forms 90% of world production and is relatively harmless. The dangers of the different types are thought to be to the physical shape of their fibres, rather than to chemical effects. The tiny, sharp fibres are thought to damage cells physically, especially their DNA, which explains their tumour-provoking properties.

'Asbestos bodies' are microscopic fibres found in the lung, coated with yellow iron-containing protein. They are not evidence of *asbestosis,* but of asbestos *exposure*: a considerable proportion of all urban dwellers have such exposure, but it is quantitatively greater in certain workers, such as laggers, shipbuilders and breakers, and in the asbestos supply and packing industries.

Farmer's lung

A pneumonia-like illness with an allergic basis, due to various moulds (especially *Micropolyspora faeni*) from damp hay. It may be an acute illness or may be a long standing condition. Rarely fatal, it may lead to permanent lung damage and severe disability. Now a scheduled industrial disease, but rarely seen in Britain now, due to changes in farm practice with hay drying and silage making.

POISONING

General features

Toxicology is a separate science in its own right, as are forensic serology and dentistry. The vast and ever-increasing number of toxic substances in the modern environment makes it impossible to offer any comprehensive survey of poisoning, but some features of immediate medico-legal importance can be identified.

First, the whole subject tends to fall naturally into two parts:

(a) the technology of analysing biological fluids and organs for toxic substances;

(b) the interpretation of the results provided by the analyst.

Laboratory analysis

The first topic has no place in this book, except to emphasise that toxicology is a task for full time experts, where the occasional dilettante is quite out of place. Even though a person may be an expert general chemist, unless he or she is constantly involved in the technology of poisons detection, their worth as an expert witness is very much reduced.

In the UK, the Home Office forensic science laboratories have the greatest expertise in criminal cases or for the coroner in accidental or suicidal poisoning. Some university departments of forensic medicine have good toxicological facilities and the area toxicological laboratories of the National Health Service also carry out drug analysis. Where a defence solicitor requires his own analysis, either private forensic or commercial laboratories, the public analyst service or some specialist laboratories in industry or the university sphere can provide the necessary expertise.

The matter of samples is vital, as the site, type and amount of biological specimen required may crucially affect the value of the analysis. The laboratory should be consulted when an analysis is required, to give guidance on the nature, storage and transport of the samples.

For example, blood samples for *alcohol* analysis must be placed into a tube containing an adequate amount of fluoride, to inhibit micro-organisms which may distort the alcohol content before analysis is carried out.

In post-mortem toxicology, sampling is also vital and gross errors can arise unwittingly if material is taken inappropriately. It has been shown in recent years, especially by Professor Derrick Pounder of Dundee, that there is a very uneven distribution of many substances in the dead body.

It is unsafe to take blood samples for many substances, especially alcohol and most drugs, from the heart, large blood vessels in the chest, neck and abdomen. This is because substances in the stomach, gut and even air passages, after regurgitation, may diffuse from those sites after death into adjacent blood vessels and the heart, giving a spuriously high result, often of high concentration.

Blood samples should be taken from peripheral veins, such as the femoral, which are remote from sources of contamination.

It should be repeated here (see 'Drowning') that fresh water drowning is accompanied by a marked rapid increase in blood volume and therefore drugs and alcohol may be diluted by as much as 50% in a post-mortem blood sample, compared to the true concentration immediately before death.

A variety of biological fluids and tissues may be used for analysis, including blood, urine, vitreous fluid from the eye (which resists post-mortem change longer than blood), stomach contents, intestinal contents, and hair (for heavy metals, etc).

Interpretation

The interpretation of results is often more difficult than the provision of a quantitative analysis result.

Owing to biological and other variations, the end result may bear little or no relationship to the amount of poison taken, and the amount needed to cause death or disability may vary enormously from person to person or even in the same person at different times. As with alcohol, the following factors have to be taken into account:

Absorption. The speed and completeness of absorption of the poison into the body (whether by mouth, inhalation or skin), will often determine whether a toxic level is attained in the blood and tissues. If the poison is eliminated as fast as it is absorbed, then no ill effects may occur.

Elimination may be by excretion of the intact toxic substance or detoxification of it by the body's chemical processes. Excretion of the original drug may be via the urine, faeces, breath or skin or a combination of all methods. The products of detoxification may also be excreted in a similar way.

The concentration ('level') in the blood represents a dynamic balance between the above processes of absorption and elimination. If the entry of the poison is faster than elimination, then a build-up will occur, which will be reflected by a rising blood level.

Once the intake of the toxic substance ceases, then elimination will cause a falling blood level, unless death supervenes, when all active detoxification and excretion cease. However, lethal damage may already have been done, which then complicates the interpretation of the analysis results. For instance, a person may take such an overdose of sleeping tablets that grave depression of the brain centres occurs. Prolonged coma may then result in death, yet once all the drug has been absorbed from the alimentary tract, the processes of elimination carry on until death. Thus a very low blood level may exist at the time of death (which is the level detected in a post-mortem blood sample) and in the absence of circumstantial evidence, the actual cause of death may be hard to substantiate. Where the victim was habitually taking therapeutic doses of the drug, then the levels measured after death may be within the therapeutic range, which makes it difficult to prove an overdose from laboratory results alone. Many drugs, such as tranquillisers and anti-depressants, pose the same problem for the pathologist and toxicologist.

Some poisons are cumulative, because their excretion is extremely slow. In these cases, even minute amounts of the substance absorbed may build up to dangerous or lethal levels. Substances such as arsenic and colchicine (autumn crocus) are in this category.

Post-mortem decay may cause some poisons to be present in misleadingly low concentration after death. Conversely, alcohol may rise after death, due to the action of yeasts and other micro-organisms on body constituents, especially if the environmental temperature is high. However, some poisons, such as metallic compounds or barbiturates, may be detected in the body many years after death.

Some toxic substances are rapidly converted into other chemicals in the body and may not be recoverable in the original form, such as the very rapid conversion of heroin to morphine. An expert knowledge of toxicological chemistry is needed for the degradation substance to be anticipated and sought in the samples.

All these factors make the interpretation of results very difficult, and it is common in fatal cases for the amount of drug or poison recovered to be less than the usually accepted fatal minimum.

Again, the published ranges for dangerous and lethal levels of the various poisons vary markedly. Owing to biological variation, the susceptibility of different people can vary greatly to a given amount of a toxic substance. Tolerance can develop from long usage, but also idiosyncrasy or sensitivity may lead to death or severe illness in amounts which should normally be innocuous.

The physical effects of poisons vary greatly according to the substance absorbed. Poisoning may occur in suicidal, accidental or homicidal circumstances and industrial exposure may give rise to civil litigation, all of which may require expert investigation and toxicological analysis. Where death has occurred, though the technical aspects of sample analysis and the production of a quantitative result, together with advice on the normal, therapeutic, toxic and usually fatal concentrations, are the province of the chemist, the *interpretation* of those results should be the function of the pathologist, clinical toxicologist or other expert medical witness.

He has to interpret the result in the light of the full findings, which may include co-existing natural disease, injuries or other modifying factors which require the bare quantitative analysis results to be viewed in a different light. The decision as to whether a certain blood or tissue level of poison caused death or disability should not be left to the analyst, though as stated above, the medical witness may often seek his advice as to conventional ranges for the particular substance under examination.

POSITIONAL OR POSTURAL ASPHYXIA

A recently recognised cause of death, most often occurring in police custody, but sometimes in accidental situations.

First named in the USA, it arose when prisoners where 'hog-tied', having their hands pinioned behind their back and their ankles tied. They were placed face down in vehicles and found to be dead within minutes.

Further cases were then recognised in other countries, where prisoners, especially large or obese, were left face-down with their wrists handcuffed behind their back, sometimes in police vehicles or in police stations.

Death is due to restriction of the ability to breathe, as the weight of the body is upon the front of the chest and the arms are not available to assist lifting the trunk from the floor. As a consequence, inhalation is restricted and oxygen lack may develop. Existing heart disease or inebriation worsens the situation, but is not essential.

Postural asphyxia may also occur when a person gets stuck in an inverted or jack-knifed position, such as attempting to climb through a fanlight window; other deaths have occurred during masochistic practices (qv) where bondage or bizarre positions, sometimes inverted, lead to restriction of breathing.

POST-MORTEM ENTOMOLOGY

The study of the infestation of the dead body by insects and other fauna is a very specialised subject, its expertise confined to only one or two zoologists in the UK.

There are many pitfalls in interpretation and even expert forensic biologists and pathologists cannot claim much specialist knowledge in estimating the time since death on the basis of the infestation.

Factors such as the ambient temperature, the season and, above all, the actual species and variety of sarcosaprophagous insect involved, always require the best opinion possible.

The stage of maturation of certain fly maggots, usually *Diptera*, may be used as an aid to estimating the time since death of infested bodies. Both live and alcohol-acetic-acid preserved maggots should be submitted for this examination.

Main infesting insects are the blue-bottle (*Calliphora*), green-bottle (*Lucilia*) and the house-fly (*Musca*). Beetles, moths and larger beetles may also be present at later stages.

Most common insect to infest the cadaver is the common blue-bottle. Eggs may be laid shortly after death (or even before if the victim is debilitated or comatose), but only in daylight and above 12°C temperature. The eyes, nostrils and mouth are the most common sites, or any wounds upon the skin. The blue-bottle favours fresh tissue rather than putrefied bodies. Small maggots may appear within 8–14 hours of egg laying, these being called the first 'instar'. The speed of hatching depends upon environmental temperature. An instar is a stage in the life history between two successive castings of the outer skin of the maggot. The first instar persists for another 8–14 hours, then the skin is cast to form the second instar of larger maggots, which live for 2–3 days. The third instar lives for six days, after which the insect pupates in a quiescent phase for about 12 days. The first empty pupa may be seen after about 22 days. The blue-bottle larva possesses an enzyme which liquefies tissues, so that numerous holes appear in the skin and the maggots can spread deeply into the tissue. This hastens putrefaction. Blue-bottles are active in the environment from early spring until late autumn. The green-bottle is similar in almost all respects to the blue-bottle as far as the life history is concerned.

The common house-fly (*Musca domestica*) is less common on bodies, the house-fly favouring putrid matter and manure. However, bodies are attacked on some occasions, the eggs hatching in about 12 hours. The first instar lasts for 36 hours, the second for 1–2 days and the third for 3–4 days.

The rationale of using maggot infestation as an index of the time of death gives a minimum time dependent upon the stage of maturation. However, various generations of maggots may be present at the same time, due to successive egg layings.

Other insects may assist over the longer period and even the absence of certain fauna, either on the body or in the underlying ground, may be of significance in timing death.

It is emphasised that the assistance of an expert entomologist is necessary.

PREGNANCY

Signs of pregnancy

(a) Cessation of menstruation.

(b) Breast changes – swelling, darkening and prominence of tubercles of nipple.

(c) Morning sickness – variable.

(d) Softening and congestive coloration of neck of womb.

(e) Palpation signs ('ballotment') of enlarging womb.

(f) Enlargement of womb – rises out of the pelvis by eighth week, reaches umbilicus by 24th week, at full term is under the ribs.

(g) X-ray confirmation – never performed except for urgent medical reasons because of potential malformation dangers of radiation to foetus in early pregnancy.

(h) 'Quickening' of foetal movements and contractions of womb.

(i) Laboratory tests. Many available, depending on change in hormones during pregnancy. Reliably positive from about 12–15 days after conception.

(j) Foetal heart sounds heard through stethoscope.

(k) Ultrasound and other imaging techniques.

Duration of pregnancy

Can be a matter of considerable importance in divorce, inheritance, etc.

The average length is calculated from the date of the last missed period to the birth and is 280 days (40 weeks, or 10 lunar months). Variations can occur due both to length of pregnancy itself and to the length of the menstrual period, but 10 days either way is the usual maximum divergence, except where early birth occurs from some obstetrical cause. In most women, birth will take place at the time of what would have been the 10th menstrual period, but as conception usually takes place some 10 days after the onset of the period, the actual length of gestation is nearer 270 days. Sperm cannot survive for long in the female genital tract, but fertilisation may occur up to a day or so after intercourse.

All births before 38 weeks are premature and all over 40 weeks are delayed.

Consideration of short pregnancies must take into account a comparable degree of immaturity in the infant. A 24 week foetus can survive with modern medical care.

The maximum length of gestation is uncertain, though 354 days has been verified medically and several leading cases have accepted a long period: Gaskill (1921) – 331 days; Hadlum (1948) – 349 days; Wood (1949) – 346 days, though Preston-Jones (1951) was rejected at 360 days.

PROCURATOR FISCAL

In Scotland, there is no coroner system, the investigation of certain categories of death being the duty of the Procurators Fiscal, to whom such deaths are reported by police, doctors, the public and Registrars of Births and Deaths. Though a Procurator Fiscal can investigate any death which he thinks requires it, the following is the advisory list published by the Crown Office:

(a) any death uncertified by a doctor;

(b) any death caused by an accident arising out of the use of a vehicle, including an aircraft, ship or train;

(c) any death arising out of industrial employment, by accident, industrial disease or industrial poisoning;

(d) any death due to poisoning;

(e) any death where the circumstances would seem to indicate suicide;

(f) any death where there are indications that it occurred as a result of medical mishap;

(g) any death resulting from an accident;

(h) any death following abortion or attempted abortion;

(i) any death apparently caused by fault or neglect on the part of another person;

(j) any death occurring in legal custody;

(k) any death of a new-born child whose body is found;

(l) any death (occurring not in a house) where deceased's residence is unknown;

(m)death by drowning;

(n) death of a child from suffocation (including overlaying);

(o) any death which may be the sudden infant death syndrome;

(p) where the death occurred from food poisoning or infectious disease;

(q) any death as a result of burning, scalding, fire or explosion;

(r) deaths of foster children;

(s) any other death due to violent, suspicious or unexplained cause;

(t) any death where a complaint from the next of kin is received by a Health Board or NHS Trust and the complaint is about the medical treatment with a suggestion that it might have contributed to the death of the patient.

There are special provisions concerning deaths associated with medical care, including:

(a) deaths which occur unexpectedly having regard to the clinical condition of the deceased;

(b) deaths which are clinically unexplained;

(c) deaths seemingly attribitable to a therapeutic or diagnostic hazard;

(d) deaths which are apparently associated with a lack of medical care;

(e) deaths which occur during the actual administration of an anaesthetic, local or general;

(f) deaths which may be due to an anaesthetic.

When apprised of a death, the Procurator Fiscal makes further enquiries via the police, his only form of investigative agency. There is no exact parallel to the English 'coroner's officer' but investigations are carried out on the Procurator Fiscal's behalf by uniformed or plain clothes officers, seconded for duty as 'sudden death officers'. The CID may be involved where necessary. The police make investigations in all cases except those concerning anaesthetic deaths, for which there is a special procedure.

Certain categories of death, such as criminality, suicide, medical mishap, those of police officers in accidents, fires and explosions, and cases involving a continuing public hazard, etc, must be reported by the Procurator to the Crown Office.

Details of the Procurator Fiscal's procedures are contained in Crown Office regulations.

PULMONARY EMBOLISM AND DEEP VEIN THROMBOSIS

Blood clot (more accurately 'thrombus') may form in veins, almost always those in the deep veins of the calf of the leg – much less often in other sites, such as the pelvis (even where there is pelvic vein thrombosis, there is usually also deep vein thrombosis (DVT)).

This DVT is very common, but usually causes no ill-effects apart from swelling and pain in the leg, which may be absent in many cases. If a part becomes detached, it is conveyed through the veins to the right side of the heart and thence to the lungs via the pulmonary arteries. Branching of the pulmonary arteries provides the first obstruction to the thrombus, which lodges at the first intersection too small to allow its passage. If large, the clot will block the major branches and cause rapid death from obstruction of the circulation (*pulmonary embolism*). If smaller, the fragments will pass further into the lung, causing non-fatal symptoms or even having no apparent effect. They may cause local areas of lung damage due to deprivation of the blood supply, called *pulmonary infarcts*.

This pulmonary embolism (PE) is a common condition and a frequent cause of sudden death after a variety of causes, such as surgical operations, fractures of the leg, injuries of many types and prolonged immobility in bed.

Figure 35:   **Pulmonary embolism**

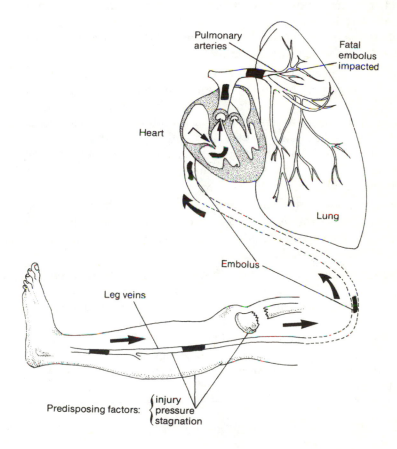

Certain drugs have a variable risk of encouraging DVT, such as oestrogens, including oral contraceptive pills, though the risk is usually very small and is only revealed in large statistical analyses.

Pulmonary embolism is often unsuspected by doctors and is the cause of death most frequently undiagnosed before an autopsy is performed. Fewer than half the deaths from pulmonary embolism have been anticipated by clinicians, when confirmed by post-mortem examination. DVT may present no signs and therefore the subsequent pulmonary embolism may be quite unexpected. If DVT is recognised and especially if small pulmonary infarcts have occurred, then the administration of anti-coagulant drugs such as heparin may prevent further DVT and potential pulmonary embolism. Failure to do so has resulted in many medical negligence actions.

Pulmonary embolism may occur at any time after trauma or operation, etc, but is most common at about two weeks following injury. However, any period from a day or two to several months is possible, though with a progressively longer interval, it becomes harder to attribute the embolism directly to the injury, as about one-fifth of all fatal pulmonary emboli occur in the absence of the usual precipitating factors.

It is therefore a matter of probabilities as to the causal relationship of an operation, injury or bed rest to a fatal embolism and this has profound medico-legal connotations. For example, where criminal proceedings arise from a death due to pulmonary embolism following a traffic accident or an assault, it has to be shown that the fatal outcome was due to the effects of the injury causing DVT and hence pulmonary embolism. As many emboli come 'out of the blue', this causal relationship is difficult to establish 'beyond reasonable doubt'.

If the pulmonary embolism occurs, say, two weeks after the injury, then the connection is strongly suspected, though never absolutely provable. If it is delayed until two months, then it is very much more difficult to prove the link between injury and death.

The age of the thrombus, both that in the lungs and that remaining in the deep veins, is of vital importance as, if it can be shown to pre-date the injury, then the causal relationship is destroyed. Unfortunately, dating such thrombi is very difficult and uncertain, even on microscopic examination: expert advice is needed. Opinions as to date may vary between experts and in any case cannot be measured with any accuracy, except during the few days following commencement. At a later stage, a time scale must be measured at best in weeks.

Predisposing factors for deep vein thrombosis

Increased clotting tendency of the blood, occurring as a natural defensive mechanism after injury (including surgical operation).

Stagnation ('stasis') of blood in the veins due to bed rest during immobility caused by injuries, fractures, coma, etc. This stasis is due to minimal muscle action, which fails to massage the blood back from the legs.

Pressure on the calves of the legs during immobility in bed: this causes obliteration of the veins and direct passive trauma to their walls.

Local tissue damage to muscles and veins, as in injuries and fractures of the legs.

Certain drugs, such as oral contraceptives, etc.

These factors are present in patients who have had surgery or tissue trauma or who are confined to bed for other reasons, yet DVT and hence pulmonary embolism can frequently occur in apparently healthy and mobile persons, 10–20% having none of the predisposing factors just mentioned.

RAPE

In most jurisdictions, the essential feature of rape is penile penetration. If this cannot be proved, then only a lesser sexual offence can be maintained.

Medical evidence of penetration

Recovery of semen from the depths of the vagina. Deposition of semen upon the vulva or thighs can occur from intra-crural ejaculation (between the thighs). Pregnancy is well known to occur from such external ejaculation and therefore subsequent pregnancy is not strict proof of vaginal intercourse (see 'Semen').

Injury to the female genitalia is strong evidence of forcible intercourse, though penetration by fingers or some instrument may produce the same signs. Also over-enthusiastic voluntary intercourse may cause some damage, though rarely as severe as in rape.

Injuries associated with rape may include the following:

Reddening, swelling and bruising of the vulva. These may also be signs of energetic voluntary intercourse, especially in difficult circumstances of clandestine love making, but severe degrees are inevitably the result of rape, especially in children.

Rupture of the hymen. This membrane may be naturally prominent or almost absent. The orifice may be wide enough to allow intercourse without rupture or may be completely imperforate. In the usual circumstances it is torn during first deep intercourse. If recent, within a day or two, there will be slight bleeding and reddened inflammatory reactions at the site of the tear. The hymenal tear soon heals and subsequent intercourse usually leaves no further signs. Childbirth normally obliterates the remnants of the hymen. Rupture or permanent dilatation of the hymen may occur from the use of tampons for menstruation or from manual masturbation (see 'Hymen').

Injuries to the vaginal wall. These may occur externally at the back, edge of the orifice of the vagina, adjacent to the anus. A tear may occur from violent penetration or from disparity of size of the vaginal opening and the penis. This may be seen in adult intercourse with a young girl or child, but can occur at later ages. It is almost never a sign of voluntary intercourse, except in marked disproportion of organ size. The tear may extend backwards into the anus and may cause a severe injury, especially in a child. Other injuries may occur to the internal walls of the vagina. These may vary from bruising and abrasions to lacerations. Fatal tears may occur in violent rape and in rape upon children. The vagina may be split in a child by a large adult penis and the peritoneal cavity entered, with death or severe illness from haemorrhage

Figure 36:   **Female external genitals**

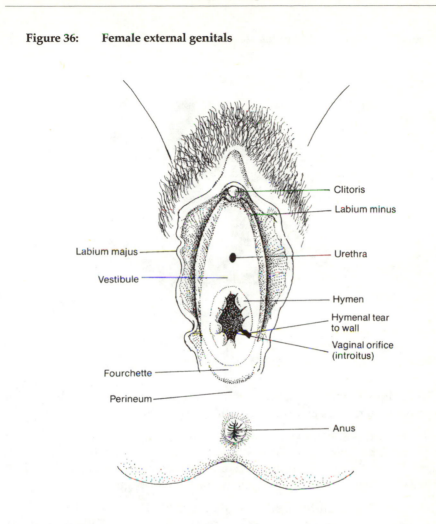

and peritonitis. The posterior fornix (the upper cul-de-sac beyond the neck of the womb) may be torn by a penis of much greater length than the immature vagina. Lesser degrees of damage may occur to any part of the female organs, from friction from either penis, fingers or mouth. The usual signs of such injury include bruising, swelling, redness and abrasions.

Venereal infections may be discovered on medical or forensic laboratory examination. Occasionally, such infections may be matched bacteriologically with a similar infection in the suspect, though this is not absolute proof of penetration. The infection is usually gonorrhoea. HIV infection may occur, but diagnosis may be delayed as even on blood testing, sero-conversion may take several months.

Figure 37:   Relationship of female genital organs

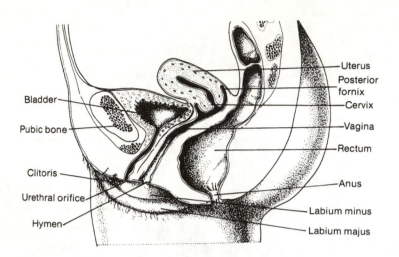

Other signs found on medical examination are not those indicative of penetration, but may assist in corroborating sexual activity.

Injuries on the thighs, buttocks and abdomen. Finger-nail scratches on the inner side of the upper thighs are especially significant, from efforts to force open the legs. Finger-tip bruises in the same area and on the buttocks and small of the back also suggest forcible clutching of the woman or girl.

Scratches and bruises on the buttocks, shoulder blades, backs of thighs and calves may also suggest forcible contact with the ground. Where relevant, soiling by dirt, earth, leaves, etc, may be found on the skin or clothing in these areas.

Blood or semen stains on the thighs, pubic hair, abdomen or buttocks may be recoverable and afford valuable forensic science evidence.

Hairs foreign to the girl may be recovered from her pubic hair or clothing.

Marks on the breast are relatively common, including finger bruises, nail scratches and bites. Mouth marks may accompany bites, being typically oval groups of small haemorrhages called 'suction petechiae'. Other bites may be found on the neck, abdomen and pubic area, but naturally may occur in voluntary sexual intercourse.

Anal and oral intercourse may be without consent: the appropriate swabs and other samples may reveal semen, though this is unlikely in the mouth except in rape associated with murder. The injuries to the anus are described under 'Sodomy'.

REFLEX CARDIAC ARREST

See 'Vagal inhibition'.

RIB FRACTURES

There are 12 pairs of ribs, all attached by joints to the vertebrae of the thoracic spine at the back; all but the lower two pairs are joined directly or indirectly to the breast bone (sternum) in front. The ribs are joined together by thin continuous sheets of muscle, the 'intercostals'.

In breathing, the ribs hinge forwards and upwards on inspiration, thus expanding the volume of the chest cavity and drawing in air.

Fractures of ribs are relatively common and, if not too extensive, are not dangerous to life. They commonly occur during cardiac massage and artificial respiration. Hazards are:

(a) *flail chest,* where numerous rib fractures, usually on both sides at the front, prevent the bellows function described above and impair the breathing ability;

(b) *penetrating fractures,* where broken rib ends stab or tear the underlying lung and cause a pneumothorax (air in the pleural cavities between ribs and lung) preventing respiration.

Pressure or impact on the front of the chest, such as impact with a steering wheel or fascia in car crashes – or stamping in an assault, can cause anterior fractures, often running in a line down the outer side of the front of the chest. This is often called the *anterior axillary line,* if in line with the front of the armpit, or *mid-clavicular line* if in line with the centre of the collar bone. Further back, they may be in the *posterior axillary line,* which is midway around the side of the chest.

Posterior fractures are not common in adults except from a violent impact such as a vehicle strike on a pedestrian or a fall from a height.

In infants, posterior fractures are commonly seen in child abuse, sometimes in a vertical line parallel to and near to the spine, where the back of the rib angles in to its attachment. This is typical of side to side pressure, as when the small infant is gripped under each armpit by adult hands and squeezed.

The child often survives and a line of 'callus', that is, lumps of calcium due to the healing process, may be seen visually at post-mortem or on X-ray skeletal survey, as a 'string of beads', often on both sides.

Controversy surrounds anterior rib fractures in infants, as they are very rare, due to the pliability of soft bone and gristle – the defence claim, that they may be due to resuscitation, as in adults, is difficult to substantiate.

RIGOR MORTIS

Stiffening of the muscles after death. Due to complex chemical changes associated with permanent oxygen lack and accumulation of lactic acid. This leads to conversion of the contractile proteins of the muscle into a stiff gel, which persists in this state until the onset of putrefaction causes softening.

Although rigor mortis develops uniformly throughout the body, it usually becomes first apparent in the smaller muscles, due to the lesser mass involved. Thus, it appears first in the muscles of the face and jaw, the limbs stiffening later, though in no fixed order.

As a measure of time since death, rigor is very unreliable.

Like all chemical processes it is temperature-dependent. In warm conditions, rigor mortis appears quickly and passes off more quickly, due to the early onset of decomposition. In the cold, it may be delayed markedly and in freezing conditions, may not appear at all (though actual freezing of the body fluids in extreme frost may cause stiffening). When a cold body is brought into a warmer environment, then true rigor may quickly appear.

In average temperature conditions, rigor may be detected within 2–6 hours and be generally present within the first 8–12 hours, though very wide variations can occur.

Fully developed rigor may last in 'average' conditions for a further 24 hours and then begin to fade during the next day. The old rule of thumb that 'rigor takes 12 hours to come on, lasts for 12 hours and takes 12 hours to pass off' can be relied upon only for its unreliability!

Rigor frequently is present up to the third or fourth day and may still be detectable after a week in some cases, especially in cold conditions. It is impossible for rigor and signs of decomposition to co-exist.

Virtually every textbook will quote a different range and all can be justified due to the lack of constancy of this labile phenomenon. An analysis by Mallach of opinions in textbooks and medical papers over a long period showed variations of between 30 minutes and seven hours for the onset of rigor; of 2–20 hours for full rigidity; and 24–96 hours for persistence of full rigor.

The time to fade from full rigor varied from 24–192 hours, so it can be seen that the evidential value is slight.

One fairly reliable fact about rigor is that it comes on much more rapidly after death from electrocution – and also tends to appear quickly after severe exertion just before death.

In children and frail, old people, it is frequently faint and transitory, depending to a considerable extent on the amount of muscle mass present.

As an index of time since death, it has very limited value and any opinion giving an exact time or a range of units of less than 3–5 hours during the first day is an untenable over-interpretation.

A more justifiable rule of thumb is that if a body is flaccid and warm, it has probably been dead less than six hours; if flaccid and cold, it has been dead more than about 2–3 days. If cold and stiff, it is likely to have died between half a day and two days earlier.

Cadaveric spasm

This is a very rare form of rigor mortis which is said to come on instantaneously at death, though some authorities deny its existence.

It is ill-understood, but invariably associated with sudden, violent death in circumstances of intense exercise or emotion. Battle casualties may show such spasm but, in civilian practice, it is very occasionally seen in deaths such as drowning, where in the death agony, the victim seizes a branch or weeds in an attempt to save himself. These may then be found clutched tightly in the hand before ordinary rigor could develop. Very rarely, a suicide may grip a pistol in such cadaveric spasm, though the forensic implications are more relevant to crime fiction than to legal practice.

SCALDS

Burns due to moist heat from hot liquids or vapours; usually superficial with no deep tissue destruction as in many dry burns. Danger due to area involved, rather than depth.

Effects from pain, primary shock and loss of function: later effects from disturbances of fluid balance through weeping skin areas, infection of skin, or intercurrent infections such as pneumonia. More serious in old people.

The *'Rule of nine'* calculates area involved by assuming each limb to be 9% of total body area, front and back of chest each 9%, front and back of abdomen each 9%, remaining 9% formed by head, neck, perineum, etc (see 'Burns').

Adults have poor outlook for survival if more than 40% burned, much less in old people. Children may survive more than half total area being burned.

Scalding is usually accidental, but may be deliberate in child abuse. Both time and temperature contribute to scalding: water at only about 50°C may cause scalds if applied for long enough, as in a hot bath.

The temperature decreases rapidly away from the point of initial contact and scalding is thus less severe towards the periphery, when the liquid is splashed. This does not apply to immersion. Splashes may be visible by the shape of the scalds. Redness and blisters are the common signs of scalding. Clothing protects almost completely against splashes, the scalds being confined to exposed areas.

SCALP WOUNDS

Profuse bleeding occurs from wounds on the very vascular scalp, though rarely dangerous to life. Simultaneous injury to contents of skull is the major danger. Scalp wounds may bleed considerably after death, especially if head left in dependent posture (see also 'Head injury').

Forensic importance in the possibility of identification of causative weapon. Fine detail of wounds obscured by interposition of hair, but general pattern may be imprinted, for example, hammer-head, large spanner or metal bar.

Confusion may arise between blunt instrument and cutting weapon, as former may cause sharply incised wound because of crushing effect over underlying hard skull. Differentiated by slightly bruised edges, fibrous strands crossing wound depths and intact hairs in blunt injury, compared to true cutting weapon.

Swelling of the scalp more prominent than wounds elsewhere, due to the vascularity and the unyielding skull beneath, which prevents downwards pressure of a haemorrhage under the skin. The scalp may accumulate a massive collection of blood (haematoma) up to 3 cm thick.

Figure 38: Sharp and blunt scalp wounds

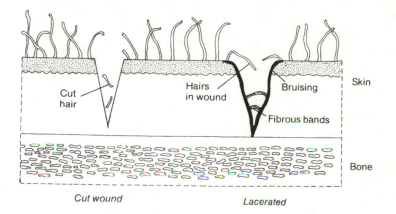

SCARS

Healed injuries of the skin, either from trauma or surgical operations. Composed of fibrous tissue covered with new epithelium (skin cells). The latter does not carry the usual skin appendages such as hair or sweat glands.

Scars of surgical incisions or of simple cuts consist of a thin segment of fibrous tissue binding the opposing edges of the defect. More extensive scars, such as those of burns, may be irregular in shape and depth, often wrinkled and bound down at intervals to underlying structures.

Scars pass through a sequence of changes after the initial injury:

(a) the wound is first filled with blood clot and serum which loosely binds the edges together. Within hours, healing begins and new skin is visible in a day or two;

(b) depending on the width of the wound, the blood clot becomes 'organised', that is, new blood vessels and young fibrous tissue covered with new skin grow across the surface under the most superficial layer of the scab of dried blood, which eventually falls off to reveal the new skin;

(c) the young fibrous scar is at first red in colour, then bluish, and gradually becomes pale over many months until it reaches a final silvery pink stage. This is dependent upon the size of the defect, but it usually is complete within 6–12 months.

Many factors affect the speed of scar formation, such as age and health of the patient, the presence of infection in the wound and the size and position of the wound. Vitamin deficiencies and other ill-understood personal variations make exact dating of a scar impossible within wide limits. Once the white-silver stage is reached, no change occurs for rest of life.

Scars cannot be removed, but a wide scar can be reduced to a narrow linear scar by careful restorative surgery.

The presence or absence of a skin scar is sometimes of vital forensic importance in identification of a person, alive or dead (for example, the *Tichborne* and *Crippen* cases). Old scars may be very difficult to differentiate from skin creases. In the living, brisk rubbing will cause the adjacent skin to redden, but not the scar. In the dead, microscopic examination and staining techniques will reveal an absence of elastic fibres, sweat and sebaceous glands at the site of the scar.

SEMEN

The male procreative fluid consists of the essential cellular elements, the spermatozoa and the fluid medium in which they are dispersed. The former are formed in the two testes from precursor parent cells in the seminiferous tubules. This process takes about 60 days to maturation. Mature sperms are stored in the epididymis, adjacent to the testis in the scrotum. Here they are in a minimum of fluid and are not mobile, being in a state of suspended animation.

When orgasm occurs, the epididymis voids part of its contents along each vas deferens, the tubes which lead up from the scrotum to the neck of the bladder. Here the primary fluid is diluted with a much larger volume of secretion from the two seminal vesicles and the prostate gland, which contribute the larger part of the bulk of the ejaculate. These glands add fructose and other chemical substances, which immediately activate the spermatozoa and make them motile, so that they can compete to seek and fertilise the female ovum in the uterus.

The constituents of the semen form the basis for forensic tests for seminal stains. A very high content of the enzyme acid phosphatase is detectable on screening tests. The most satisfactory legal proof that a stain is seminal is the microscopic identification of sperm, either heads or intact sperms with tails. However, with the increase in vasectomised men, lack of sperm may lead to greater dependence on chemical and serological tests for semen. Antibodies to semen can be used to detect semen by immunological techniques which are quite specific, and the advent of DNA technology allows definite identification of the semen against blood or other tissue samples from an individual, replacing the older blood group and other tests.

The examination of garments for seminal stains by the use of ultra-violet light is a useful screening test, but is by no means specific as pus, urine, blood and other biological fluids may also give positive fluorescence.

SEXUAL INTERCOURSE

The signs indicating that sexual intercourse has taken place may be recent or late (see also 'Rape').

Recent intercourse

Semen in the vagina may be absent if no ejaculation, or a condom used.

Vasectomy removes spermatozoa from the semen, but the chemical tests remain positive.

Evidence of recent tearing of the hymen. Bleeding, slight swelling, redness and a tear which usually extends to the wall of the vagina (see 'Hymen'). However, intercourse can occur without hymenal damage when that structure is lax or has a large aperture.

Tear of the perineum (bridge of skin between the back edge of the vaginal orifice and the anus) can only be caused (apart from childbirth) by over-dilatation of the introitus (vaginal opening) by either a penis or the forcible insert of fingers or some object, usually in a child or young girl. All these agents are evidence of over-stretching of the vaginal orifice, but not necessarily by a male organ. It is impossible for the perineum to be torn by normal activities such as jumping or falling, etc. An injury to the crutch might cause generalised damage to the area, but the isolated tear of the perineum can only arise from overstretching of the vaginal opening.

Previous intercourse

Widely dilated vagina and vulval orifice are likely to be due to habitual intercourse and/or childbirth, but are not inevitably due to this. Conversely, the usual appearance of a closed vaginal opening has no significance either way.

Even a single act of intercourse can tear the hymen into a condition which is not then altered significantly by further intercourse, though the hymen tends to become less prominent as time goes by and may be almost eliminated by childbirth. Within a day or so after first intercourse, the bleeding, swelling and raw edges of the hymenal tears become healed (see 'Hymen').

Evidence of current or previous pregnancy is strong evidence of intercourse, though many pregnancies have arisen from extra-vaginal sexual relations (see also 'Rape').

SKELETAL IDENTIFICATION

The forensic examination of bones is a common task for pathologists and a series of questions needs to be answered in a logical sequence.

Are the remains bones?

Sometimes artefacts such as stones, wood, etc, may be assumed by lay persons, including police, to be bones. A plaster facsimile used by medical students was another false alarm seen by the author.

Are the bones human?

Where substantial remains or fragments are recovered, anatomical recognition is sufficient, the necessary knowledge of anatomy depending on the amount of material. Where small pieces are involved, expert anatomical or even veterinary opinion is needed. If visual recognition fails, then the forensic laboratory can determine the species by serological tests, in which extracts of the bone are matched against immune sera from various animals. For this to succeed, the remains can rarely be older than five or 10 years since death. However, recent advances in DNA technology have allowed sex and personal identity to be determined even on very old bones.

If human, what sex are they?

Apart from DNA, this is entirely an anatomical exercise and depends on the nature and amount of the recovered remains. If a skull or pelvis is available, sexing is about 95% certain. Long bones such as thigh also have good sexual characteristics, as do the lower spine and the shoulder blade and breast bone. Before puberty, the sexual differences are slight or absent.

What age was the person at death?

Age determination (qv) decreases in accuracy with increasing maturity. The age of the foetus can be determined within weeks, and that of a child to within months. Using expert dental techniques (see 'Identification'), the age of an infant may be determined in ideal circumstances with an accuracy of days or weeks.

Up to the age of about 20, ageing is relatively accurate. The eruption of the teeth (milk and permanent), the appearance of ossification centres ('epiphyses') at the ends of bones, the fusion of these epiphyses with the main bone and other maturing processes offer much information. In middle age, the evidence is much less, but changes in the pubic symphysis of the pelvis, wear pattern of the teeth, etc, can assist. Radiological evidence of the remodelling of the internal structure of some bones, such as the neck of the femur, is useful in specialist hands.

The closing of the seams (sutures) in the skull has fallen into disuse in recent times, but some authorities say that the fusion on the inside of the cranium is relatively accurate, to within a decade up to 60 years.

In old age, very little accuracy is possible, apart from general senile appearances of toothless jaws, more fragile bones, etc.

What height was the deceased?

See 'Stature, estimation of'.

What is the race?

Less exact data is available, but shovel-shaped front teeth in mongoloids, longer thigh bones in negroid, different facial bone pattern in negroids and mongoloids may assist.

Any individual identifying features?

Healing fractures with calcified 'callus' may match a known injury. The dating of such healing is impossible within wide limits. Old deformities from congenital defects or polio, etc, may be detectable. Surgical intervention to the bones from old infections or fractures may be seen (prostheses such as metal pins, replaced joints, etc).

Radiologically, bones may be matched with pre-existing X-rays in some instances, especially if some unusual feature exists. The skull is usually unique, as are frontal sinuses (qv) and can give absolute identity match if pre-mortal X-rays are available. In all skeletal identification problems, the services of an expert are needed, including forensic pathologist, anthropologist, dentist, anatomist, radiologist and laboratory scientist.

SKULL FRACTURES

A fracture of the skull is usually no danger to life in itself (except when fragments of a depressed fracture may press upon or penetrate the brain). In most cases, the fracture is merely an indicator of substantial trauma to the head and the same force which fractured the skull may also cause internal brain damage, which is the essential and dangerous lesion.

About 25% of fatal head injuries have no fracture of the skull, yet the brain damage caused death.

Types of fracture

Fissured or linear

A relatively simple fracture line running in a straight or curved direction. If this line crosses a major meningeal artery rupture of the vessel may give rise to an extradural haematoma (qv).

Depressed

Here one or more fragments may be tilted downwards to press upon or penetrate the membranes or brain. In certain circumstances, especially in the temporal area, such a depression may eventually give rise to epilepsy (qv).

Pond fracture

A circular fracture, often depressed centrally, due to a focal impact. It may have concentric circles and radial lines, suggesting spider-web shape. A blow from a round-headed hammer, etc, may cause such a fracture.

Comminuted fracture.

Multiple fracture lines causing complete separation of bone fragments, sometimes with gross destruction of contour of head and pulping of underlying brain. Seen in railway and traffic accidents or where repeated violent blows from a blunt instrument are applied to the head.

Horizontal fracture

A heavy blow or blows on the side of the head may cause a horizontal fracture to run around the circumference of the head, with secondary fracture lines remote from the point of impact; seen particularly in infants subjected to impact on the head.

Contre-coup

A fall onto the back of the head may cause contre-coup (qv) fractures of the thin bone over the eye sockets at the opposite end of the skull, always associated with brain damage on the undersurface and tips of the frontal and temporal lobes.

Figure 39: Types of skull fracture

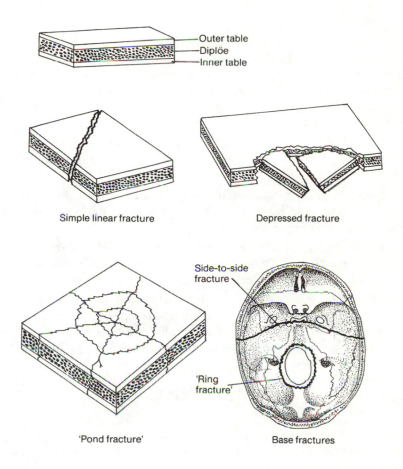

'Pond fracture'   Base fractures

Ring fracture

A fall onto the feet from a height may cause a 'ring fracture' of the back of the skull around the *foramen magnum*, where the force transmitted up the spinal column implodes the top of the spine into the skull.

Hinge fracture

Hinge fracture of base of skull is common in severe head injury, often from impact on either side of the head. A fracture line often crosses a line of weakness on the floor of the skull, usually across the middle fossae through the pituitary fossa. This is the so called 'hinge' or 'motor cyclist's fracture' but can be seen in any heavy impact on the skull. This fracture may cross half the skull or may traverse it completely, thus hinging the base of the skull into two movable halves.

The force necessary to fracture a skull is hard to evaluate, but is less than generally thought. In the case of infants, much discussion and controversy exists as to the height from which a child must be dropped to cause a skull fracture, though a more vital question is the force needed for brain damage or intracranial membrane bleeding.

Weber in Germany (1985) showed that passive falls in dead infants from only 80 cm (32 in) onto a firm floor caused fractures in all cases and even dropping from a similar distance onto various padded surfaces also sometimes caused fractures.

The question sometimes arises, in adults, as to whether a thin skull allows fractures to occur with less force. The answer must be in the affirmative, though it does not appear to be a major factor.

Skull fractures do not necessarily occur at the point of impact – they can be remote from this, but usually on the same side of the head. Lines of structural weakness determine the actual site and extent of the fractures.

An impact on the side or top of the head commonly causes an obliquely downward fracture of the side of the skull (the temporo-parietal area), which may turn inwards across the base of the skull if the force is great. An impact on top of the head may cause fractures of both sides, especially in infants.

SMOTHERING

Another indefinite term in the 'asphyxia' category, usually employed to indicate death from mechanical obstruction of the external air passages (nose and mouth).

Death can ensue rapidly with no classical signs of asphyxia (qv), which are now outdated, leaving no physical signs to be demonstrable at autopsy.

Suffocation, where proven, may occur from soft material, such as a pillow being forcibly held over the face – or where an incapacitated person, such as those drunk, drugged or suffering from an epileptic fit, lies face down on a soft surface. The weight of the head plus sealing of the mouth and nostrils with saliva, vomit, etc, prevents ingress of air.

Most of these deaths leave no objective post-mortem signs, such as facial congestion, cyanosis or petechiae, which are usually due to constriction of the neck causing damming of the blood return through the neck veins.

Another well known cause is a plastic bag over the head, a not uncommon method of suicide. Here congestive petechial signs are virtually always absent, so if the bag is removed by someone before the body is found, then no cause of death is apparent.

Suffocation was formerly wrongly indicted as a frequent cause of 'cot death' (qv) (sudden death in infancy – SIDS), where it was for centuries called 'overlaying', meaning the suffocation of an infant in bed with an adult. Though it is likely that some presumed SIDS are maternal suffocations, this can never be proved pathologically (unless there is physical damage to the mouth and lips), yet some doctors illogically allege that they can determine this as a cause of death, usually by misreading the frequent appearance (70%) of petechiae on the intra-thoracic organs of true SIDS, as evidence of 'asphyxia'. Recently it is being claimed by some pathologists that the presence of patchy haemorrhage in the lungs is an indicator of suffocation rather than true SIDS, but this supposition is untenable.

Where considerable pressure has been applied to the face and nose of a victim, either by a hand or enveloping fabric, there may be bruising of the lips, especially inside, where they are forced onto the teeth. Patchy whitening of the lower face, due to irregular but normal post-mortem hypostasis (qv), especially in children, must not be mistaken for evidence of suffocating pressure, as it has been in the past by inexperienced or biased doctors.

SODOMY

Strictly, the active element in male homosexuality: the passive recipient of anal intercourse is the 'pederast', though etymologically this should refer to young boys. The whole activity is also termed 'buggery'. These terms have come to be used less exactly.

The passive recipient may show signs of either acute penetration or chronic participation in anal intercourse. Where recent, possibly forcible penetration has occurred (especially in young boys), the anal margins may be reddened, inflamed or bruised. There may be a split in the margin of the anus, with bleeding or signs of infection or healing if examination is delayed. The orifice may remain dilated and the sphincter muscle may be incontinent. There may still be signs of lubricant, if the act was voluntary. Forensic examination of swabs from the anus and rectum may reveal semen, lubricant and possibly venereal infection.

Care must be taken in interpreting the degree of dilatation of the anus in dead bodies where sodomy is suspected: after death, the anus may relax markedly, especially in children, and give the spurious appearance of dilatation. Such an appearance should only be accepted if other signs of penetration also exist.

Where the recipient is an habitual pederast, the anus may be permanently dilated and lie at the bottom of a funnel-shaped depression, though this appearance has been exaggerated in former textbooks and is often merely an anatomical variation seen in control cases. The skin of the surrounding area may be thickened and glazed, with a loss of the usual abrupt margin between skin and pink mucous membrane at the edge of the anus, though there are other innocent causes for this, such as chronic infections. The sphincter may be permanently incontinent. Lubricant, semen and evidence of venereal infection may be found.

The active partner or assailant may show little or no signs of penetration, as in rape cases, unless violence has occurred. The glans penis may be reddened, abraded or bruised, especially at the edges of the corona (margin of the glans). Rarely, the frenulum (band of fibrous tissue under the glans) may be damaged. Lubricants, such as jelly, Vaseline or even hair cream may be recovered by forensic examination and faecal soiling or even blood may be seen.

SOLVENT ABUSE

(See 'Glue sniffing')

SPLEEN

Organ the size of a small fist, hidden under the lower rib margin in the left upper part of the abdomen. Not vital to life, concerned with elimination of unwanted red cells and bacteria in the bloodstream and with immunity production. Main forensic importance is rupture due to blunt injury to the abdomen, common in assaults (especially kicking) and traffic accidents.

It is a soft, pulpy organ within a thin fibrous capsule. Injury can split the capsule and lead to severe haemorrhage into the abdominal (peritoneal) cavity. Prompt surgical removal needed to avoid fatal internal blood loss. There may be a delayed rupture due to blood accumulating beneath the intact capsule, which then tears some hours after injury, allowing a latent period with little or no clinical signs.

A spleen enlarged by disease (such as malaria) is much more vulnerable to injury.

SPONTANEOUS COMBUSTION

A persistent myth, centuries old, which claims that a living human body can spontaneously burst into flames and be consumed.

There are numerous cases on record, familiar to most forensic pathologists, where a body has been found with part or even most of the corpse consumed by fire, with little or no fire damage to the immediately adjacent surroundings.

However, virtually all these cases occur near a hearth where there is an updraught; there is always some source of ignition, such as fire or cigarette; and the victim is often an alcoholic. Even so, some cases are remarkable, in that only a pair of feet in unburnt slippers may remain; or there is a hole burned through the carpet and floorboards with no surrounding conflagration.

Experiments have shown that human fat, wrapped around fabric as a wick, can burn away completely in a current of air; it is however, hard to understand how much of a skeleton can vanish, given that even formal high-temperature cremation may not destroy large bones.

STAB WOUNDS

The most frequent method of homicide in the UK. Stab wounds are incised wounds in which the depth is greater than the width. Most stabs are caused by a knife or similar weapon such as a chisel, screwdriver or ice pick, but slivers of glass, metal rods, circular prods and even wooden stakes can inflict stab wounds, either homicidally, suicidally or accidentally.

The depth of penetration, as opposed to a slashed wound, increases the risk of damaging some vital internal structure, usually in the chest or abdomen, the most common danger being internal haemorrhage. In the chest, the heart, lungs and great blood vessels form the most lethal target.

Features

Skin wound. Appearance may be deceptive, as the elasticity of the skin may cause the ends of the wound to come together, with some gaping of the centre, so that the length is less than the width of the blade after withdrawal.

Also, with a tapering blade, its width at the estimated point of maximum penetration must be correlated with the wound length. Conversely, the skin wound may be longer than the blade width, due to 'rocking' of the knife in the wound. The angle of withdrawal may be different to that of penetration, also

Figure 40:   Characteristics of knife wounds

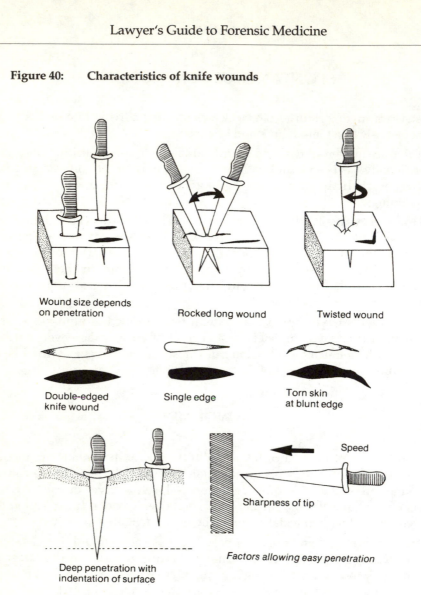

Wound size depends on penetration

Rocked long wound

Twisted wound

Double-edged knife wound

Single edge

Torn skin at blunt edge

Speed

Sharpness of tip

Deep penetration with indentation of surface

Factors allowing easy penetration

causing the wound to enlarge. If the blade is twisted before withdrawal, a 'V-shaped' wound may result.

Also, re-introduction after partial penetration, perhaps at a different angle, may further complicate the interpretation. Where one end of the wound is sharply cut and the other blunt, it may be inferred that a one-edged weapon was used, but there are fallacies in this interpretation. Even a blunt edge may cause the skin to split, leaving a sharp end. When the blade is forcibly driven up to the hilt, an abrasion or bruise may be imprinted on the skin around the wound, though this is not seen very often.

Depth. A knife may inflict a wound deeper than the total length of the blade, due to deformation and indentations of the surface with a forcible stab, especially in the pliable abdomen. Even the rib cage may momentarily indent, allowing the tip to reach a point deeper than that measured at autopsy.

Direction. Caution must be used in interpreting the angle of approach of the knife, from a study of the orientation of the track in the body. The posture of the victim at the time of infliction cannot be assumed to be upright and forward facing in every case. A wound apparently inflicted downwards into the chest, for example, may have been made horizontally into the chest of a crouching victim. Neither can the orientation of each wound in a multiple stabbing be related to a static victim, as turning and twisting of both victim and assailant can lead to great variation in the relative positions of each.

Degree of force. Invariably an issue in homicide, being related to determination and intent, but one very difficult to quantify, other than in terms like 'slight, moderate or forceful'. Very subjective descriptions often applied with little relation to actual situation. Pathologists should never employ pejorative terms such as 'frenzied', as this imputes a state of mind impossible to determine from post-mortem appearances and which lies in the realm of psychiatry.

Experiments have shown that:

(a) the most important factor in penetration is the sharpness of the extreme tip of the blade. With a very sharp tip, a knife can be introduced up to the hilt by the pressure of only one finger;

(b) speed of approach. A rapid stab will penetrate the skin with minimal force (like a dart) whereas the same knife pressed slowly against the surface will require far more effort for penetration;

(c) the skin acts as an 'elastic reservoir' – it is the most resistant tissue apart from bone or cartilage and once punctured, the knife will slide into the chest or abdomen without further force being required, as if penetrating the membrane of a drum. Thus a deep wound is not necessarily a 'savage blow' in the chest or abdomen;

(d) in the frequent defence of 'falling on the knife', such a mechanism is easily possible and does not require a sharp-tipped knife to be supported on the hip or elsewhere. The momentum of a falling body will allow transfixion to occur before the inertia of the knife and supporting hand allow them to be pushed backwards;

(e) the edges of the knife above the tip are of little importance in facilitating entry. Once the tip is through, the rest easily follows;

(f) factors such as senile skin and different areas of the body have little relevance in ease of penetration, compared to the two major factors of tip sharpness and speed of entry.

STATURE, ESTIMATION OF

In the living, direct measurement is available. In the intact corpse, a similar method gives an approximation to the live height, but due to relaxation of the muscles and changes in the spinal discs, etc, there may be a discrepancy of at least 2.5 cm (1 in) with the living stature. The dead body usually lengthens within this range.

Where a decomposed or mutilated or skeletalised body is the subject for measurement, the stature must be estimated indirectly. This is best done by an accurate measurement of limb bones, especially the thigh bone (femur), though the shin (tibia) or upper arm (humerus) may be used. Where a complete skeleton or decomposed body is available, this method may be supplemented by direct measurement, but considerable inaccuracies are involved due to loss of spinal discs and cartilage or disconnection of the axial skeleton and limbs in the putrefied body.

Using long bones, reference can be made to established anatomical tables such as those of Pearson or Trotter and Glesor, or Dupertuis and Hadden. These given a margin of error to be expected using the method, which may be up to 5 cm (2 in).

Potential errors exist because of:

(a) *inaccuracies in measuring the isolated bone*, including whether joint cartilage persists. Specific parameters must be adhered to and special equipment such as an osteological board used for measurement;

(b) *racial and sex errors* cannot always be compensated for – the tables were constructed for certain ethnic groups and may not be strictly applicable to different material;

(c) *improving nutrition*, in modern communities, causes the older tables to be no longer applicable to contemporary body dimensions.

All these factors may combine to introduce appreciable errors when attempting to extrapolate total stature from a single bone. As a very rough approximation, the length of the femur (thigh bone) can be taken as 27% of the total body length and the tibia (shin bone) about 22%.

STATUS LYMPHATICUS

Sometimes known also as 'status thymo-lymphaticus', this hypothetical entity is now virtually of historical interest only and is regarded as untenable as an explanation of sudden death.

In vogue in the first part of this century, the alleged condition consisted of a persistence of the thymus gland in adults (a gland in the upper part of the chest normally shrinking at puberty), together with over-profuse lymph glands and lymphoid tissue in the body and under-development of the large blood vessels, especially the aorta.

Persons (usually younger adults) with this condition were thought to be especially prone to sudden death from relatively trivial causes, which left no signs to be demonstrable at autopsy. The syndrome was often confused or linked with 'vagal inhibition' (qv). After some energetic debate and controversy in the medical press between the wars, the existence of status lymphaticus fell into disuse.

Most forensic pathologists would agree that no such condition can be substantiated on morphological grounds, though sometimes an autopsy reveals a persistent thymus and prominent lymphoid tissue in a victim of an obscure sudden death. However, it seems very doubtful whether any statistical support could be found to substantiate the hypothesis. The syndrome has been invoked mostly to explain deaths under anaesthetic and during relatively minor operations, for which there might be better explanations.

STERILISATION

The inhibition of procreative ability by surgical operation. May be irreversible or reversible, the latter sometimes spontaneously.

In the male, usually achieved by 'vasectomy', which involves tying and cutting each *vas deferens*, the ducts which convey sperm from the testes to the neck of the bladder. This process does not significantly reduce the volume of ejaculate, which is formed mainly by the prostate gland and the seminal vesicles.

Vasectomy is a simple surgical procedure performed under local anaesthetic without the necessity of admission to hospital. A temporary complication may be the formation of a haematoma (collection of blood) at the operation site.

Occasionally, the vas deferens may spontaneously rejoin and allow fertility to be restored. Following vasectomy, other contraceptive methods must be continued for up to three months or until semen samples are shown to be permanently free from viable spermatozoa. About 1% of vasectomies revert and occasionally a negative sperm test at three months may become positive again later, for reasons not yet adequately explained.

In the female, a similar sterilisation technique may be performed on the fallopian or uterine tubes which convey the ova from the ovaries to the womb, these being tied and transected on each side. This may be done by open operation or via 'laparoscopy', an instrument being introduced through a small incision. Sterilisation may also be performed during operations for other gynaecological conditions, including termination of pregnancy and by hysterectomy.

Naturally, sterilisation is an inevitable by-product of many gynaecological operations, especially hysterectomy (removal of the womb or removal of both ovaries or uterine tubes). However, the removal of one ovary and the opposite tube need not lead to sterility, as ova can cross the abdominal cavity to reach the other tube.

Like the vas deferens, occasionally, tied uterine tubes may spontaneously re-open and both circumstances have given rise to litigation for negligent technique where an unwanted pregnancy has resulted. This is more frequent when the tubes are blocked by metal clips, rather than being cut through surgically.

STILL-BIRTH

Any child which has issued forth from its mother after the 24th week of pregnancy and which did not, at any time after being completely expelled from its mother, breathe or show any other signs of life (Births and Deaths Registration Acts). The original legislation, such as the 1953 Act, laid down 28 weeks' gestation, but in other legal contexts, due to improved obstetrical care, this has been reduced to 24 weeks – though even less mature foetuses of 22 or even 20 weeks may be born alive and some survive.

Unless witnessed by a doctor, midwife or other responsible person, the retrospective diagnosis of a still-birth is difficult, unless maceration (signs of death *in utero*) or gross malformation is present (see 'Live birth').

A still-birth must be registered before disposal: the special still-birth certificate can be completed by a doctor or midwife, if they were either present at the birth or examined the body afterwards (an unsatisfactory means of determination). If both were present, the doctor has precedence over the midwife in signing the certificate.

In the absence of such a certificate, a statutory declaration by an informant may be accepted, though this is rare.

The causes of still-birth are varied and often obscure. Even autopsy cannot reveal a cause in a significant proportion – and cannot be decisive even about the fact of still-birth within the narrow definition given above (see 'Live birth').

The most common cause certified for still-births is 'placental and cord conditions', with disease and malformation of the foetus and diseases and abnormalities of pregnancy as other major reasons.

STOMACH

Primary receptacle for food, in which acid digestion takes place. When complete, the exit from the stomach (pylorus) opens to allow contents to pass into duodenum, where bile neutralises the acid and alkaline digestion begins in intestine.

The *timing of death from stomach contents* is highly unsatisfactory. Very misleading opinions have been offered by pathologists, as the rate of digestion is almost useless in determining the time since the last meal. Fluid passes very rapidly through the stomach, so food plus a large volume of liquid will leave the stomach quickly.

(a) There is great individual variation and even the same person has varying rates at different occasions.

(b) The type of food varies the rate, for example, high carbohydrate hastens and fatty substances slow the speed of stomach emptying.

(c) Physical and emotional stresses can retard or completely stop digestion.

Thus, even if the time of the last meal is known, the autopsy appearances of the stomach contents, both quantitatively and qualitatively are not a reliable guide to the time since death, especially if that was preceded by a period of injury, fear or other stress. Only in a sudden, unexpected death can any approximate conclusions be drawn, but even these vary within wide limits. Where disability, coma, etc, exist, food may remain undigested for days until eventual death.

In normal physiological circumstances, an 'average' meal may remain in the stomach for two to four hours, before gradually seeping through the pylorus. But the whole concept of timing death by this means is fraught with error. More useful is the nature of food found at autopsy, if still recognisable; this may be related to the content of a known meal and thus death can be presumed to have taken place after that particular meal and before the next scheduled meal.

Certain drugs may be recognisable in stomach contents, especially those with a strong smell, like cyanide, phenols or alcohol. Others may be coloured, like the blue of amytal capsules or the red of Seconal. Actual tablets, powder or capsules may be visible.

The condition of the stomach lining may be significant, for example, erosion from corrosive substances like acids, alkalis, or less irritative poisons like aspirin or some alkaline barbiturates. Shallow acute ulcers, often with bleeding, may be seen in hypothermia (qv) or stress conditions such as head injuries. Chronic alcoholism may cause gastritis, with thickening, corrugation and mucous coating of the lining. A perforation of a gastric ulcer is an acute surgical emergency, as the release of acid contents into the abdominal cavity may cause sudden collapse and rapid death from chemical peritonitis.

STRANGULATION
(See also 'Asphyxia')

Pressure on the neck, either manual or by ligature. Manual strangulation sometimes called throttling (qv).

The old view that it caused death or disablement merely by 'cutting off the air' is now recognised to be untenable. Great medico-legal significance in the mechanisms, which are complex and variable.

Features

When the neck is compressed, the following factors may operate:

Obstruction of the large veins (jugulars) which return blood from the head to the heart. The pressure inside the veins is low and only slight pressure is required to impede or obstruct the flow. This leads to 'backing up' of blood in the face and head, seen as congestion and blueness (cyanosis) due to accumulation of deoxygenated blood in the skin.

Prolonged unremitting pressure for at least 15–30 seconds leads to rupture of over-distended small veins in skin, lips and eyes, leading to petechial haemorrhages (qv) and frank bleeding from nostrils and ears.

This is due to rise of pressure in the veins, because arteries (which are not obstructed at this level of squeezing) are pumping blood into the head, and this blood cannot escape down the neck. Also oxygen lack in the vein walls may contribute, though this is a minor and rather doubtful factor.

The haemorrhages in the whites of the eyes (petechiae) are thus mainly a sign of venous obstruction, not central oxygen-lack due to 'cutting off the air' at the windpipe.

When the neck is constricted, these changes develop progressively as time goes on, but the actual length of time necessary for their production varies considerably and is not capable of being exactly determined. It probably takes in excess of a quarter of a minute for eye petechiae to appear and often much longer. Dogmatic opinions are common, but ill-founded on fact. The completeness and constancy of the pressure on the neck, together with individual variations, prevent accurate estimation of this minimum time, which is often of legal importance in relation to intent and determination.

Pressure on the great arteries in the neck (the carotid arteries which supply blood to the head and the brain). The pressure of blood inside these is far higher than in the veins and consequently total obstruction requires far more effort. If both right and left carotid arteries are obstructed, almost immediate unconsciousness will occur due to deprivation of oxygenated blood to the brain.

Figure 41: **Strangulation**

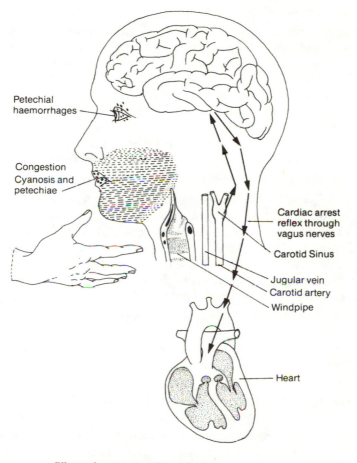

Effects of pressure on the neck
1 Carotid sinus pressure – vagus nerve stimulation – cardiac arrest
2 Carotid artery blockage – unconsciousness
3 Jugular vein blockage – congestion and haemorrhages
4 Airway blockage – oxygen lack

Continuous pressure for more than 3–5 minutes (an unlikely scenario) could cause irreversible brain damage, but probably death from reflex cardiac arrest (see below) would occur long before this point.

Carotid sinus pressure. Where the carotid arteries divide in the upper part of the neck into internal and external carotids, there exists on each side a sensitive pressure receptor called the *carotid sinus,* together with adjacent nerves in the sheath of the artery. These monitor blood pressure, and operate a bio-feedback system to regulate blood pressure, but a sudden squeeze or impact upon these can lead to drastic slowing or even stoppage of the heart – the so called 'vagal inhibition' (qv).

This is a common cause of death in pressure on the neck, especially in manual strangulation, and can occur instantly when the neck is gripped. Reflex nerve impulses go from the carotid sinuses and sheath via the glosso-pharyngeal nerves to the brain stem, where they stimulate the tenth cranial nerve nucleus. This initiates impulses down the vagus nerves to the heart and can slow or stop it altogether. A more acceptable name than vagal inhibition for this common mechanism is *'reflex cardiac arrest'*. In its pure form, it accounts for at least half the deaths from manual strangulation and may account for the remainder, even if it is delayed until sufficient time has passed for the congestive-petechial signs to appear.

Obstruction of the air passages was classically held at one time to be the only cause of death. In fact sufficient compression to stop the air flow of the stiff, rigid cartilage of the larynx or windpipe (trachea) is very difficult. A more usual mechanism is for the larynx to be lifted up so that the tongue blocks the back of the throat. In any event, pure deprivation of air can be survived for many minutes, during which death from one of the other mechanisms above is more likely to occur. Fractures of the hyoid bone or laryngeal cartilages are indicators only of pressure on the neck and not of the mechanism of death (see 'Hyoid bone').

There is thus an opportunity for a number of causes to operate during strangulation.

If the face is pale at death, then by definition, the carotid/cardiac reflex mechanism must have occurred, as death was too rapid for any of the congestive changes to have taken place.

If the face is congested and petechial haemorrhages (qv) are present, then sudden immediate cardiac arrest could not have occurred in the early period of strangulation, probably about 15–30 seconds minimum duration.

No maximum time can be inferred, as a shift of the strangling fingers or tightening of the grip may cause carotid pressure to supervene at any point along the 'congestive-asphyxial' path and the pathological appearances cannot indicate any time period.

From pure (and exceptionally rare) obstruction of the air passages, death would not be expected to occur for at least several minutes and numerous cases of failed near-strangulation have indicated that a prolonged period of throttling can be survived. Many of the survivors had gross congestive changes in the face, indicating that their survival was due to a lack of the carotid reflex mechanism.

This mechanism is more likely to occur in manual strangulation, due to the focal impact of finger-tips into the groove in front of the sternomastoid muscles where the arteries lie, but it can often occur in ligature strangulation. It is very common in hanging, due to the sudden jerking impact of a fall affecting the carotid structures.

It must be emphasised again that evidence of physical damage to the neck structures, especially the larynx, is evidence only of violence to the neck and not to an asphyxial mechanism.

Sometimes, actual evidence of carotid trauma can be found by careful dissection of the arteries, revealing tears of the inner lining of the wall.

The most significant forensic point, especially from the aspect of the defence in a criminal trial, is that signs of pressure on the neck with a pale face means rapid death, whilst congestion and haemorrhages mean a delayed death, though a time factor is impossible to state with any accuracy, but is probably in excess of 15–30 seconds.

SUBARACHNOID HAEMORRHAGE (OR HAEMATOMA)

Bleeding beneath the arachnoid, the inner layer of the two membranes covering the brain. Common condition, with frequent medico-legal connotations, occurring as follows:

General head injuries

As part of any head injury in which the brain surface is damaged; often occurs with associated subdural bleeding.

Ruptured cerebral (berry) aneurysm

As a natural disease due to rupture of a cerebral artery, usually at the base of the brain. Most often, the rupture is due to leakage or bursting of a (berry) aneurysm of the Circle of Willis (qv), but in about 15% of cases, no aneurysm can be demonstrated at either operation or autopsy.

A less common cause is bleeding from a congenital anomaly of the blood vessels on the surface of the brain, such as an angioma (a benign tumour of blood vessels) or other vascular malformation.

Subarachnoid haemorrhage from a ruptured cerebral aneurysm is a common cause of sudden collapse and is frequently fatal, especially in younger and middle-aged adults. As women have less coronary artery disease in this age group, it is a relatively frequent cause of sudden death in women of child-bearing age, the other causes being pulmonary embolism or a complication of pregnancy.

Cerebral aneurysms (qv) are often called 'berry' or 'congenital' aneurysms, though the actual aneurysm is not congenital. Rather there is a weakness of the wall of an artery where a junction occurs in the Circle of Willis, due to congenital, perhaps embryological, factors. This weakness is subject to increasing internal stress as the blood pressure rises in middle age, so that a swelling develops, usually at a junction of two vessels. This balloons and may eventually burst, causing blood under arterial pressure to escape into the subarachnoid space. Extra exertion, such as sport or sexual intercourse, may raise the blood pressure sufficiently to cause the rupture, but it can occur spontaneously during rest. Emotion and physical exertion seem to be factors in raising blood pressure and increasing blood flow.

It is usually claimed that alcohol enhances the onset and severity of a subarachnoid bleed, but there is little physiological proof of this. The claim that it dilates cerebral blood vessels seems irrelevant in relation to the larger non-muscular vessels at the base of the brain and the walls of the aneurysm itself.

As mentioned below, where subarachnoid bleeding is associated with trauma, the latter is usually sustained in a scenario where alcohol is much in evidence, such as a bar brawl or public house fight. This does not mean that the pharmacological action of alcohol is relevant, only that fighting and drink usually go together.

It has also not been proven that direct injury to the head can precipitate a rupture, due to the deeply situated and well protected site of the Circle of Willis. However, rupture during or soon after a fight, assault or even threat of violence may well be related to the emotional and physical stress involved, with a consequent adrenaline response and a rise in pulse rate and blood pressure.

The symptoms of a ruptured cerebral aneurysm and consequent subarachnoid haemorrhage may vary from severe headache to sudden, rapid death. A victim may fall to the ground and die on the spot from a massive bleed. However, many patients have premonitory smaller bleeds and may recover spontaneously. Others may be operated upon, the surgeon often being able to clip the bleeding vessel and effect a complete cure.

Traumatic subarachnoid haemorrhage

A very important topic in relation to fatal assaults.

This type of subarachnoid haemorrhage commonly occurs from trauma specifically applied to the upper part of the side of the neck, though impact on the back or side of the head can also cause the same internal damage. This can cause a rupture of one of the arteries forming part of the *vertebro-basilar system* at the base of the brain.

The two *vertebral arteries* come up tunnels in the sides of the vertebrae of the spinal column in the neck and then penetrate the dural membrane that lines the skull and spinal canal, to enter the base of the skull through the large hole (*foramen magnum*) where the spinal cord emerges.

The left and right vertebral arteries then join together on the base of the brain to form the single *basilar artery*, which supplies blood to the rear of the brain, which includes the vital centres for breathing, etc.

A blow on the side of the neck (usually below the ear) or less often on the side of the head, can suddenly rotate and incline the head in such a way as to stress the arteries of the vertebro-basilar system and cause a rupture, giving rise to a subarachnoid haemorrhage, which can be rapidly fatal.

Such a blow need not be of great magnitude, though it has to be substantial.

It can be delivered by a blunt weapon or by a kick; it is unusual for a fist blow to cause this tear, though it is not impossible. A fall onto a flat surface cannot cause the injury, but if the fall is onto some projection, then it can occur.

The mechanism of traumatic subarachnoid haemorrhage is ill-understood. It was formerly thought always to be due to tearing of a vertebral artery outside the skull, in the tunnel in the uppermost (first) cervical vertebra and that the blood then tracked through the dural membrane into the subarachnoid space. The rapidity and volume of blood inside the cranium made this hypothesis unlikely, and it is now widely accepted that there is a tear of the vertebral or basilar artery or one of their branches within the cranium – even if there also happens to be a concomitant small bleed outside the skull in the upper part of the extracranial vertebral artery.

The difference is academic from a legal aspect – the injury is due to trauma to the neck or head, whatever the mechanics of the bleed.

In practical terms, it may be difficult or impossible for the pathologist to identify the bleeding point, which may be obscured by blood clot and impossible to preserve intact during removal of the tissues at autopsy.

Various techniques are used, including post-mortem radiography after injecting the vessels with radio-opaque fluid; better is the slow decalcification of the neck and lower skull bones, which takes weeks, then careful dissection of the vessels. Even then, it may not be possible to identify the actual bleeding point.

Death may occur very rapidly – typically, after a fracas in the street or bar, a man is struck on the neck and collapses to the floor, being dead when emergency services attend. The reason for such rapid death is obscure, but seems to be due to sudden release of blood around the vital centres in the brain stem, which the vertebro-basilar system supplies.

SUBDURAL HAEMORRHAGE (OR HAEMATOMA)

Bleeding between the inner and outer membranes of the brain, that is, below the *dura* and above the *arachnoid*. Always caused by injury to the head, even though this might be so trivial as to pass unnoticed, especially in old people.

The source of the bleeding is from the veins which cross the subdural space from the surface of the brain to reach the venous sinuses – large blood channels in the dura.

Subdural haemorrhage (SDH) is most common in infancy and old age, but can occur at any time of life where there is a head injury. Unlike extradural haemorrhage (qv), subdural haemorrhage commonly occurs without fracture of the skull.

In infants, it is a common finding in alleged child abuse and was the major component of the original description by Caffey in 1946. Many clinicians and some pathologists always attribute SDH to violent shaking, but it is now clear that impact of the head from a blow or fall is much more common, even if the scalp and skull show no injury from contact with a flat surface or object. Subdural haemorrhage is the most common cause of death in child abuse (qv).

The pressure on the brain may cause neurological signs and symptoms and eventually death from raised intracranial pressure affecting the vital centres in the brain stem. However, many SDHs are relatively small and the real danger is from actual direct brain damage and brain swelling, often with *diffuse axonal injury* (qv), the SDH being a concomitant indicator of trauma to the head.

In old people, subdural haemorrhage is not uncommon, due to the senile shrinkage of the brain which increases the width of the subdural space and makes the fragile vessels more vulnerable due to stretching and shearing stresses. Often found at autopsy as an incidental finding in old persons. May then be a 'chronic' subdural haemorrhage, the haemorrhage (also called a 'haematoma') persisting for months or years. May be symptomless or giving rise to false diagnosis of 'stroke' or senile dementia. May have been caused by a trivial head injury which is not recorded in the clinical history.

An old subdural haemorrhage, at whatever age of victim, is brown in colour due to altered blood pigment and after weeks or months, may have a thick fibrous capsule. In infants especially, the age of an SDH may be of vital legal importance (as in the *Louise Woodward* case in Boston, Mass), because of access and alibi issues for the time of injury.

A fresh SDH is dark red, and this will not change to naked-eye inspection for at least a few days when a brownish tinge appears, though no rigid time scale can be applied.

Figure 42: **Position of subdural haemorrhage**

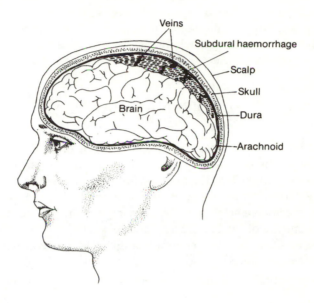

On microscopic examination, no change can be seen for at least 36 hours, when by special stains for the iron-containing pigment haemosiderin, granules of iron may be seen not earlier than this time.

Progressively from then, signs of absorption and healing appear, but again no definite time sequence can be established within wide limits.

An acute subdural haemorrhage is common in all types of head injury, whatever the age of the victim – seen especially in blunt trauma and traffic accidents. Death from pressure on the brain may be averted by surgical intervention – holes are drilled in the skull to evacuate the blood clot, but there is often associated brain damage which itself may be fatal.

After a head injury, there is often a latent interval (after a short period of concussion (qv)) before blood accumulates either in the extradural position or subdurally. The length of this 'lucid interval' is very variable, from a few minutes to many hours or even days in the subdural haemorrhage of older victims.

A 'thin-film' subdural haemorrhage has little clinical significance, being very common in all sorts of trivial head injury. Only when substantial enough to cause generalised or localised pressure on the surface of the brain (due to being confined within the rigid skull), does it present a danger to life. However, even minor degrees of subdural haemorrhage are often associated with other types of intracranial damage, such as brain bruising, lacerations, oedema (brain swelling) or deep haemorrhages and injury to the brain.

An SDH may re-bleed at a later date, either spontaneously or after a second episode of trauma, sometimes minimal in severity. This is of great importance in child abuse, where the second bleed may occur during the custody of a different carer, as in the *Woodward* case.

SUDDEN NATURAL DEATH

Most sudden or rapid unexpected deaths from natural causes are due to a catastrophe in the cardiovascular system, even if topographically situated in some major organ such as the brain. Where death is virtually instantaneous (a 'drop-down' death) the cause can only be in the heart, due to a sudden cardiac arrest. Even massive strokes, pulmonary embolism, etc, do not kill as quickly as sudden failure of the heart. Sudden unexpected death is most often due to cardiac causes and the most common single reason is coronary artery disease (qv) in men in Western-type society.

Sudden natural death in women of child-bearing age (15–50) is likely to be due to:

(a) a complication of pregnancy, such as abortion, ectopic pregnancy;

(b) pulmonary embolism from deep leg vein thrombosis;

(c) subarachnoid haemorrhage from a ruptured berry aneurysm;

(d) heart disease of various types.

Coronary artery disease in women was formerly one or two decades later than in men, due to the protective effects of female hormones, but in recent years has developed earlier, probably due to an increase in smoking.

Common causes of sudden natural death

Cardiovascular

(a) Coronary artery disease (qv). Coronary thrombosis and myocardial infarction are pathological subconditions of the general disease. Often called 'ischaemic heart disease', ischaemia being a reduced blood supply, but this term is not quite synonymous with coronary artery disease, as hypertensive heart disease and some types of valve lesion are also ischaemic.

(b) Valve disease, especially aortic stenosis. This is a common disease, especially in elderly men. The aortic valve becomes narrowed and stiffened by chalky deposits, restricting the pumping outflow and reducing the pressure in the coronary arteries.

Figure 43:   **Common causes of sudden natural death**

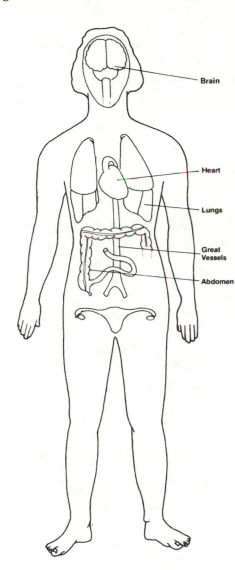

		Relative incidence
Brain	Sub-arachnoid haemorrhage	++
	Cerebral haemorrhage	+
	Epilepsy	
Heart	Coronary artery disease	+++++
	Hypertensive heart disease	+++
	Aortic stenosis	++
	Myocardiopathies	
Lungs	Pulmonary embolism	+++
	Haemoptysis (TB or tumour)	
	Asthma	
	Viral pneumonia	
Great Vessels	Atheromatous aneurysm	+++
	Dissecting aneurysm	++
	Syphilitic aneurysm	
Abdomen	Perforated viscus	+
	Mesenteric embolism	+
	Gastrointestinal haemorrhage	
	Abortions	
	Ruptured ectopic pregnancy	

(c) Hypertensive heart disease – strain on the heart due to working against a high peripheral pressure (see 'Blood pressure').

(d) Congenital heart disease, depending on the type and severity, may be relatively rare cause of sudden death, usually in young people. Surgical correction has greatly reduced this category.

(e) Cardiomyopathy and myocarditis (qv) – relevant in younger adults.

(f) Aneurysm of aorta (qv) – common cause in older people, when rupture occurs.

Nervous system

(a) Subarachnoid haemorrhage (qv) from a ruptured berry aneurysm or brain artery: important cause in young to middle-aged.

(b) Cerebral haemorrhage (qv).

(c) Cerebral thrombosis – rarely cause of sudden death, but leads to a 'stroke'.

(d) Epilepsy (qv) – can cause sudden death, even if no actual fit or status epilepticus at the time.

Abdominal causes

(a) Massive gastro-intestinal bleeding from peptic ulcer, oesophageal varices in cirrhosis of liver or, rarely, cancers.

(b) Perforation of the gut, either a peptic ulcer of stomach or duodenum, or cancer or diverticulosis of large intestine.

(c) Complication of pregnancy, such as massive haemorrhage from abortion or ectopic pregnancy.

Chest causes

(a) Haemorrhage (haemoptysis) from lungs or air passages, due to tuberculosis or cancer.

(b) Bronchial asthma – sudden death can occur even if no acute attack or status asthmaticus present: formerly, many deaths were due to toxic effects on heart of broncho-dilator sprays.

An appreciable number of sudden deaths in young to middle-aged adults reveal no cause at post-mortem (see 'Obscure autopsy'). These must be ascribed to sudden failure of the heart muscle from occult causes and have to be recorded as 'unascertainable'.

SUFFOCATION

A variety of the asphyxial group of conditions, though the nomenclature is unsatisfactory. Usually taken to mean deprivation of air supply to the lungs, either from absence of respirable gas in the atmosphere (such as entering a. room exhausted of oxygen by a gas fire or a pit or silo filled with carbon dioxide) – or mechanical obstruction of the mouth, nose or air passages, though the latter is often called 'smothering' (qv).

Though included in the rather vague category of 'asphyxia', death from suffocation may be so rapid as to exclude oxygen lack, for example, a child may die quickly if a plastic bag is pulled over its head or a worker may drop dead on entering a chamber devoid of oxygen. Here cardiac arrest is precipitated by some ill-understood vagal reflex, rather than pure oxygen deprivation.

TATTOOS

Performed by pricking pigments under the skin with a manual or electric needle. The permanency depends on the skill of the operator and on the nature of the pigment. The red colour tends to diffuse in time; more so than the black, which is particulate carbon rather than a dye.

A tattoo is permanent unless the skin and underlying subcutaneous tissue are removed, either surgically or by scarring by some injurious means, such as deep burning or corrosive substances.

Tattooing can transmit several diseases, especially virus hepatitis and syphilis.

Forensically, the main interest of tattoos is in identification of both living and dead. They survive most injuries except deep burns. Superficial burns may obscure tattoos, but when the burned epidermis is removed at surgical cleansing or autopsy, the tattoo survives in the deep layers of the skin.

Even moderate degrees of post-mortem decomposition, as in drowning, do not destroy tattoos, which can be seen when the peeled layers are removed. Only when actual putrefaction of all tissues begins do they become indiscernible.

Tattooing of persons under 16 is illegal in Britain, under the provisions of the Tattooing of Minors Act 1969.

THROMBOSIS

Coagulation of blood within the vessels during life. Often called 'clotting', but this strictly means the coagulation of blood after it is shed from the body, outwith the blood vessels.

Thrombosis is a complex mechanism involving many factors in both the blood itself and the vessel wall. Thrombus consists of fibrin (an insoluble protein formed by precipitation of a soluble precursor, fibrinogen) mixed with red blood cells and also 'platelets', tiny cell fragments which circulate in the blood. These help to initiate the clotting process by providing substances which convert fibrinogen to fibrin; they also mechanically plug any small defects in the vessel wall to stop leakage.

The thrombus, the actual clot in the vessels, is laid down in successive strata, made up of layers of fibrin, red and white blood cells and platelets. The strata represent chronological layers of deposition; in large thrombi, such as in an aortic aneurysm, they are called the 'lines of Zahn'.

Thrombi may occur in arteries or in veins. Precipitating factors may be stagnation of blood, as in deep vein thrombosis; local damage to the vessel wall, as in an injury; an increased propensity of the blood to coagulate after tissue damage anywhere in the body; or to degenerative changes in the vessel wall, especially atheroma (see 'Coronary artery disease').

Estimation of the duration of a thrombus since formation is complex and inexact. It depends upon naked eye and microscopic evaluation, dependent upon the expertise of the pathologist. Differentiation of ante mortem thrombus from post-mortem clot is less difficult, but where ante mortem thrombus forms very soon before death, then microscopy is needed, and if the coagulation is peri-mortal then a reliable answer may not be possible.

Thrombosis in veins leads to danger of pulmonary embolism (qv) and, in arteries, leads to death of the tissues supplied by the thrombosed vessel, due to deprivation of blood supply. Examples include myocardial infarction and gangrene of the foot, also 'strokes' due to thrombosis of brain arteries.

THROTTLING

An imprecise term, usually indicating manual pressure on the neck, rather than due to a ligature (garrotting). 'Manual strangulation' is a preferable term (see 'Strangulation').

THYROID GLAND

A gland in the neck, just below the larynx. It consists of two fleshy lobes, one on either side of the windpipe, connected by a narrow isthmus.

It is an important endocrine gland, its main function being the production of thyroxine, an iodine-containing compound which is vital in controlling the rate of metabolism. Enlargement of the gland is common due to a variety of causes including overactivity and iodine deficiency.

Overactivity of the gland leads to hyperthyroidism, also known as exophthalmic goitre or Graves' disease. Here there is over-excitability, raised heart rate, flushing, prominence of the eyes and danger of heart failure. Removal of part of the gland is one treatment, though anti-thyroid drugs have greatly reduced the need for surgical operation. The latter has important medico-legal aspects, in that the recurrent laryngeal nerve, which controls speech, may be damaged during operation and may lead to an action for surgical negligence.

Reduced function of the thyroid is more common. If it occurs in infancy, the child is a cretin, being dull, sluggish and mentally retarded. If acquired during adult life (most common in older women), it leads to hypothyroidism or 'myxoedema', so called from the thickened appearance of the skin, especially the face. Loss of eyebrow hair, mental sluggishness, sensitivity to cold, coarsening of the features, thickening of the skin of the hands and thinning of head hair are typical. The blood vessels are said to be more fragile and haemorrhages may occur more readily.

Persons so affected are much more likely to suffer hypothermia (qv). There are also mental changes ('myxoedema madness') which may have medico-legal consequences. Treatment is by the administration of thyroxine or thyroid extract.

Behind or embedded within the thyroid gland are the tiny *parathyroid* glands, usually four in number, which have a vital role in controlling calcium metabolism. Negligence actions have occurred because these have been inadvertently removed or damaged during thyroid operations.

TIME SINCE DEATH

This is one of the most important, yet most inaccurate and controversial topics in forensic medicine. For many years, numerous pathologists have conducted research and published methods of improved techniques in estimating the time since death, but the procedure is still fraught with uncertainties.

Most methods ultimately depend upon the rate of cooling of the body, as chemical changes are mediated by temperature, including rigor mortis, enzyme changes and other chemical estimations. The various aspects are discussed under the following entries – see 'Cooling of body', 'Decomposition of dead body', 'Hypostasis', 'Post-mortem entomology', 'Rigor mortis' – but as a general observation, it can be said that most methods tend to underestimate the time, rather than overestimate it.

No estimate given in units of less than one hour is realistic, even quite close to the time since death; indeed, one of the most widely used methods (Henssge) gives a minimum bracket of ± 2.8 hours.

As the probable interval lengthens, so does the potential error increase. Estimations based on temperature are only valid during the first day after death in temperate climates.

The environment is all-important in attempting to estimate the time. Unfortunately, in the criminal circumstances where the information is most vital, accurate corroboration is often lacking to allow the doctor to check his methods. Also the temperature, air currents, winds, humidity, etc, of a scene of death may vary widely before the body is discovered, introducing unknown errors.

It is unrealistic for a doctor to offer a single time as his estimate of the time of death: a 'bracket' should be given, stating the most likely minimum and maximum extent of the period during which death probably took place.

Other methods of estimating the time of death include potassium analysis of the vitreous fluid from the eye – an inexact method, but potentially useful when the body has been dead for more than a day or so.

Residual electrical activity in the muscle is recommended by some authorities, but requires special equipment and expertise.

The use of stomach contents (qv) for timing death has severe limitations.

See overleaf for Henssge nomogram method.

Figure 44: **Henssge's nomogram**

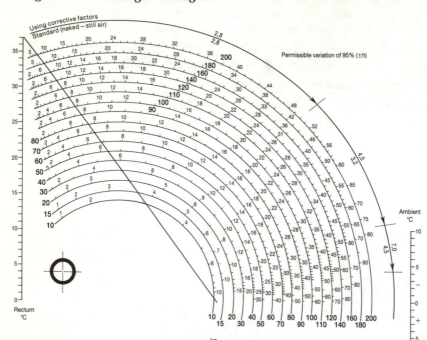

Henssge's nomogram method for estimating the time since death from a single rectal temperature, where the environmental temperature is below 23°C. The nomogram expresses the death time (t) by:

$$\frac{T_{rectum} - T_{ambient}}{37.2 - T_{ambient}} = 1.25 \exp(B\ t) - 0.25 \exp(5B\ t); B = -1.2815(kg^{-0.625}) + 0.0284$$

The nomogram is related to the chosen standard, that is, naked body extended lying in still air. Cooling conditions differing from the chosen Cooling conditions differing from the chosen standard may be proportionally adjusted by corrective factors of the real body weight, giving the corrected body weight by which the death time is to be read off. Factors above 1.0 may correct thermal isolation conditions and factors below 1.0 may correct conditions accelerating the heat loss of a body.

How to read off the time of death:

(a) connect the points of the scales by a straight line according to the rectal and ambient temperature. It crosses the diagonal of the nomogram at a special point;

(b) draw a second straight line going through the centre of the circle, below left of the nomogram, and the intersection of the first line and the diagonal.

The second line crosses the semicircles which represent the body weights.

At the intersection of the semicircle of the body weight, the time of death can be read off.

The second line touches a segment of the outermost semicircle. Here can be seen the permissible variation of 95%.

Example: temperature of the rectum 26.4°C; ambient temperature 12°C; body weight 90kg.

Result: time of death 16 ± 2.8 hours. Statement: the death occurred within 13.2 and 18.8 (13 and 19) hours before the time of measurement (with a reliability of 95%).

Note: if the values of the ambient temperature and/or the body weight (see corrective factors) are called into question, repeat the procedure with other values that might be possible. The range of death time can be seen in this way.

Requirements for use:

(a) no strong radiation (for example, sun, heater, cooling system);

(b) no strong fever or general hypothermia;

(c) no uncertain* severe changes of the cooling conditions during the point between the time of death and examination (for example, the place of death must be the same as where the body was found);

(d) no high thermal conductivity of the surface beneath the body.**

* Known changes can be taken into account: a change of the ambient temperature can often be evaluated (for example, contact the weather station); use the mean ambient temperature of the period in question. Changes by the operations of the investigators (for example, taking any cover off) since finding the body are negligible: take the conditions before into account.

** Measure the temperature of the surface beneath the body too. If there is a significant difference between the temperature of the air and the surface temperature , use the mean.

Empiric corrective factors of the body weight:

Note: for the selection of the corrective factor in any case, only the clothing or covering of the *lower* trunk is relevant. Personal experience is needed; nevertheless, this is quickly achieved by consistent use of the method.

Dry clothing/ covering	In air	Corrective factor	Wet through clothing/covering Wet body surface	In air	In water
		0.35	naked		flowing
		0.5	naked		still
		0.7	naked	moving	
		0.7	1–2 thin layers	moving	
naked	moving	0.75			
1–2 thin layers	moving	0.9	2 or more thick	moving	
naked	still	1.0			
1–2 thin layers	still	1.1	2 thick layers	still	
2–3 thin layers		1.2	more than 2 thick	still	
1–2 thick layers	moving or	1.2	layers		
3–4 thin layers	still	1.3			
more thin/thick	without	1.4			
layers	influence	...			
		1.8			
thick bedspread		...			
+ clothing combined		2.4			

TRAFFIC ACCIDENTS

The type of injury varies widely according to the location of the victim, that is, pedestrian, cyclist, motor-cyclist, car driver, front-seat passenger or rear passenger and with the use or absence of safety equipment.

Pedestrians

Worldwide, pedestrians are the most frequent victims of road accidents, comprising over half of the estimated million deaths and 15 million injuries. In Britain, about 28% of deaths are pedestrians (1980–90), but only 19% in the USA. For each death there are about eight significantly injured pedestrians. About 84% are struck by the front of a vehicle; nearside impact is more common than offside in the UK.

Injuries can be divided into *primary* and *secondary* injuries.

Primary injuries

Impact due to initial blow from vehicle, frequently on legs by bumper bar, or hip region from frontal grille or bonnet edge. Larger vehicles, such as trucks or buses, may make primary impact higher on body, which affects later events.

Where a car strikes the legs, because this is below the centre of gravity of the body, the upper part is often rotated towards the oncoming vehicle and the victim is lifted up onto the bonnet. Severe injuries may then occur from striking the windscreen, which may shatter, or striking the windscreen pillar or upper rim. Severe head injuries may occur from this impact.

By now, the car is almost invariably decelerating, but the body having acquired forward momentum by being lifted up, continues to move forward, sliding off the front or side of the bonnet to receive secondary injuries from hitting the ground.

Secondary injuries

Further injuries may occur from being run over either by the same car before braking is complete or by an adjacent vehicle. If the victim is not lifted onto the car, he may be projected forwards (and later run over) or thrown obliquely to the side. In any event, secondary injuries, frequently more lethal than the primary impact, may occur. The most common is a head injury from striking the ground or nearby structures. Other secondary injuries include fractured pelvis and ribs and limb fractures.

Localised injuries may occur from door handles, mirrors, headlamp rims, mascots, etc, though deliberate improvements in car design have reduced the number of such projecting hazards.

A considerable proportion of pedestrian victims are found to have a significant level of alcohol in their blood.

What was the speed of the vehicle?

An estimate of the speed of a vehicle is sometimes requested, based on the injuries suffered by the pedestrian. This cannot be done, in spite of some claims by medical experts. Death can occur at speeds as low as 15 mph, yet other pedestrians have survived high speed impacts. The injuries depend on the part of the body struck and other variables. Scooping-up onto the bonnet can also occur at speeds as low as 15 mph.

An estimate of speed is only sometimes possible by the evaluation of non-medical evidence, such as skid-marks and vehicular damage.

Motor cyclists

These suffer injuries to each extremity of the body, head injuries being sustained in 80% of fatalities. The usual sequel of events is forward projection from the machine on impact. The rider strikes the ground or other obstacle head first and, at high speed, the crash helmet affords little chance of survival. At lower speeds it makes an appreciable difference, largely by presenting a smooth surface to the ground so that deceleration can be relatively gradual. Thus any projection on the helmet, such as a peak, defeats the object.

A typical injury has been called the 'motor-cyclist's fracture', being a side to side crack across the base of the skull due to violent impact on the side of the head. A ring fracture of the base is also common, as is a broken neck.

Leg injuries occur when the lower limbs are trapped under the falling machine. As in all traffic accidents, the danger of subsequent injuries from other vehicles (especially on high speed roads such as motorways) is not sufficiently appreciated. Another injury occurs when a motor-cyclist drives under the back of a truck, known as 'tailgating' – severe head or neck injuries, or even decapitation, may occur.

Pedal cyclists

Because of the lower speeds, the gross head injuries seen in motor cyclists are not so common, but are still frequent, though crash helmets are increasingly being worn. The primary impact from a car or truck may cause lower rib or pelvic fractures, but most damage occurs from secondary injuries due to being projected or falling from the unstable machine.

Vehicle occupants

The injuries differ according to the position of the victim in the car, the front seat passenger being the most vulnerable. However, statistically, the driver is most often injured, due to the fact that he is so frequently the only occupant.

Rear-seat passengers have less chance of death or severe injuries, though after the use of seat belts by front-seat occupants became mandatory, and the fitting of air bags more common, the proportion of death and serious injury to those in the back increased. This led to the compulsory use of rear seat belts.

Children in the front seat, either alone or on the lap of an adult, have a disproportionately high injury rate, and in many European countries, it is illegal for them to occupy this position.

Injuries to the front seat passenger

In one series of fatal accidents, 55% of front-seat passengers suffered fractured skulls, as against 42% of drivers. Spinal neck injuries occurred in 35% of passengers and 30% of drivers. Passengers suffered brain damage in 64%, drivers in 53%.

As most car accidents consist of a frontal impact, there is usually violent deceleration. If an unyielding object is struck, the deceleration equals the contact speed of the car and if two vehicles collide, the 'G forces' equal the sum of their speeds.

This gross deceleration lifts the unbelted passenger from the seat and projects him forwards. The first contact is usually the knees, lower legs or thighs against the parcel shelf or fascia, depending on the car design. This may cause abrasions, lacerations or fractures to the legs.

Then the upper part of the body folds forwards, but still rises as a whole and may be smashed against and/or through the windscreen. The body may be completely ejected through the glass and land in the road, to suffer secondary injuries and perhaps running over. Alternatively, the head may strike the rim of the windscreen or side pillar or 'A-frame', causing severe lacerations and head injury. The shattered toughened glass leaves characteristic abrasions on the face, resembling multiple V-shaped or Y-shaped abrasions and lacerations.

The deceleration commonly causes a 'whiplash' injury (qv). The head is thrown violently down on the neck in a frontal impact 'hyperflexion' and a fraction of a second later, when the vehicle stops, the head swings back over the seat, causing a 'hyperextension' stress, which is more dangerous than hyperflexion. This cracking whiplash effect can dislocate or fracture the spine, either in the neck region (cervical) or back region (thoracic or dorsal). The vertebrae can be crushed or displaced, with the danger of distorting the spinal canal, spinal cord injury and paralysis (tetraplegia or quadriplegia) (qv).

Safety equipment

The use of a restraint harness, head rest or air bag reduces the dangers.

A diagonal shoulder-plus-lap strap seat belt reduces mortality by about 25%. The head rest reduces the hyperextension risk of whiplash, but none of these compromise devices purports to reduce all injuries.

The protective functions of a seat belt are:

(a) to prevent or reduce the contact with the windscreen and fascia;

(b) to retain the person in the vehicle if the side door bursts open, as commonly happens, with the risk of ejection and secondary injuries and running over by other vehicles, especially on motorways;

(c) the significant stretching of the belt fabric increases the deceleration time and reduces the G forces on the body; and

(d) the considerable total area of the seat belt in contact with the body spreads the deceleration forces over a greater area of the body, compared to dissipation of the same force over a small zone, which would cause severe or fatal injury, especially on the head.

Both driver and front seat passenger may be injured if the engine and transmission, even the front suspension, are intruded backwards into the passenger compartment – and if the roof or sides are imploded towards them. In these instances, the seat belt is obviously of no protective value.

Head rests prevent backward hyperextension, which contribute to neck injuries, but like seat belts, cannot prevent forward hyperflexion.

Air bags momentarily prevent forward movement of the upper part of the body and keep the occupant off the windscreen and fascia; this also prevents hyperflexion neck injuries to some extent.

There are injuries reported from air bags, including friction burns to the face and, rarely, fatalities.

Injuries to drivers

These are less common than those to passengers alongside them, due probably to (a) the slight warning due to greater concentration on road conditions, with subsequent bracing before impact; and (b) the protection afforded by the steering wheel.

Though the steering wheel can inflict its own injuries on the driver, it is still more of an asset than a liability, acting as a brace and preventing so much forward projection. However, the wheel can crush ribs, breast bone, chest and abdominal contents. Especially when broken, the wheel spokes can cause gross injuries to the heart and lungs. Modern wheels are made to telescope or concertina on their shaft and are thus less lethal, but injuries to the organs of the chest and upper abdomen, such as a torn liver, are more common in drivers than in passengers.

The drivers may sustain fractures of arms from bracing on the steering wheel, and of legs or pelvis from pressing on the foot pedals at the moment of impact.

Rear-seat passengers

Fatalities less common than in the front seat occupants, but there are still potentially lethal risks. The passengers may be projected forwards onto the front seat occupants or even thrown through the windscreen. Injuries from interior fittings, such as door handles, window winders, mirrors and lights may occur, especially as, if the car overturns, the occupants may be whirled around the periphery of the compartment. Ejection may also occur, sometimes through the rear window.

Side-impact injuries

Naturally the occupants on the side of impact will suffer most, but the vehicle may be overturned and all may be injured. Trapping due to distortion of the passenger compartment may occur. The use of side impact reinforcement systems in modern cars reduces, but cannot eliminate, injuries from this cause.

Fire is relatively uncommon in car crashes, in spite of the arguments formerly made by anti-seat belt protesters. A Canadian survey showed that only 24 out of 1,297 motor car accident victims died of burns – of these, only three were in passenger seats.

TRANSPLANTATION OF ORGANS AND TISSUES

Transplants may be:

(a) a *homograft*, when tissue from the same person is moved to another site, for example, skin grafts or a digit moved to replace damaged or maldeveloped fingers. No legal problems apart from usual informed consent and no problems with tissue rejection.

Auto blood transfusion is another example, when blood taken from a Jehovah's Witness patient before operation is returned to them when required;

(b) a *heterograft*, where part of another person (or even animal) is transplanted. The oldest and most frequent is blood transfusion, but now also includes corneae of eyes, kidneys, hearts, liver, lung, pancreas and bone marrow.

Tissues or organs may be from (a) live donors, usually a relative, or (b) from a dead donor (cadaveric transplantation).

Live donation requires fully informed consent from a mentally competent adult; though no special legal requirements exist, it is ethically desirable that time be allowed for a full explanation to be given to the donor of the potential risks so that he may, if he so wishes, obtain further medical and, possibly, spiritual advice. The issue revolves mainly around the donation of one of a paired organ (usually kidney) where the possibility of future failure of the remaining organ might endanger health or life. Naturally, it is illegal to remove a vital non-paired organ, even with consent, as, in even the most emotive circumstances of a parent wishing to donate to a mortally sick child, such a procedure would be homicide.

Since scandals surrounding the commercial exploitation of donors emerged, the Human Organ Transplant Act 1989 established strict rules over the procedure and set up a Regulatory Authority to police them.

Where the donated tissue is easily regenerated (for example, blood donation) no legal problems arise. It is highly unusual for an adult to give permission for donation from a child, but in the case of blood or bone marrow, which again is quickly regenerated, such donation does occur, especially when a close relationship such as a twin or sibling is involved.

Nb: the guiding principle in live donation is that the benefit to the recipient should exceed the possible harm to the donor by a considerable margin.

Cadaveric transplantation is, naturally, the only source of unpaired organs, such as the heart, and is the largest source (in Europe) of paired organs such as the kidney. In Britain, the legal aspects of cadaveric donation are regulated by the Human Tissue Act 1961 (qv) and most other jurisdictions have similar legislation. It is in this context that definitions of death and brain death (qv) are of importance.

Further legal problems have arisen over the possible transmission of infective diseases such as HIV, hepatitis and CJD (Creutzfeldt-Jakob Disease) (qv).

HIV-contaminated blood products given to haemophiliacs and growth hormone from human pituitaries contaminated with CJD gave rise to extensive litigation in recent years; corneal grafts have also inadvertently been taken from infected donors.

In all but homografts, great care and technical expertise must be employed to obtain the best possible compatibility between donor and recipient tissues. This invokes highly complex tissue typing to avoid rejection of the donated organ. Apart from the best possible matching of tissue types, energetic immunosuppressive measures with drugs are carried on after transplantation. An exception is corneal grafting, the longest established technique for solid tissue transplantation, where such problems are minimal. In this instance, there is also little complication relating to moment of death, as corneal grafts can be taken from the cadaver up to a day or so after death.

In the cases of other organs, such as kidney, speed is of the essence and in Europe a centralised data bank (Eurotransplant) of waiting potential recipients is maintained on computer, ready to be matched immediately with new donor material. In Britain, this service is based in Bristol.

Some religious sects, notably Jehovah's Witnesses, have strong objections to any form of transplantation, including blood transfusion. Whilst adult members are entitled to withhold consent for such procedures, controversy surrounds their refusal to allow life-saving measures to be applied to their children. Formerly, it was usual for the child to be rapidly taken into care, by a court being convened at the bedside, but this has fallen into disuse and now the opinion of two doctors acting in good faith seems sufficient against the success of any possible civil action for assault. The same would apply to the urgent treatment of an adult religious objector, if he was unconscious and *in extremis*: doctors who employed life-saving measures, such as blood transfusion, would be supported by their medical protection organisations in the defence of any subsequent suit for assault, but every case differs and the ethical, and even political, climate on this matter is ever-changing.

TRAUMA AND DISEASE

The role of trauma in the causation of disease is a potent source of medico-legal argument and in many cases the problem is insoluble. However, it must be emphasised that the probability of an injury giving rise to disease varies greatly according to the type of disease under discussion and there can be no generalisation possible in this respect.

If injury be held to include certain toxic or irritative states, as well as direct trauma, then the field of positive causation is greatly widened. For example, it will then include such things as chemical carcinogenesis, which is the inducement of tumours, such as the well established connection between asbestos and mesothelioma or the malignant diseases caused by radiation.

Returning to the possible effects on human tissues of direct injury, the probability of such an effect has been greatly exaggerated in the past, with unwarranted conclusions being drawn in many places, usually because of the prospect of financial compensation. Though there are certain diseases where a connection, on the balance of probabilities, is thought to exist, such a connection is usually incapable of absolute proof, as all these diseases are well known to occur quite spontaneously. For example, although the association of asbestos exposure and mesothelioma tumour is well recognised (and included in the schedule of industrial diseases), it must be remembered that 15% of all mesotheliomata occur without any apparent asbestos exposure.

Coronary artery disease

Though claims are commonly made that death or disability from coronary artery disease ('heart attacks') are due to injury or over-exertion, this claim must be carefully analysed.

There is no evidence whatsoever that injury or exertion can *cause* the underlying disease, that is, trauma and effort play no part in the aetiology of coronary atheroma. However, in a person who already has coronary artery disease, it cannot be denied that over-exertion may precipitate an acute episode in the natural history of the disease, usually myocardial infarction or death from ventricular fibrillation or cardiac arrest (qv).

Recent research has confirmed the association between exertion and sudden cardiac death. Mittleman in the USA investigated 1,228 patients with acute myocardial infarction and showed there was a sixfold increase in incidence during or within one hour of heavy physical exertion. In Germany, Willich researched 1,194 patients and showed a doubling of risk. Both surveys showed that the risk was greater in those who were normally sedentary.

Trauma very rarely causes a coronary episode, unless there is substantial direct injury to the front of the chest. Sudden over-exertion, such as the lifting of a heavy weight or a sudden stress beyond the usual physical capabilities of the person, may precipitate some form of exacerbation of the cardiac condition, as stated above. However, it must be emphasised that sudden cardiac deaths are so common in the absence of trauma or effort, that no real prospect of absolute proof can be hoped for in maintaining that the untoward result was directly related to the injury or effort.

Other types of heart disease

Diseases such as hypertension, aortic valve disease and aortic aneurysms, etc, have similar relationships to injury and effort, there being no evidence that the latter can give rise to the basic disease, but it must be admitted that a sudden strain might precipitate complications of the disease. This is especially so if the effort or stress of the injury causes a sudden rise in blood pressure, which may cause rupture of an atheromatous plaque in a diseased coronary artery or of an aneurysm or precipitation of death from valvular disease or hypertensive heart disease. The fact that such diseases frequently cause death or sudden disability, in the absence of such special circumstances, reduces the cause and effect relationship considerably.

Tumours

The relationship between malignant disease and injury is a frequent source of controversy. In general, there is very little evidence indeed to allow such a causal connection to be made, except where chemical or long standing irritative states exist. For instance, a cancer of the bladder may well follow exposure to aniline in an industrial worker and this is well recognised. Again a person with asbestosis of the lungs has a high probability of contracting lung cancer and those exposed to asbestos may much less frequently develop a mesothelioma though, as mentioned earlier, some 15% of mesotheliomata are unrelated to asbestos.

Physical trauma is much less likely to lead to tumours, except in a direct manner, where a jagged tooth may cause years of irritation, bleeding and infection upon the tongue and lead to a cancer. However, it is inconceivable that a single act of injury could give rise to a tumour, though this is often alleged. Most allegations have arisen because the detection of a tumour appears to date from shortly after the traumatic incident. However, in almost all cases, the attention drawn to the injured part is instrumental in bringing to light the existence of the tumour which must have pre-existed in almost all cases. A blow on a part of the body may draw attention to a previously unnoticed lump, or the temporary signs of the injury may render the first signs of the tumour apparent.

Certain criteria, known as 'Ewing's postulates', must be satisfied before any connection can be maintained (though, even then, there is no scientific way of proving anything other than a possibility):

(a) the tumour must arise exactly at the site injured;

(b) definite and substantial trauma must be proved;

(c) the tumour must be confirmed pathologically;

(d) the tissue at the site must have been healthy before the trauma;

(e) a reasonable interval – neither too long or too short – must elapse between the time of the trauma and the appearance of the tumour; and

(f) though not one of the Ewing's original postulates, there should be some good scientific reason for ascribing the tumour formation to the injury – and this is rarely possible.

The interval necessary is also a difficult matter. Though few would accept anything less than months, the upper limit may be very long. For instance, mesothelioma from asbestos may take 15–20 years to appear.

Brain tumours have presented many problems in relation to head injury, but there is no good evidence that a causal relationship exists. This statement must be modified according to the type of tumour, as growths of the membranes (meningiomata) may have a slightly better chance of establishing a cause-and-effect relationship than growths of brain itself, such as a 'glioma'. Courville, who is one of the best authorities on the subject, has come to the invariable conclusion that in no case, evaluated from a clinical or pathological viewpoint, has a glioma proved to be of traumatic origin. As head injuries are so common in the general population, it is inevitable that tumour formation and a history of trauma must frequently coincide. It should be remembered that over 10% of a non-tumour-suffering population can recall a significant head injury.

Infections

Here, the possibility of trauma being related is far greater, depending upon the circumstances. Due either to an injury penetrating and carrying infection into the wound, or because tissue damage renders the body more susceptible to ever-present contamination, then the possibility exists in greater or lesser degree according to the circumstances. Again, expert evidence is required to evaluate the site, timing and other pathological factors, which might relate the injury to the infection.

Damage to a limb, for instance, may give rise to osteomyelitis (infection of the bone) or a chest injury may rekindle a healing or dormant tuberculous condition. Each case must be considered upon its particular circumstances, but the chances of connecting infection to injury are far greater than with tumours.

Epilepsy

The onset of fits after a focal head injury (almost always a localised skull fracture and/or brain damage) is well established, but direct evidence of a local area of injury in a site that neurologically can be related to the fits must be produced, as well as assurance that no fits were suffered before the head injury. It is difficult or impossible to differentiate the usual types of 'idiopathic' (that is, of unknown cause) epilepsy from post-traumatic epilepsy unless there are localising signs which correspond to the area of injury. Some types of fits may be so localised, such as temporal lobe epilepsy, where there may be olfactory or gustatory manifestations. In addition, the use of electro-encephalography (EEG) may localise the focus of origin of the fits. A depressed fracture, even when healed, may cause local pressure or irritation to the surface of the brain, which may be correlated with the focus of the fits to substantiate the claim of traumatic epilepsy. The age of onset may be significant, as it is less likely for a person of mature years to begin idiopathic epilepsy, when there is a definite injury present consistent with the production of fits. The whole matter needs the most expert neurological advice for resolution.

The possibility that a pre-existing disease actually caused or contributed to the accident, which in turn led to the trauma, must be considered. This is especially the case in fatal instances, where dependants claim that some stress or injury caused death and the subject himself is not available as a witness or for clinical examination.

The problem arises even more often in relation to insurance and compensation claims concerning transport accidents, where the relative role of pre-existing disease, such as coronary occlusion or hypertension, is difficult to assess in retrospect as a potential cause of the fatal accident.

TRAUMATIC ASPHYXIA

An inappropriately named condition, where the most florid signs of 'asphyxia' are seen. It is almost always accidental, due to pressure immobilising the chest wall and preventing breathing movements. Very occasionally it can be homicidal, as in 'Burking', named after Burke and Hare, where the killers sat upon the chests of drunken victims to obtain cadavers for anatomical dissection.

Accidents, such as burial in earth, mud, sand, silo contents, grain bunkers, etc, may cause fixation of the chest, even though the mouth and nose are above the surface. It is the most common cause of multiple deaths in crowd accidents where collapse of barriers and crushing of the victims (such as Hillsborough, Ibrox Park, Heisl Stadium and Bolton football disasters) leads to packing together of bodies so that the chest movements are restricted.

Another cause is the pinning of drivers beneath vehicles, especially agricultural tractors, which now must have a safety roll-bar or cab to guard against this particular accident.

The common factor is fixation of the chest by external pressure, even though the air passages are unobstructed at the nose and mouth. As the ribs cannot move and the diaphragm cannot descend, no air can be drawn into the lungs. The frustrated violent attempts to breathe and the impairment of blood return to the chest, which is normally assisted by movements of the thorax, causes gross congestion in the face and neck above the level of the collar bone. This area becomes red or purple in colour and numerous petechial haemorrhages (qv) appear in the eyelids, whites of the eyes and skin of the face. Sometimes bloodshot whites of the eyes bulge through the lids, giving the most classical example of asphyxia – more correctly called 'congestive signs' due to impaired return of blood through the large veins to the heart.

VAGAL INHIBITION (REFLEX CARDIAC ARREST)

This term fell into considerable disrepute as a consequence of overemployment in past years as a rather loose excuse to explain many deaths where no positive findings could be obtained by autopsy. However, using discretion and reasonable criteria, the concept has genuine validity. Part of its fall from grace resulted from confusion with 'status lymphaticus' (qv), an even more nebulous entity used to explain obscure sudden deaths.

In essence, vagal inhibition is a convenient and exact term describing sudden heart stoppage due to excessive nervous stimulation of the heart via the vagus nerve, which is the paired (10th) cranial nerve which leaves the base of the brain and courses down the neck, through the chest to terminate in the abdomen. It supplies many organs and structures with 'parasympathetic' nerve fibres, which is part of the 'autonomic nervous system'. This is not under voluntary control and performs a myriad of functions concerned with the workings of blood vessels, glands, heart, etc. The other component of the system is the 'sympathetic' nervous system, which is in balanced opposition to the parasympathetic system.

The medico-legal significance is profound, in that any sudden unexpected stimulus to many parts of the body can cause a burst of nerve impulses to pass down the parasympathetic via the vagus, so slowing or stopping the heart. In contrast to sympathetic nerve activity (the 'flight or fight' response which releases adrenaline and directly speeds up the heart), vagus impulses slow the heart and in excess, can stop it altogether.

The type of stimulus which can trigger this vagal reflex includes sudden cooling of the skin, as in falls into cold water; the abrupt entry of cold water into the back of the throat or air passages; touching or dilation of the neck of the womb as in abortions; and forensically most important, sudden pressure on the neck (qv). The latter causes nervous discharges to originate in the carotid sinuses, which causes sudden death in a large proportion of strangulations, rather than an asphyxial death.

The likelihood of vagal inhibition is heightened when the victim is pre-sensitised by emotional tension. For instance, very apprehensive patients have died instantly on having teeth extracted or small operations performed under local anaesthetic. The woman undergoing an abortion may die the moment the cervix of the womb is touched or dilated. Other cases are on record where student 'rags' have caused death when the skin was touched with ice in a mock execution. Professor Keith Simpson records a case where a woman died instantly on rapidly gulping a glass of cold water and every pathologist has cases where similar events have occurred, leaving no traces at post-mortem examination. Even a horrific or nauseating sight has caused sudden death and the potential categories of such events are without limit.

However, for such an explanation to be acceptable, the following criteria should be applied:

(a) no demonstrable abnormalities sufficient to cause death at autopsy (see 'Obscure autopsy');

(b) the circumstances of the death allow of some situation such as described above to have been present: unfortunately, in many cases, the death is not witnessed; and

(c) no other more convincing explanation is forthcoming.

Where negative autopsy findings are combined with a completely unhelpful history, it is more satisfactory to admit that the cause of death was 'unascertainable' than to invoke vagal inhibition. It has been the lack of this caution that has allowed an otherwise reasonable explanation to fall into disrepute and even ridicule.

VERTEBRAL ARTERY INJURY

See 'Subarachnoid haemorrhage'.

VITAL REACTION

A term indicating the response of living body tissues to injury.

By definition it can only occur during life and is therefore an index of ante mortem injury. This is of considerable importance in forensic medicine in (a) attempting to establish that an injury was inflicted before death; and (b) possibly estimating the time of infliction before death.

The rather absolute acceptance of ante-mortem versus post-mortem infliction has become more indistinct in recent years, as it has become apparent that death is a *process*, not an *event* and that injuries inflicted at or around the time of death ('peri-mortal') may not be so easily differentiated. It has been found, for instance, that white blood cells (leucocytes), which may be attracted to injured tissue, can remain mobile for many hours after the cessation of the heart and breathing, the conventional markers of life or death.

It is also apparent that the cellular response to injuries, with migration of white blood cells and other tissue cells, is much more irregular than formerly thought; some undoubtedly ante mortem injuries may be without such a cellular response for a long time after wound infliction.

The vital reaction may be sought by the naked eye, microscopic histological examination, or histochemical or other chemical means.

Naked eye evidence includes the signs of inflammation, viz, reddening and swelling. The edges of a wound or burn will usually show these signs if sufficient time has elapsed before death supervenes. A minimum time is hard to quantify, but is usually of the order of several minutes in the case of burns, and longer in wounds.

Histological examination. Using conventional histological methods, by preparing stained sections of tissue for examination under the microscope, the most important signs of vital reaction are oedema (swelling) and hyperaemia (dilatation of blood vessels), which are rather indeterminate signs. The best criterion is the appearance of migrant white blood cells (leucocytes) into the injured part. The first cells to appear are the polymorphonuclear leucocytes and may be seen from a number of minutes to a few hours after injury. Unfortunately, their appearance is most irregular and if death occurs within a short time (up to many hours) then none may be visible.

Chemical and histochemical tests. More recent research has shown that enzymes and other substances such as histamine and serotonin (all mediators in the inflammatory reaction, which is a precursor to healing) may appear within a few minutes after injury, in the zone adjacent to the main damage. The area of actual tissue destruction may lose its pre-existing enzyme content.

This is an area of ongoing research, some of which is only just appearing in routine practice in the more advanced forensic centres. However, many of these sophisticated new enzyme techniques have not been adopted into general use, due to their unreproducibility by those who did not develop the methods.

WHIPLASH INJURY

Spinal damage caused by violent bending and then straightening of the vertebral column. The most common cause is a traffic accident involving motor car occupants. Sudden deceleration from a frontal impact, or acceleration from impact in the rear, causes the head to swing back and forth, resulting in severe stresses to bones and joints of spine caused by the inertia of the heavy head. This may result in fracture and/or dislocation of the spinal joints of the neck and upper chest.

There may be local damage to bones and joints of the spinal vertebra, with subsequent fractures, dislocations, pain and tenderness, but the major danger is injury to the spinal cord at the level of the injury, which may result in nerve damage, paralysis or even death.

The legs may be paralysed (paraplegia) or all four limbs (tetraplegia or quadriplegia). If the injury is high in the neck (above 3rd–5th vertebrae) the nerves which control breathing may be damaged and death ensue from respiratory paralysis.

Lesser degrees of injury may damage the nerve roots that pass out from the spinal canal, with impairment of motor function (movement) of parts of the upper limb or of sensory function leading to numbness, tingling, etc.

In addition to damage to the spine and spinal cord, a severe whiplash of the chest region may damage the aorta, which is attached to the front of the spine where the aortic arch becomes the descending aorta. The aorta may be completely transected at this point or may show one or more transverse tears in its lining due to whiplash stress: death from fatal internal bleeding may result (see 'Aorta').

RECOMMENDED READING

Adelson, L, *The Pathology of Homicide*, 1974, Springfield, Illinois: Charles Thomas.

Denny, R, *None for the Road – Understanding Drink-Driving*, 1997, Crayford: Shaw.

Di Maio, V and Di Maio, K, *Forensic Pathology*, 1989, New York: Elsevier.

Evand, KT and Knight, B, *Forensic Radiology*, 1981, Oxford: Blackwell Scientific.

Knight, B (ed), *Estimation of the Time Since Death*, 1995, London: Edward Arnold.

Knight, B, *Forensic Pathology*, 2nd edn, 1996, London: Edward Arnold.

Knight, B, *Legal Aspects of Medical Practice*, 5th edn, 1992, London: Churchill-Livingston.

Knight, B, *Simpson's Forensic Medicine*, 11th edn, 1997, London: Edward Arnold.

Mason, JK, *Forensic Medicine for Lawyers*, 3rd edn, London: Butterworths.

Mason, JK (ed), *Pathology of Trauma*, 2nd edn, 1993, London: Edward Arnold.

Mason, JK and McCall Smith, E, *Law and Medical Ethics*, 1983, London: Butterworths.

McLay, WDS (ed), *Clinical Forensic Medicine*, 2nd edn, 1996, London: Greenwich Medical Media.

Polson, C, Gee, D and Knight, B, *Essentials of Forensic Medicine*, 5th edn, 1985, Oxford: Pergamon Press.

Walls, H and Brownlie, A, *Drink, Drugs and Driving*, 2nd edn, 1985, London: Sweet & Maxwell.

Whittaker, D and Macdonald, F, *A Colour Atlas Of Forensic Dentistry*, 1989, London: Wolfe Medical.

INDEX